Italian-American Students in New York City, 1975–2000

A Research Anthology

Nancy L. Ziehler

EDITOR

JOHN D. CALANDRA ITALIAN AMERICAN INSTITUTE

QUEENS COLLEGE, CITY UNIVERSITY OF NEW YORK

STUDIES IN ITALIAN AMERICANA
VOLUME 3

John D. Calandra Italian American Institute
Queens College, CUNY
25 West 43rd Street, 17th floor
New York, NY 10036

ISBN 0-9703403-5-4
ISBN 978-0-9703403-5-1
Library of Congress Control Number: 2011931830

To all the students, researchers, administrators, and production personnel who have had a hand in this publication.

CONTENTS

Foreword

Among the many things I discovered soon after my arrival at the John D. Calandra Italian American Institute was a treasure trove of early studies on Italian Americans. This research had been conducted by a number of CUNY faculty—"Calandra Scholars," as Dr. Ziehler rightfully baptizes them in her preface, even though two of the essays date back to before the Institute's founding, in 1979, what was first known as the Italian American Institute to Foster Higher Education.

Together with Dr. Ziehler's keen introduction, these essays constitute a window onto the past, of how the Italian-American student negotiated his or her ethnicity during a time when issues of ethnicity, gender, and race were being raised at numerous levels and in various venues across the country.

These studies address many of those issues. The down side, however, was that, except for two articles—one co-authored by Pierre Tribaudi and Dr. Ziehler, the other by Drs. Joseph Scelsa and Vincenzo Milione—none of these essays saw the light of day at the time of their completion; they remained unpublished and hence not part of a greater national discourse on ethnicity. This book thus brings to the public's attention, and in a sense gives second life, to the significant findings that these Calandra Scholars had adroitly unearthed within a four-decade span.

It is the very shedding of light on this sector of Italian America that proves so significant and necessary; and we must continue to unearth other aspects of the Italian-American community for the purpose of (1) revisiting our history, and (2) taking possession of it. It is a record rich with achievement and success. It is also a record of sad and tragic events and episodes that have befallen turn-of-the-twentieth century Italian Americans.

Like other southern Europeans, Italians were initially perceived as non-white in this country. And while it is true that blacks constituted the largest group of people lynched, Italian immigrants have the dubious distinction of being the largest group lynching, which took place in New Orleans in 1891. In addition, the alliance between Italy, Germany, and Japan during World War II placed many of those immigrants on an enemy aliens list. One unspoken consequence was the loss of the subsequent generation's linguistic inheritance. "Don't speak the enemy's language," clamored innumerable posters and public announcements during that time. Further still, Italians were underutilized in numerous professions over the years and—while in more recent times, when it now seems Italian Americans have become *white* and thus respected members of the upper middle class—things have not improved as one might have wished.

These are some of the reasons we need to revisit our history. Let us not forget that, according to what we might surmise from the behavior of some in the entertainment world, Italians are sometimes still fair game for ridicule in the public arena. We cannot always take for granted that we enjoy all the benefits of those who inhabit on a daily basis that world of white privilege. This is still not the case in spite of the wonderful successes of those past and present, including former Speaker of the House Nancy Pelosi, who broke both ethnic and gender boundaries. Joey of *Friends*, George of *Seinfeld*, and the Romanos of *Everybody Loves Raymond* are examples of what might be considered recent negative portrayals of Italian Americans in the medium of television.[1]

A collection of essays of this sort accomplishes a number of things. First, it gathers those voices that have interrogated significant areas of Italian America and presents them, finally, to the public in the formal venue that is this book. In so doing, it contributes to the general discourse

---

[1] Remedy to some of the above was sought out and obtained by individuals in the past. The late New York state senator John D. Calandra and colleagues took it upon themselves to investigate the treatment of Italian-American faculty, staff, and students at the City University of New York (CUNY) in the 1970s, since there had been numerous complaints about the treatment of Italian Americans within that institution. The finding was that Italian Americans were indeed underutilized and underrepresented at all levels university-wide. The immediate result was then Chancellor Kibbee's proclamation (December 9, 1976) that Italian Americans were to be considered a protected class throughout CUNY, with all the rights and privileges of federally recognized affirmative action groups. Another result was the eventual formation of the Italian American Institute to Foster Higher Education, in 1979, which, over the years, has been transformed, in both size and mission, into the John D. Calandra Italian American Institute, a university-wide, research institute under the aegis of Queens College, CUNY. The 1979 Institute was founded primarily to foster higher education among Italian Americans through academic and career counseling especially, and impart, to Italian Americans and non-Italian Americans alike, knowledge of the culture of Italian America. Over the years, the mission broadened to include social, psychological, and demographic research on Italian Americans both within and beyond the walls of CUNY. Today, these earlier research components are buttressed by an equally rigorous sector of academic cultural activities that range from lectures to symposia to film series. Such an institute dedicated to Italian Americana, be it the original structure of 1979 or the more expanded unit of today, is a unique entity. No other center or institute in the Americas or in Italy (the exception being the Fondazione Giovanni Agnelli of Turin) approaches its magnitude and the possibilities therein.

on ethnicity in this country, thus infusing it with an Italian-American hue. Third, it is de facto an act of "cultural transmission" of certain aspects and characteristics of Italian America. We need to be sure that those who follow, the younger generation, are aware of our culture, past and present. They can indeed have access to such knowledge. People need to be there to impart the information necessary for such cultural awareness. This includes teachers and professors on all levels. Such a strategy for success is twofold: (a) lessons on Italian America need to form part of the various K-12 curricula around the country; (b) professors in colleges and universities need to include aspects of Italian Americana in their various courses and, especially at the graduate level, in their seminars.

We must, in the end, embrace our culture more fully. We cannot continue to engage in a series of reminiscences that lead primarily to nostalgic recall. Instead, we need to revisit our past, reclaim its pros and cons, and reconcile it with our present. We need to figure out where we came from, ask questions of both ourselves and the dominant culture, and continue to champion our Italian-American cultural brokers—i.e., artists and intellectuals—of all sorts so that they can continue to engage in an Italian-American state of mind, if such is their choice.

Ultimately, all of this is dependent upon our strengthening the foundation of Italian Americana, by recapturing a stronger sense of *amor proprio* and combining it with our abilities—financial, performative, aesthetic, intellectual—in order to document, maintain, transmit, and further promulgate Italian-American culture. This book constitutes a cornerstone to this new foundation.

ANTHONY JULIAN TAMBURRI

Professor and Dean, John D. Calandra Italian American Institute

Preface

The John. D. Calandra Italian American Institute[1] of Queens College, City University of New York (CUNY), is pleased to present *Italian-American Students in New York City, 1975–2000: A Research Anthology.* Most of these works, either presented at annual conferences of the American Italian Historical Association or distributed locally within the New York State Legislature and the CUNY community, have not been made available to the general public.

Culling more than thirty years of scholarship, the aim of this publication is two-fold. First and foremost, the substantial amount of data contained within this *Research Anthology* is intended to address a gap in the vast body of multicultural counseling literature pertaining to students of diverse populations, their cultural contexts and respective sets of values, customs and needs. Indeed, very little research has been published about Italian-American students since the onset of multiculturalism approximately forty years ago.

Second, in keeping with professional guidelines and ethical mandates to learn about racially and ethnically diverse populations (ACA, 2005; APA, 2002), the *Research Anthology* can be used by readers to develop a preliminary understanding about a specific white ethnic population whose experiences may differ substantially from their own and that of the "standard American culture" (Chavez and Guido-DiBrito, 2000). Small samples, methodological limitations, and dated publications notwithstanding[2], knowledge gained through the respective literature reviews and research findings can raise awareness of this group's specific cultural context and serve as an ethnic backdrop for those working as counselors, psychologists, or educators of Italian-American students.[3]

---

[1] See Calandra Institute website for complete history and range of services offered: www.qc. cuny.edu/calandra

[2] Methodological issues will not be addressed or critiqued herein, but left to each individual reader.

[3] As always, we are cautioned to avoid fitting the unique experiences of individuals into stereotypical profiles based on race, ethnicity or any distinguishing variable (Sue and Zane, 1987), therefore, a suggested and most appropriate use of this volume is to cultivate an appreciation and heightened sensitivity to a specific ethnic population as recommended by professional policy statements.

Contributors to the volume include past and present faculty members from various colleges across CUNY, as well as Calandra Institute personnel and Calandra Scholars.[4] In each case, the motivation to engage in ethnic research originated not from ethnocentrism, but from the contributors' deep interest in the population and its well being along with their core belief that "true multiculturalism must be inclusive of the full range of ethnic groups that compose the society; and that ethnicity is a cultural, not a biological phenomenon" (Vecoli, 1996, p. 13). Further, since Italian Americans were designated an affirmative action category for CUNY in 1976[5], the contributors largely sought to illuminate and understand the distinct issues faced by these students in order to develop appropriate targeted interventions to effectively assist them. Taken together, their collective works will provide the reader with an appreciation of the meanings, contexts, and helping strategies that underlie the term "protected class" as it relates to Italian-American students at CUNY.

As you peruse the *Research Anthology* you will notice that chapters are separated into three parts. In order to set the table for the ten reports that follow it, Part I consists of a brief essay concerning the confusion of race and ethnicity as constructs in social science literature, explicating how this confusion, among other factors, resulted in the absence of Italian Americans from multicultural counseling literature. Select findings from studies contained in the *Research Anthology*, which may surprise readers unfamiliar with the Italian-American community, will be presented to illustrate the importance of including research focused on Italian Americans, or any ethnic group residing in the United States for that matter, in mainstream multicultural publications. Part II comprises the bulk of the collection and provides demographic and psychoeducational profiles of undergraduate students enrolled across CUNY (Krase and Fuccillo, 1975; Krase, 1978; Castiglione, 1982; Krase, 1983; Blumberg and Lavin, 1985; Perrone, 1986), as well as investigations exploring career variables (Perrone, 1986), and the family versus career dilemma among Italian-American female law school students (Battista, 1988). Part III contains more recent investigations regarding the high school dropout rate of Ital-

---

[4] Calandra Scholars: a term used to describe researchers and graduate students from various educational institutions who consulted with the Calandra Institute for research assistance.

[5] Affirmative Action Directive Memorandum from Chancellor Robert J. Kibbee sent to CUNY Council of Presidents, December 9, 1976. This correspondence designated all Italian Americans as a protected class or an affirmative action category within CUNY.

ian-American teens in New York City (Scelsa and Milione, 1990), possible causes (Tribaudi and Ziehler, 2002), and what was done to ameliorate the problem (Milione, De Rosa, and Pelizzoli, 2002). All of the reports are presented as discrete chapters and appear as originally written by their principal investigators with the exception of minor edits. Permission to reprint the materials was obtained from each author.

Using a human development perspective, one may wonder why research on young adults precedes that of adolescents in this volume. The choice to present the material in this order is based on chronology. In other words, the higher education studies are presented in Part II because they preceded research on Italian Americans in NYC secondary schools by at least fifteen years. Hence, all entries flow in order of their publication dates allowing readers to trace the history of Italian-American student development in New York City from 1975 to 2000.[6]

References

American Counseling Association. (2005). *Code of Ethics.* Alexandria, VA: ACA.

American Psychological Association. (2002). *Guidelines on Multicultural Education Training, Research, Practice, and Organizational Change for Psychologists.* Washington DC: APA.

Battista, G. L. (1988). "Family vs. Career: A Dilemma for the Italian-American Woman of the '80s." In J. V. Scelsa, S. J. LaGumina, and L. F. Tomasi (Eds.), *Annual Conference of the American Italian Historical Association, Vol. 21, Italian Americans in Transition* (pp. 115–123). Staten Island, New York: American Italian Historical Association.

Blumberg, A. and Lavin, D. E. (1985). "Italian-American Students at the City University of New York: A Socioeconomic and Educational Profile." Unpublished manuscript, City University of New York, Office of Institutional Research and Analysis and the Italian American Institute.

Castiglione, L. (1982). "A Demographic Study of Italian-American College Students Attending the City University of New York." Unpublished manuscript, Queens College, City University of New York, Italian American Institute to Foster Higher Education.

Chavez, A. F. and Guido-DiBrito, F. (2000). "Racial and Ethnic Identity and Development." In M. C. Clark and R. S. Caffarella (Eds.). *An Update on Adult Development Theory: New Ways of Thinking About the Life Course: New Directions for Adult and Continuing Education, No. 84* (pp. 39–47). San Francisco: Jossey-Bass Publishers.

Krase, J. (1978). "Italian-American Female College Students: A New Generation Connected to the Old." In B. B. Caroli, R. F. Harney, and L. F. Tomasi (Eds.), *Annual Conference of the American Italian Historical Association, Vol. 10, The Italian American Immigrant Woman in North America* (pp. 246–251). Toronto, Canada: Multicultural History Society of Ontario.

Krase, J. (1983). "Educational Attainment and Educational Values: Italian-American Generations." Revision of paper presented at the American Italian Historical Association XV Conference, "Italian Americans Through the Generations: The First 100 Years." October 29–31, 1982, St. John's University, Jamaica, NY.

---

[6] Generalization of findings to groups of Italian-American students beyond the geographical locale of New York City and from divergent socioeconomic backgrounds is not recommended.

Krase, J. and Fuccillo, V. J. (1975). "Italian-Americans and College Life: A Survey of Student Experiences at Brooklyn College." Unpublished manuscript, Brooklyn College, City University of New York, Department of Sociology and Center for Italian American Sudies.

Milione, V., De Rosa, C. T., and Pelizzoli, I. (2002). "Italian American High School Dropout Rate: How Are We Doing?" Retreived from Queens College, City University of New York, John D. Calandra Italian American Institute website: http://qcpages.qc.cuny.edu/calandra/research/pdf/2000hsdropout.pdf.

Perrone, J. (1986). "Italian-American Students at CUNY: A Psychoeducational Profile." 1986 Faculty Fellow report, City University of New York, Office of Student Affairs and Special Programs, Italian American Institute.

Scelsa, J. V. and Milione, V. (1990). "Statistical Profile of Educational Attainment Including High School Dropout Rate Indicators for Italian-American and Other Race/Ethnic Populations: United States, New York State, and New York City." In H. E. Landry (Ed.) *Annual Conference of the American Italian Historical Association, Vol. 23, To See the Past More Clearly: The Enrichment of the Italian Heritage* (pp. 1–18). Austin, Texas: Nortex Press.

Sue, S., and Zane, N. W. S. (1987). "The Role of Culture and Cultural Techniques in Psychotherapy: A Critique and Reformulation." *American Psychologist, 42,* 37–45.

Tribaudi, P. and Ziehler, N. L. (2002). "Stress Patterns in Adolescents: A Focus on Italian Americans." *The Italian American Review, 9,* pp. 39–71.

Vecoli, R. J. (1996). "Are Italian Americans Just White Folks?" In M. J. Bona and A. J. Tamburri (Eds.), *Annual Conference of the American Italian Historical Association: Vol. 27, Through the Looking Glass: Italian and Italian American Images in the Media* (pp. 3–17). Staten Island, New York: American Italian Historical Association.

PART ONE
Introduction

Italian Americans in Social Science Research: The Issue of Race and Ethnicity

NANCY L. ZIEHLER

The purpose of this chapter is to set the stage for the essence of the book, specifically the ten research reports that follow. Initially, I will discuss factors found in two academic disciplines that may have resulted in the exclusion of research about Italian Americans from mainstream multicultural publications. Next, since the studies in this *Research Anthology* revealed patterns and psychological issues in Italian-American students that emerged as distinct from the general student population in New York City, I will address the importance of expanding multicultural counseling literature to include diverse white ethnic groups, in this case Italian Americans. It is my contention that including and disseminating such knowledge will benefit everyone. Not only will such inclusion serve to raise awareness and cultural sensitivity among professional counselors, psychologists and educators, but students will also become the beneficiaries of interventions and strategies designed to assist them.

Readers may be surprised to learn that interest pertaining to Italian-American students in New York City was spawned as a result of the Civil Rights Movement, when Italian Americans at CUNY realized that they shared many of the same issues voiced by oppressed groups (Elmi, 1996).[1] However, while the studies within this *Research Anthology* commenced over thirty-five years ago, soon after the multicultural revolution in the helping professions began, none of the research reports can be found in mainstream publications along side of those concerning students of color and other minority ethnic groups. If assimilation had given way to cultural pluralism in the United States, why was research on Italian

---

[1] Elmi (1996) contains a complete history of the Italian-American struggle for social justice at CUNY from 1970-1994. Issues protested by Italian Americans included: under-representation of Italian-American faculty and staff at CUNY; denial of tenure and promotional opportunities; inequities in the allocation of student financial aid, resources for student organizations, acceptance into SEEK and College Discovery programs; budget cuts directed at Italian language and Italian studies programs at CUNY; and counseling that was insensitive to the needs of Italian-American students.

Americans excluded from multicultural social science literature? Several explanations may account for this fact; we will briefly consider two possibilities, located in sociology and counseling psychology.

One explanation for the dearth of published research on Italian Americans and other white ethnic groups in the US may be found in sociological theories of assimilation. Overall, these theories maintained that as generations of white ethnics progressed over time in the United States, they would lose what was culturally specific to their group while blending into and adopting the culture of the dominant white European-American society (Alba, 1985 and 1992; Gans, 1979 and 1992; Glazer and Moynihan, 1970; etc.). The beliefs of these and other authors infiltrated academe, exerting a huge impact on social science research. Many in academic circles began to view the study of white ethnic groups as Eurocentric and politically incorrect.[2] While it was acceptable to study people of color, the movement toward greater diversity seemed to render research on white ethnics unacceptable. On a personal note, in my twenty-five years as a counselor at CUNY, I have known several professionals who wished to conduct Italian-American social science research but refused to do so for fear of jeopardizing their academic careers.

The paucity of research on Italian Americans in social science publications can also be attributed to widespread confusion in the use of race and ethnicity as constructs in counseling psychology, specifically multicultural counseling research. Although many studies claimed to examine ethnicity, race and ethnicity were frequently confounded terms; this mix-up resulted in methodology that used the terms interchangeably (Cokley, 2007; Helms, 1996 and 2007). Under these conditions, researchers employed data collection practices that routinely stratified samples according to race but not ethnicity. For example, in their review of multicultural adolescent stress literature, Tribaudi and Ziehler (2002) noted, "most studies that labeled themselves 'multicultural' performed only standard data comparisons of gender and race. Although these studies attempted to examine ethnicity, race and ethnicity were used synonymously" (p. 41).

As a result, white research participants were treated as a homogeneous population based on skin color regardless of their specific cultural, socioeconomic, or ethnic group membership. This practice was also em-

---

[2] For a discussion concerning the backlash in American academe against ethnicity in white groups, particularly Italian Americans, see Vecoli, 1996.

ployed in early studies that investigated Asian, Black, and Hispanic populations. Despite their distinct ethnic group memberships, with accompanying sets of cultures and opportunities, research participants were grouped according to race, and racial categories were studied as homogeneous entities. It was not until the 1990s that multicultural counseling scholars began to address several related conceptual and methodological issues concerning race and ethnicity, thus writing extensively to clarify the differences between race, ethnicity, racial identity, and ethnic identity in future research (Betancourt and Lopez, 1993; Cokley, 2007; Helms, 1996 and 2007; Helms, Jernigan and Mascher, 2005; Helms and Talleyrand, 1997).

With regard to Italian-American students, Krase and Fuccillo (1975) were the first researchers in this *Anthology* to point out the limitation of racially stratified data collection practices.

> Italian Americans are given little opportunity to identify themselves as such; as a result, they are frequently grouped with a larger category of "white students" or a residual one of "others." It becomes impossible therefore to derive any useful data about Italian Americans given the present system by which it is collected (p. 1).

Several authors whose works appear in the present volume drew attention to this methodological weakness (Castiglione, 1982; Krase and Fuccillo, 1975; Scelsa and Milione, 1990; Tribaudi and Ziehler, 2002). While some highlighted the limitation and others did not, the totality of their work represents a collective and courageous effort to transcend it. Overall, their assertion is that, although similar to the dominant US culture in skin color, Italian Americans comprise an ethnic subculture characterized by a distinct set of values, traditions, and needs that warrants research and further understanding. These studies are not meant to deny or minimize the societal benefits experienced by Italian Americans as a result of white skin privilege; rather, they are intended to suggest that ethnic groups can experience privilege and, concurrently, endure unique challenges, stressors, and forms of oppression obscured by white skin privilege and racial categorization.

The relevance of research practices based on racial categorization rather than ethnic group membership is called into question by Italian-American students themselves who, according to the data, do not identify themselves by race. For example, when subgroups of Italian-American male and female high school students were compared with those of mixed Italian-American ancestry, it was found that none of the subgroups preferred to be identified by racial background alone (Tribaudi and Ziehler, 2002). Most strikingly, not even one respondent, including those of mixed racial and ethnic backgrounds, identified him or herself by race. Dissatisfaction with the blanket term "white" is also found among college students in two published studies. Mitrano (1999) interviewed twenty-five Italian-American students at Central Connecticut State University about their ethnic identity and found them "to question the assimilation-ist model's assumption that they are all simply 'white folks" (p. 99). In another qualitative study that used semi-structured interviews with a small number of undergraduate and graduate students, the undergraduates consistently reported that they were seen as "white" by faculty and campus administrators while their ethnicity was overlooked (Ziehler and LaRusso, 2000). Furthermore, classification as white seemed to have negative effects on these students. They described themselves as "invisible" and their accompanying narratives were characterized by feelings of alienation and lack of connection to their campus. The results of these studies seem to suggest that Italian-American students are expressing a need to be seen and researched as ethnic, rather than racial group members.

Ethnic identification and its importance to Italian Americans is underscored by the number of student research participants who identified themselves as Italian or Italian American when given the opportunity to do so. For example, Krase and Fuccillo (1975) reported that out of 290 students surveyed, 45.9% identified themselves as Italian, 35.2% identified as Italian American, 11.3% identified as American Italian, while only 5.2% identified as American. In two subsequent analyses of the same data to determine the impact of generation in the United States on ethnic identification, Krase (1978) reported that "to 92.2% of the female students and 89.1% of the male students "Italian" is a major component of their ethnic identity" (p. 249). This was regardless of the fact that 63.4% of the students' fathers and 72.2% of their mothers were born in the United States (Krase, 1983). "What is of greatest significance in these responses is the small proportion who answered 'American' alone in any case, and the high proportion who answered 'Italian'" (Krase, 1983, p. 19). Further support for the importance of ethnicity to Italian-American college students as unrelated to generational status is found in a dissertation conducted by Sterzi (1988) at the Graduate Center of City University of New

York. Sterzi found that although Italian-American undergraduate students were structurally and culturally assimilated to mainstream society, their ethnic attitudes were not related to generation and were fairly favorable to the maintenance of Italian ethnicity for the entire sample.

While these studies seem to illustrate at least the nominal importance of ethnic identification among Italian-American college students in New York City, they do not inform us about the actual meaning of ethnic identity in their lives. Further research, such as the qualitative inquiry conducted by Mitrano (1999), is needed to explore the meaning of ethnic identity, how it is constructed, and how it is psychologically and symbolically expressed by Italian-American students. What is clear, however, is that in the general conversation regarding race and ethnicity, ethnicity and ethnic identification loom as salient constructs in the lives of Italian-American students, whereas racial identity seems much less significant to their inner experience of self. This conclusion alone is a potent stimulus for further investigation and an important reason to expand multicultural counseling literature to include research on Italian Americans. Let us now consider some others.

As social scientists, we can all agree that research serves various functions. On the most basic level, it can be used to gather descriptive facts about a population from which a demographic profile can be constructed. On another level, it can be used to confirm or validate patterns that counselors and educators observe in their everyday interactions with members of specific populations. On a deeper level, research has the potential to illuminate what was previously unseen or unknown, thereby uncovering new information and creating further knowledge about the population. Finally, in the event that demographic, confirmatory, or exploratory research findings reveal unproductive patterns or issues of psychological concern, research can also be used as a basis to develop specific interventions to assist students.

The studies included in the *Research Anthology* functioned to create demographic and psychoeducational profiles, confirm patterns, uncover new information, and trigger the development of programs designed to address the educational and emotional needs of Italian-American students in NYC. Professionals working with this population need to be prepared with an awareness of this literature so that they, too, can deal with Italian-American students in an enlightened and culturally sensitive manner. Although spatial constraints preclude a content analysis of the complete array of data, the importance of publishing research on Italian-American students in multicultural counseling literature will be demonstrated through a brief discussion of select findings. Thus, results from one demographic, one confirmatory and one exploratory study will be presented, as well as one intervention program that was developed to assist students as a direct result of the confirmatory research referred to in this discussion.

While Italian-American students had become the largest single white ethnic group at CUNY in the late 1970s and early 1980s, very little was known about them. In order to determine their basic demographic characteristics, Blumberg and Lavin (1985) compared Italian Americans with other white and minority students in a longitudinal study that followed the academic careers of 11,625 freshmen who entered CUNY in the fall of 1980. Analysis of the data revealed the following socioeconomic and educational profile.

In terms of socioeconomic circumstances, Italian-American students presented themselves as traditional college students; they were younger, single, and more likely to be living with their parents. Compared to other students groups, Italian Americans were less likely to have multiple sources of financial aid; at the community college level they were less likely to have any financial assistance at all. The absence of financial assistance does not automatically translate into economic advantage, however. Although 75% of these students were not in the lowest surveyed income bracket, their reported family incomes supported a larger number of people thereby offsetting what appeared to be an income advantage. Additionally, in another demographic study contained within this volume, Castiglione (1982) found that most Italian-American students did not receive any guidance concerning grants and financial assistance in high school; a lack of information may account for their absence of financial assistance. Finally, these students placed a great deal of emphasis on paid employment (Castiglione, 1982; Blumberg and Lavin, 1985). Those enrolled at senior colleges were employed about as equally as other white students; those enrolled at community colleges, however, were more likely to be working part-time than either minorities or other white students.

Pertaining to educational factors, Italian-American students came from backgrounds in which their parents were significantly undereducated, especially in terms of college attendance. Thus, they were more likely than the other student groups to represent the first generation of their families to attend college and their educational aspirations were reported at levels well below those of minority and other white students. For instance, while 30% of minority and other white students aspired to a Ph.D. or its equivalent, only 18% of Italian Americans indicated the same. At the undergraduate level, Blumberg and Lavin (1985) found that despite adequate levels of academic preparedness to attend senior colleges, 60% of all Italian-American students were enrolled at community colleges. Most of them maintained a vocational orientation to education with 75% reporting their first reason to attend college was to get a better job.

Reflecting on the socioeconomic and educational patterns of Italian-American students described above, Gambino (1987) discussed their possible negative effects on success in college. He noted, "these patterns work against optimum academic careers . . . (and) make it more difficult for Italian-American students to be involved in and integrated in the total campus experience enjoyed by many other students" (p. 88). Thus, the profile constructed by Blumberg and Lavin (1985) depicted students who were doing well, but were heavily burdened by factors other than coursework. Updated demographic studies are needed to determine how and if the profile may have changed over the last twenty-five years.

Moving beyond demographic characteristics, Perrone (1986) went on to explore the interior experiences of students at CUNY. Among several other variables including personal values and locus of control, Perrone surveyed the major stressors experienced by Italian-American students. The data revealed that, compared to an aggregate sample of non-Italian-American students, Italian-American males and females reported very high levels of stress and anxiety. In contrast to their non-Italian-American counterparts, Italian-American males placed a very high value on working and earning an income; they also linked work with a psychological sense of independence. Perrone noted possible detrimental effects of these stressors on Italian-American males at CUNY.

> These attitudes linking work, pay and independence, unfortunately, may cause some of these students to overload themselves and coupled with the usual and expected academic concerns and pressures of achievement oriented students, create a source of distress for them. Counselors have often observed this as the precipitating cause for "dropping out," academic failure or stress-related physical and psychological effects (p. 61).

Italian-American females were found to experience greater stress and anxiety than both their male counterparts and males and females in the general student population. Forty to fifty percent admitted that the following stressors were personal problems for them: feeling depressed or sad, feeling anxious and uptight, feeling lonely, eating too much, not getting enough exercise and being overweight. Perrone concluded,

> Even allowing for some significant sampling error, it is alarming to consider the number of Italian-American women in the general CUNY student population who may be experiencing the same feelings of anxiety, loneliness and depression. This finding alone supports a greater need for effective counseling services and focused student service programs for these women (p. 64).

According to Gambino (1987), Italian-American females at CUNY "are, in a phrase, very unhappy" (p. 92). Updated research is needed to determine current stressors and stress levels experienced by Italian-American students of both genders and in comparison to various racial and ethnic group samples across CUNY.

Research on Italian-American adolescents was noticed in the early 1990s when census data was extrapolated to confirm what educators had suspected for quite some time, namely a disturbingly high dropout rate among these teens in New York City. Scelsa and Milione (1990) found that, although Italian-American teens were doing well on a nationwide and New York State level, one out of every five NYC Italian-American teens dropped out of high school, a rate of 21% or the third highest rate in NYC.

As a result of these findings, Calandra Institute and community-based programs were initiated to reverse the trend. The programs included: culturally sensitive outreach counseling in select NYC high schools to increase interest in higher education and recruit students into CUNY; AMICI, an early intervention mentor project (in conjunction with the NYS Mentor Program, founded by Matilda Cuomo, former First Lady of New York State) for at risk junior high school students; parent training meetings; and citywide seminars and conferences hosted by the Calandra Institute and various community organizations to raise the awareness of educators, counselors and the general public about this disturbing pattern.[3]

---

[3] For a further elaboration of these programs and counseling interventions, see Elmi, (1996); and Milione, De Rosa, and Pelizzoli (2002).

Based on concepts central to effective multicultural counseling, the initiatives mentioned above were each designed with cultural responsiveness at their very core. Cultural responsiveness in the context of counseling is described as "counselor responses that acknowledge the existence of, show interest in, demonstrate knowledge of, and express appreciation for the client's ethnicity and culture and that place the client's problems in a cultural context" (Atkinson and Lowe, 1995, p. 402). There is strong support for the effectiveness of cultural responsiveness as a counseling strategy with ethnic minority clients. In their review of outcome studies that examined the effects of culturally responsive versus culturally non-responsive counseling, Atkinson and Lowe (1995) reported that culturally responsive counselors were rated more positively on credibility and several therapeutic relationship measures than culturally non-responsive counselors. In addition, the authors cited evidence that culturally responsive counseling "results in greater client willingness to return to counseling, satisfaction with counseling, and depth of self disclosure" (p. 403).

In a follow-up study concerning the dropout rate, Milione, De Rosa, and Pelizzoli (2002) examined data from the 2000 US Census and found that the dropout rate among Italian-American high school students in NYC had declined dramatically. Down from 21% in 1988 to 12.1% in 2000, Italian-American teens now had one of the lowest dropout rates in NYC. Furthermore, this statistic represented the largest decline of all racial and ethnic population groups in NYC since 1988. The authors concluded that the package of specifically designed interventions, including culturally responsive counseling, mentoring and community outreach, proved successful in lowering the dropout rate of Italian-American high school students in NYC. Future research in the area of culturally responsive counseling with Italian Americans may inform and further enhance counseling practice with this population of white ethnic students.

Each of the ten reports presented in the *Research Anthology* demonstrates the necessity to conduct multicultural studies that examine students belonging to distinct ethnic groups, as opposed to racial categories. For example, were it not for the comparative dropout study conducted by Scelsa and Milione (1990), a huge problem among Italian-American teens may have gone unnoticed by the general public and, worse, the high dropout rate may have continued or even escalated over time. In light of the counseling profession's contextual mission to embrace and expand diversity, it is suggested that future reports concerning Italian Americans must appear in mainstream multicultural publications to heighten awareness and cultural sensitivity among all helping professionals. Finally, it is hoped that widespread access to the materials contained within this volume will stimulate future research on Italian-American students in NYC and other locations across the country.

References

Alba, R. D. (1985). *Italian Americans: Into the Twilight of Ethnicity*. Englewood Cliffs, NJ: Prentice-Hall.

Alba, R. D. (1990). *Ethnic Identity: The Transformation of White America*. New Haven: Yale University Press.

American Counseling Association. (2005). *Code of Ethics*. Alexandria, VA: ACA. American Psychological Association.

American Psychological Association. (2002). *Guidelines on Multicultural Education, Training, Research, Practice, and Organizational Change for Psychologists*. Washington DC: APA.

Atkinson, D. R., and Lowe, S. M. (1995). "The Role of Ethnicity, Cultural Knowledge, and Conventional Techniques in Counseling and Psychotherapy." In J. G. Ponterotto, J. M. Casas, L. A. Suzuki, and C. M. Alexander (Eds.), *Handbook of Multicultural Counseling* (pp. 387–414). Thousand Oaks, CA: Sage Publications, Inc.

Betancourt, H., and Lopez, S. R. (1993). "The Study of Culture, Ethnicity, and Race in American Psychology." *American Psychologist*, 48, 629–637.

Blumberg, A. and Lavin, D. E. (1985). "Italian-American Students at the City University of New York: A Socioeconomic and Educational Profile." Unpublished manuscript, City University of New York, Office of Institutional Research and Analysis, and the Italian American Institute.

Castiglione, L. (1982). "A Demographic Study of Italian-American College Students Attending the City University of New York." Unpublished manuscript, Queens College, City University of New York, Italian American Institute to Foster Higher Education.

Chavez, A. F., and Guido-DiBrito, F. (2000). "Racial and Ethnic Identity and Development." In M. C. Clark and R. S. Caffarella (Eds). *An Update on Adult Development Theory: New Ways of Thinking About the Life Course: New Directions for Adult and Continuing Education*, No. 84 (pp. 39–47). San Francisco: Jossey-Bass Publishers.

Cokley, K. (2007). "Critical Issues in the Measurement of Ethnic and Racial Identity: A Referendum on the State of the Field." *Journal of Counseling Psychology*, 54, 224–234.

Elmi, F. N. (1996). "The Invisible Minority: A History of the Italian-American Struggle for Justice and Equality at the City University of New York." 1993–1994 Faculty Fellow report, Queens College, City University of New York, John D. Calandra Italian American Institute.

Gambino, R. (1987). "Italian American Studies and Italian Americans at the City University of New York: Report and Recommendations." 1986–1987 Faculty Fellow report, City University of New York, Office of Student Affairs and Special Programs, John D. Calandra Italian American Institute.

Gans, H. J. (1979). "The Future of Ethnic Groups and Cultures in America." In H. J. Gans (Ed.), *On the Making of Americans: Essays in Honor of David Riesman* (pp. 193–220). Philadelphia: University of Pennsylvania Press.

Gans, H. J. (1992). "Comment: Ethnic Invention and Acculturation, a Bumpy-line Approach." *Journal of American Ethnic History*, 12, 42–52.

Glazer, N. and Moynihan, D. P. (1970). *Beyond the Melting Pot*. Cambridge: MIT Press.

Helms, J. E. (1996). "Toward a Methodology for Measuring and Assessing Racial as Distinguished from Ethnic Identity." In G. R. Sodowsky and J. C. Impara (Eds.), *Multicultural Assessment in Counseling and Clinical Psychology* (pp. 143–192). Lincoln, NE: Buros Institute of Mental Measurement.

Helms, J. E. (2007). "Some Better Practices for Measuring Racial and Ethnic Identity Constructs." *Journal of Counseling Psychology*, 54, 235–246.

Helms, J. E., Jernigan, M., and Mascher, J. (2005). "The Meaning of Race in Psychology and How to Change It." *American Psychologist*, 60, 27–36.

Helms, J. E. and Talleyrand, R.M. (1997). "Race is Not Ethnicity." *American Psychologist*, 52, 1246–1247.

Krase, J. (1978). "Italian-American Female College Students: A New Generation Connected to the Old." In B. B. Caroli, R. F. Harney, and L. F. Tomasi (Eds.), *Annual Conference of the American Italian Historical Association, Vol. 10, The Italian-American Immigrant Woman in North America* (pp. 246–251). Toronto, Canada: The Multicultural History of Ontario.

Krase, J. (1983). "Educational Attainment and Educational Values: Italian-American Generations." Revision of paper presented at the American Italian Historical Association XV Conference, "Italian Americans Through the Generations: The First 100 Years." October 29–31, 1982, St. John's University, Jamaica, NY.

Krase, J. and Fuccillo, V. J. (1975). "Italian-Americans and College Life: A Survey of Student Experiences at Brooklyn College." Unpublished manuscript, Brooklyn College, City University of New York, Department of Sociology and Center for Italian American Sudies.

Milione, V., De Rosa, C. T., and Pelizzoli, I. (2002). "Italian American High School Dropout Rate: How Are We Doing?" Retrieved from Queens College, City University of New York, John D. Calandra Italian American Institute website: http://qcpages.qc.cuny.edu/calandra/research/pdf/2000hsdropout.pdf.

Mitrano, J. R. (1999). "The Garbage Can Model of Ethnic Identity Formation: A Case Study of Generation X Italian Americans." *Italian American Review*, 7, 83–103.

Perrone, J. (1986). "Italian-American Students at CUNY: A Psychoeducational Profile." 1986 Faculty Fellow report, City University of New York, Office of Student Affairs and Special Programs, Italian American Institute.

Scelsa, J. V. and Milione, V. (1990). "Statistical Profile of Educational Attainment Including High School Dropout Rate Indicators for Italian-American and Other Race/Ethnic Populations: United States, New York State, and New York City." In H. E. Landry (Ed.) *Annual Conference of the American Italian Historical Association, Vol. 23, To See the Past More Clearly: The Enrichment of the Italian Heritage* (pp. 1–18). Austin, Texas: Nortex Press.

Sterzi, G. (1988). "Ethnicity, Socialization, and Academic Achievement of Italian-American College Students at the City University of New York." Doctoral dissertation, Graduate Center, City University of New York. *Dissertation Abstracts International, 50,* 2209.

Tribaudi, P. and Ziehler, N. (2002). "Stress Patterns in Adolescents: A Focus on Italian Americans." *The Italian American Review, 9,* 39–71.

Vecoli, R. J. (1996). "Are Italian Americans Just White Folks?" In M. J. Bona and A. J. Tamburri (Eds.), *Annual Conference of the American Italian Historical Association: Vol. 27, Through the Looking Glass: Italian and Italian American Images in the Media* (pp. 3–17). Staten Island, New York: American Italian Historical Association.

Ziehler, N. L. and LaRusso, M. G. (2000). "Italian-American Students at CUNY: An Exploratory Study of Interpersonal Conflict and Student Development." In L. Guinta (Ed.), *Dispute Resolution: An Emerging Research Agenda for the Twenty-first Century* (pp. 41–55). New York: CUNY Dispute Resolution Consortium at John Jay College of Criminal Justice.

PART TWO

Italian American Students
at the City University of New York

Italian Americans and College Life: A Survey of Student Experiences at Brooklyn College, 1975

JEROME KRASE
VINCENT J. FUCCILLO

INTRODUCTION

The task of conducting a survey of the Italian-American student population at Brooklyn College was at least one year in the making. It grew out of a series of wide-ranging discussions among the staff of the Center for Italian American Studies at the college and interested faculty and students about what could be done to improve student services, to develop programs and to inaugurate new activities that would serve the needs of this particular segment of our student body. No longer were these concerns hypothetical since the proportion of such students had since 1971 increased twofold in size (see Tables 2 and 3). Moreover, it was presumed that this group would continue to grow.

In view of these developments, there is substantial reason for improving our knowledge about these students. Statistics on various aspects of student life at the college are collected but rarely are they organized on an ethnic basis. Italian-American students are given little opportunity to identify themselves; as a result, they are frequently grouped with a larger category of "white students" or a residual one of "others." It becomes impossible therefore to derive any useful data about Italian Americans given the present system by which it is collected. Moreover, these statistics are often given in aggregated form. For our purposes, they provide little assistance in the kinds of information that we believe would be genuinely useful.

For these reasons, it was decided to develop our own questionnaire. We would construct the survey instrument, arrange for its administration, perform the necessary mechanical chores and undertake the analysis of the data.

We expected to draft a report based on this analysis and ensure that it would be widely disseminated throughout the college, the City University system, interested outside community groups and relevant governmental agencies. Such a report, we believed, was badly needed. For one thing, too little is known at present about the central characteristics of this sizable component of our student population. Program development, curricula reform, and a host of other related college activities would be immeasurably improved if more concrete information were known about the features of the clientele population for which these programs and activities are being developed. The more we know about our student population, it would seem, the more sensible will be the college planning process. Furthermore the report would assist all those who seek to provide service to students, including administrators, counselors, tutoring and remedial staffs and faculty.

The report that follows provides a general composite portrait of the Italian-American student at Brooklyn College. It offers demographic occupational and attitudinal data of various types. While it does not pretend to be comprehensive in scope, it gives a clearer indication of the central characteristics of this growing segment of our population than has to date ever been gathered, as far as we are aware.

This current report should be seen as a preliminary venture and utilizes only a small part of the available data collected in the survey. A more comprehensive analysis is planned for the coming months. We are mindful that this report may raise more questions in the minds of its readers than answers, but we believe that this is beneficial. A concerted effort to address the problems of Italian-American students is a necessary preliminary step to plans for action. The data can be found in the final section of this report. We would not wish to impose any single set of views as to the meaning of the data, but do hope that it will be employed by responsible individuals to develop their own views and conclusions.

Our own inferences, recommendations, and a number of suggestions for the appropriate policy changes, new initiatives, and actions are followed by a discussion of the methods employed in this report.

We would like to thank all those faculty and students who assisted us at various stages of this report. Special thanks goes to Mr. Ronald Caizza and Ms. Irene Ivone for their assistance with the coding. We owe a special word of thanks to all the students who took the time to complete the questionnaire. We can only hope that their efforts will not go unrewarded, as the college struggles to redefine its responsibilities and functions in the difficult years ahead.

SUMMARY OF FINDINGS

As a result of our research project we have amassed a large amount of data on Brooklyn College's Italian-American students. A large proportion of our findings are presented in the next section in the form of tables. In most cases the tables are self-explanatory and by themselves can be useful guides to learning about our Italian-American students' backgrounds, experiences and aspirations. In this section we have chosen to summarize what we feel are some of the most significant findings in the areas of opportunity for higher education and attitudes toward college and education. Finally we will offer some program and counseling suggestions as to future directions and proposals for change.

The survey and this report were both completed prior to the discontinuance at the City University of open enrollment and free tuition. We believe that our findings and recommendations therefore take on an even greater importance because of the changed situation. Not only might we be able to make informed judgments as to the effects of these changes on our present Italian-American population but also we will have a basis from which to assess the differences, if any, between pre- and post-1976 students at the college.

OPPORTUNITY FOR HIGHER EDUCATION

It is apparent that the Italian-American student has benefited from the inauguration of open admissions at City University, taking substantial advantage of the relaxation of standards for admission to attend Brooklyn College (see Table 12). In the absence of open enrollment it would appear that a significant proportion of these students would not be presently attending college. Some would of course seek admission to other institutions of higher learning in the private sector, and especially among the parochial colleges, but the vast bulk would undoubtedly move into the job market. Moreover they would find little encouragement, either in their chosen occupational fields or in their home, to pursue their education or to widen their career options. Financial constraints in addition would serve to deter even the most ambitious.

The heightened aspirations of our Italian-American students for professional careers and managerial positions is tied in part to the availability of college education. About three-quarters of our students aspire to a professional or managerial career whereas a significantly small percentage of their parents are currently employed in such occupations (see Tables 9A and 20). Approximately 63% of the fathers of our student sample have occupations in the blue-collar category with 27% employed in craft occupations; 46.6% of the mothers of our sample are employed outside of the household. Moreover, higher education continues to be the price for admission into the white-collar, professional, semi-professional and managerial occupational sectors.

Limitations imposed on the availability of college education would therefore serve not only to restrict the access by our students to these fields of employment, but would undermine the heightened aspiration levels of these students as well.

It is also clear that the continuance of a free tuition policy is an important asset for these students, a number of whom rely upon their own employment to cover personal and educational expenses (see Table 22). At least one-half of our sample are employed during the academic year, working an average of fifteen hours per week (see Table 7). About 40% of our sample comes from families of five or more, and some have other family members enrolled in college at the present time (see Table 19). This places a greater economic burden on these families, most of whom belong to the blue-collar segment of our population. It need hardly be pointed out, moreover, that this group in our society has been especially besieged of late by inordinately high rates of unemployment coupled with soaring levels of inflation.

The parents of the vast majority of our students have never attended college, and only a small handful have gone on to complete a baccalaureate degree (see Table 21). Of our sample's parents, 61.4% of the fathers and 69% of the mothers have completed at least a high school education. Only 8% of the fathers and 3.8% of the mothers have earned a college degree. Thus our students are often the first in their families to pursue a higher education. According to our findings, 69% of our sample reported that no other immediate family members (including those outside of the nuclear family) had ever earned a college degree. As a result, they are unable to rely upon parents for advice, information or other assistance on most aspects of college life. This is particularly unsettling for the Italian-American student since most of them have been regularly encouraged to rely on their families for support and advice on a wide variety of matters. With the family incapable of responding in the usual manner, the student is often thrown back on his or her own resources, in part because certain cultural traits inhibit them from utilizing the existing counseling services of the college. These services, although often seem as remote and indifferent, are nonetheless important, especially in view of the paucity of sources of institutional advice for these students who are strained by the difficulties of adjusting to a new, predictable environment.

Many of our students come from families who have only recently emigrated to the United States from Italy. Some have parents whose dominant language is Italian and, in a number of instances, this is the language that is employed in the home (see Table 8). These conditions aggravate the problems of cultural adjustment for many of our students who are now, perhaps for the first time, striving to adapt to those clusters of American values that place a high premium on higher education, professionalization, and occupational mobility. It should also be apparent that these developments, by magnifying pressure on the unity and solidarity of the Italian-American family, threaten to undermine its position as the central focus of Italian and Italian-American life.

Many of our students (38% of our sample) who express a desire to pursue a post-baccalaureate education intend to do so within the City University system (see Table 9B). By far, the major reason for this decision has to do with the matter of finances. As we have suggested, fully one-third of our students are self-supporting. A larger group works part-time to contribute to their support, while only a handful are exclusively dependent on the financial resources of their families. This makes the City University graduate school, because of its lower tuition rates than all other comparable institutions in the city, particularly attractive. In the absence of the lower tuition charged at CUNY, however, there is every likelihood that these students would simply refrain from attending any graduate school.

ATTITUDES TOWARD COLLEGE AND EDUCATION

As our survey demonstrates, Italian-American students are quite job-oriented and view their education principally from a vocational and career-based perspective (see Tables 29 and 31). This practical orientation is reinforced by parental attitudes toward higher education that range from general skepticism to overt distrust. Whatever their degree of reluctance, Italian-American families expect that a college education will prepare students for specific occupations. Moreover, the nature of these occupations is limited, being confined chiefly to those of law, medicine, teaching and business. For many of these parents, material considerations seem to be the major criteria in the evaluation of college work, degree programs and even curricular planning.

Education, especially higher education, is designed to serve some definite and often tangible purpose such as that of future employment rather than more general functions such as broadening experiences, deepening insights or enriching the quality of life.

Our students do not look upon their college education in terms of a broad social experience and the social climate of the institution seems, if not hostile, certainly distant from them. They seldom participate in extra-curricular activities at the college such as academic or social clubs, athletic events or college-sponsored sporting activities. Their free time is rarely spent at the college. Almost three-fourths of our sample report that they do not participate in the available extracurricular activities and programs on campus. Even a higher proportion report non-participation in the ac-tivities of off-campus organizations. The low levels of social participation are no doubt due in part to the considerable time that must be allocated to traveling to the campus from home. More than one-quarter of our stu-dents must travel at least forty minutes to school. Over half spend more than thirty minutes in transportation time (see Table 14B). Moreover, a good number of them are employed, on a full-time or part-time basis, and this also serves to limit greater participation in campus life.

Our students express a variety of attitudes and shades of opinion to-ward their college experiences and their contact with various aspects of the college community. While almost one-third of them do not avail themselves of the counseling services provided by the college, those that do are far from pleased by the results of these encounters (see Table 28). This negative attitude is tied, in part, to general familial views inherited by our students which disparage the role of outside institutions, seeing them as alien or at times even threatening. Powerful familially-based cul-tural norms and values thus tend to stiffen the resistance of our students to actively seek assistance, even when the need for help in academic as well as personal matters is obvious.

Clearly our students are also far from pleased with most of the other services provided by the college. However, while registration services and low-level administrators of the college are judged inadequate, Italian-American students rate the facilities and the personnel of the library very highly (see Table 28). Judgments such as these are being made in terms of some criteria, which operate either informally or in more systematic and ordered fashion. While we cannot specify with any complete precision the criteria employed or sketch the manner in which they come into play, we might suggest that our students seem particularly displeased by the impersonal quality which typifies some college services, while those services which employ more direct, face-to-face encounters are more strongly favored and appear to be more satisfying to them. Like most other college students, but especially for Italian Americans who are nurtured in the warm intimacy of their family life, bureaucratic regulations and impersonal administrators seem inflexible, stiffish and distant; these qualities, in short, are most foreign to them. As a result, their negative responses are inevitable.

On the whole, our students seem generally pleased with their course work, considering it to be both informative and relevant (see Table 28). As one might expect they express greater preference for small, more intimate classroom experiences rather than mass lecture ones (see Table 26). Although these students hesitate to meet individually with their instructors, for much the same reason that they are reluctant to tap the counseling services of the college, some do go to faculty for advice, but this is confined largely to academic matters (see Tables 24 and 25).

In general, as Table 30 reports, our students feel that they have had sufficient academic preparation in high school for college work. They feel especially well prepared in reading, and least prepared in mathematics. The students express that they feel less well prepared in writing, though perhaps this view is symptomatic of the recently noted nationwide phenomenon concerning the inadequacy of verbal skills among college-aged adults. Unfortunately the vast majority of our students do not take advantage of the college remedial and tutorial services designed to assist students to improve their writing ability and to upgrade their basic skills, (see Table 28).

We might venture to suggest a number of reasons why the tutorial services of the college are not employed more often by these students. First, the availability of these services is not sufficiently well known throughout the college. They have not been widely advertised, and thus knowledge of their existence, role and purpose are confined to a limited portion of our student body.

Second, there is a presumption that these remedial and tutoring activities are restricted to minority group students, thus discouraging others from accessing them. Finally, a lack of identification with the college as a whole, coupled with personal feelings of alienation, serve to further reinforce unwillingness by Italian-American students to use these services. Obviously, as well, they are little motivated to inform themselves about these college activities, which thus remain unknown and consequently often underutilized.

FUTURE DIRECTIONS AND PROPOSALS FOR CHANGE

At this point, we offer a few suggestions designed to improve the quality of a number of programs, activities and services at the college; provide a more supportive environment for our students; and sharpen the responsiveness of the planning process at our institution. These recommendations of course are based on a profile of the Italian-American student that is far from complete. Nonetheless the data we have gathered provides a crucial resource on the basis of which proposals for program development, curricular reform and organizational change can be more effectively fashioned and implemented. Needless to say, although at this stage we view the recommendations that follow as suggestive, we consider that they are important and that they merit active consideration.

In our view, a top priority should be assigned to the need for improvement in the areas of academic and personal counseling. In some instances we recommend a modification of the existing activities, in others we support a more significant change.

To begin with, Italian-American students in particular should be provided with adequate job and career counseling. At the same time, counselors should make a diligent effort with these students to expand their awareness of occupational opportunities and to broaden their view of the educational process so that education may be seen as something more than simply a prelude to employment. The counseling services of the college must be made more responsive to the needs and special interests of our Italian-American students. Programs and activities should be inaugurated to sensitize guidance personnel to the special demands of this segment of the college student body for not only do many of these students identify themselves as Italian Americans (see Table 17), but a striking number are able to identify what they perceive to be the unique needs, interests and dilemmas of this group. The self-awareness of the Italian-American students, with their strong sense of personal identification and their capacity to articulate needs and grievances, offers positive evidence in support of changes in the direction and structure of many of the prevailing counseling activities. We urge that more intimate formats be employed in the delivery of counseling services and that impersonal, officious, and bureaucratic student-counselor encounters be minimized. The preference of Italian-American students for face-to-face encounters makes it important to establish formats and settings of this type.

Special efforts must be undertaken to encourage Italian-American students to avail themselves of these services. A large scale, broadly based advertising campaign should be launched throughout the college using both the formal channels of communication and the informal networks. The latter are important for Italian-American students most of whom perceive that they occupy a marginal status in the college community and thus are often outside the regular formal channels. A campaign advertising the counseling services — one which stresses a growing recognition of the special needs of Italian-American students and is disseminated through the informal communication structures employed by these students — is more likely than any other undertaking to induce a positive response. It is also important to provide visible recognition of the presence and legitimate status of Italian-American students, although this matter of representation is equally pressing in other areas of college activity. The assignment of a number of Italian Americans to prominent positions within the counseling program is not unimportant and may counter an initial reluctance by these students to use these services.

We might add a brief note pertaining to the more specialized tutorial and remedial services provided by the college. Clearly they are important for some Italian-American students, although as we have noted, they are not regularly accessed. We might increase their use by wider advertising in the manner described above but, in addition, we must make a concerted attempt to de-stigmatize these activities. This is especially important for Italian-American students whose insecure status at the college makes them particularly reticent to seek any services which might, even indirectly, serve to call their academic credentials and respectability into question.

We have earlier pointed to the problem of indifference and apathy among these students toward student government fraternal groups and house plan associations. This is a reflection of a general alienation and a lack of integration into the college community as a whole. Table 29 provides some evidence of this general pattern. Italian-American students seem especially deficient when it comes to accessing a formal, institution-

alized network of contacts to facilitate this integration; hence they are often forced to rely upon their families or in the end their own personal resources. In the college setting, as we already suggested, this lack aggra-
vates problems relating to academic performance and threatens academic
success. In order to alleviate this problem, efforts must be made to construct an alternative array of integrative institutions, such as building
upon students interests, developing activities that relate more clearly to
their cultural heritage, and reducing the alien character of college. If we
are seriously committed to improving their academic success, we must
invite them to feel a part of the college and not only as commuters, encouraging their identity with the college, and minimizing the disconcert-
ing effects of their perceived isolation and alienation.

Curriculum development, lastly, is also another important area of college activity with substantial interest to our Italian-American students.
New courses must be designed for all interested in exploring the nature
of Italian heritage in the United States, broadening their perspective on
the American experience and understanding the pluralistic bases of our
contemporary society. The content of existing courses must also be modified to take account of the Italian-American experience where relevant.
For Italian-American students, these course changes and additions may
ease the tensions and conflicts that are generated by their growing sense
of self-discovery and personal awareness. Moreover, the additions and
modifications in the curriculum may encourage these students to view
the college in a more positive manner, to appreciate the accommodative
nature of the academic environment of which they are a part, and to
demonstrate to them how the structure and mandates of intellectual inquiry can be brought to bear on matters of personal and emotional interest. Curriculum reform and development is an activity that must be supported by the college, however, which must make every effort to see that
the proposed courses are widely advertised and that they be made readily available for registration at regular intervals. It is also important for
the college to publicly recognize the importance of this activity and insure
that it is accorded a top priority status. Only by means of these efforts can
Italian-American students take a step to bridge the gap that separates
them from optimal academic and personal achievement. To do any less
would be to increase the risk of failure and disappointment, and to ill
serve this important and growing segment of our student body.

TABLE 1. *Residence of Brooklyn College Italian-American Students in Brooklyn by Zip Code, Spring 1975*

ZIP CODE	PROPORTION OF SAMPLE	POST OFFICE ADDRESS
11214	11%	Bath Beach
11223	9%	Gravesend
11204	8%	Parkville
11228	7%	Dyker Heights
11234	6%	Ryder
11229	5%	Homecrest
11219	5%	Blyth Bourne
11236	4%	Canarsie
11210	4%	Vandeveer
11209	4%	Fort Hamilton
All other Brooklyn	33%	
Non-Brooklyn	4%	
	100%	

Note: Our data indicates that there is a considerable neighborhood concentration of the Italian-American student body. A substantial majority (63%) live in only 10 of Brooklyn's 37 zip code areas (see Figure 1).

FIGURE 1. *Map by Zip Code of Brooklyn College Italian-American Students, Spring 1975*

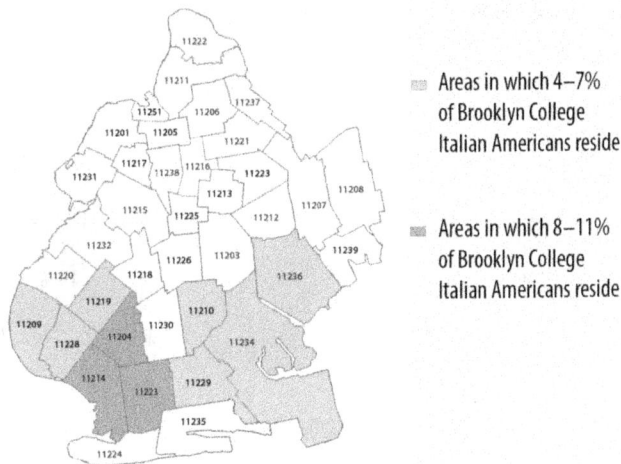

Areas in which 4–7% of Brooklyn College Italian Americans reside

Areas in which 8–11% of Brooklyn College Italian Americans reside

TABLE 2. *Class ranking of Brooklyn College Italian-American Students, Spring 1975*

LEVEL	PROPORTION OF SAMPLE
Freshman (first year)	32.1%
Sophomore (second year)	24.8%
Juniors (third year)	25.8%
Seniors (fourth year)	15.6%

TABLE 3. *Year Entered Brooklyn College Italian-American Students, Spring 1975*

YEARS	PROPORTION OF SAMPLE
Prior to 1970	4.4%
Prior to 1971	7.9%
Prior to 1972	21.4%
Prior to 1973	28.3%
Prior to 1974	29.7%
Prior to 1975*	8.3%

*Includes only spring 1975 entrants. Spring enrollment is generally much lower than fall enrollment.

TABLE 4. *College School Enrollment of Brooklyn College Italian-American Students, Spring 1975*

SCHOOL	PROPORTION OF SAMPLE
Social science	33.8%
Science	21.4%
Education	16.6%
Humanities	16.2%
Performing arts	4.1%
Other and don't know	7.9%

*Brooklyn College is divided into six schools.

TABLE 5. *Sex Distribution of Brooklyn College Italian-American Students, Spring 1975*

SEX	PROPORTION OF SAMPLE
Male	51%
Female	49%

TABLE 6. *Previous College Attendance of Brooklyn College Italian-American Students, Spring 1975*

PREVIOUS COLLEGE	PROPORTION OF SAMPLE
None	80.7%
Two year CUNY college	11.4%
Four year CUNY college	1.7%
Other colleges	6.2%
	100.0%

TABLE 7. *Employment Status of Brooklyn College Italian-American Students, Spring 1975*

EMPLOYMENT STATUS DURING ACADEMIC YEAR	PROPORTION OF SAMPLE
Employed	57.2%
Unemployed	42.8%

HOURS PER WEEK WORKED	PROPORTION OF SAMPLE "EMPLOYED"
1–10	13.0%
11–20	54.0%
21–30	22.0%
31 or more	11.0%

WEEKS PER YEAR WORKED	PROPORTION OF SAMPLE "EMPLOYED"
40 or less	29%
41 or more	71%

SUMMER EMPLOYMENT STATUS OF THOSE UNEMPLOYED DURING ACADEMIC YEAR	PROPORTION
Employed	61%
Unemployed	39%

TABLE 8. *Self-reported* Estimated Grade Point Average of Brooklyn College Italian-American Students, Spring 1975*

APPROXIMATE EQUIVALENT LETTER GRADE	GRADE POINT AVERAGE	PROPORTION OF SAMPLE
B+ to A	3.5–4.0	9.3%
B to B+	3.0–3.4	31.7%
C+ to B–	2.5–2.9	34.8%
C to C+	2.0–2.4	16.6%
	Below 1.9	2.0%
	Don't know	5.5%

*It should be noted that students, when self-reporting grades, tend to inflate them.

TABLE 9. *Long-range Occupational Goals of Brooklyn College Italian-American Students, Spring 1975*

A. NON-ACADEMIC PURSUITS	PROPORTION OF SAMPLE
Professional and managerial	73.8%
Business and administrative	1.0%
Clerical and crafts	1.0%
Undecided	24.2%

B. POST-BACCALAUREATE EDUCATION	PROPORTION OF SAMPLE
CUNY	43.7%
New York City private	25.5%
New York State public or private	6.3%
Outside New York State	7.2%
Undecided	17.3%

TABLE 10. *Immediate Plans After Graduation from Brooklyn College Italian-American Students, Spring 1975*

PLANS	PROPORTION OF SAMPLE
Graduate school	26.2%
Work	42.8%
Marriage	3.1%
Travel and miscellaneous	7.6%
Undecided	20.3%

TABLE 11. *Perceived Obstacles to Attaining Career or Professional Goals of Brooklyn College Italian-American Students, Spring 1975*

OBSTACLE	PROPORTION OF SAMPLE
None	39.3%
Ethnic or national background	16.2%
Sex	13.8%
Age	12.4%
Race	6.9%
Religion	3.4%
Physical appearance	3.1%
*Other and don't know	4.8%

*Question responded to reads: "Which of the following will present the greatest disadvantage to your attaining your career or occupational goals?"

TABLE 12. *Other Colleges to which Brooklyn College Italian-American Students Applied for Admission, Spring 1975*

TYPE OF COLLEGE	PROPORTION OF SAMPLE
Other CUNY four year	39.0%
CUNY two year	13.2%
Private New York City	29.6%
Public New York State	5.0%
Private New York State	13.2%

Note: 89% of our sample stated Brooklyn College was their first choice of CUNY colleges. Almost half of our sample applied exclusively to Brooklyn College for admission.

TABLE 13. *High Schools Attended by Brooklyn College Italian-American Students, Spring 1975*

HIGH SCHOOL	PROPORTION OF SAMPLE
Brooklyn public	46.9
Brooklyn private or parochial	44.5
Other public	3.1
Other private or parochial	2.8
No response	2.7

Note: About half of our sample (47.3%) have graduated from private or parochial high schools; 90.7% of the sample had pursued a college preparatory secondary school curriculum.

TABLE 14. *Mode of Transportation and Length of Travel Time of Brooklyn College Italian-American Students, Spring 1975*

A.	MODE OF TRANSPORTATION	PROPORTION OF SAMPLE
	Bus	55.9%
	Automobile	.9%
	Subway	8.3%
	Walk	6.2%
	Other	1.7%

B.	TRAVEL TIME TO COLLEGE FROM HOME	PROPORTION OF SAMPLE
	0–19 minutes	22.1%
	20–29 minutes	23.1%
	30–39 minutes	17.2%
	40–49 minutes	17.6%
	50–59 minutes	6.2%
	More than one hour	13.1%
	No response	.7%

TABLE 15. *Religious Preference of Brooklyn College Italian-American Students, Spring 1975*

PREFERENCE	PROPORTION OF SAMPLE
Roman Catholic	83.5%
No preference	7.9%
Jewish	2.8%
Other Catholic	1.7%
Protestant	.3%
Other and no response	3.8%

TABLE 16. *Frequency of Attendance at Religious Services of Brooklyn College Italian-American Students, Spring 1975*

FREQUENCY	PROPORTION OF SAMPLE
Once per week	34.5%
Once per month	8.3%
Important holidays only	19.3%
Once per year	7.9%
Weddings and funerals only	15.5%
Never	11.4%
No response	3.1%

TABLE 17. *Ethno-national Self-identification* of Brooklyn College Italian-American Students, Spring 1975*

ETHNO-NATIONAL GROUP	PROPORTION OF SAMPLE
Italian	45.9%
Italian and American	35.2%
Italian and other	11.3%
American	5.2%
Other	1.0%
No response	1.4%

*Question responded to reads: "Of which ethnic or nationality group do you consider yourself to be a member?"

TABLE 18. *Use of Italian Language at Home of Brooklyn College Italian-American Students, Spring 1975*

FREQUENCY OF USE	PROPORTION OF SAMPLE
Frequently	7.2%
Regularly	12.1%
Occasionally	22.4%
Rarely	6.6%
Never	51.7%

TABLE 19. *Size of Household of Brooklyn College Italian-American Students, Spring 1975*

NUMBER IN HOUSEHOLD	PROPORTION OF SAMPLE
3 or less	19.9%
4	34.5%
5	25.2%
6	11.4%
7 or more	7.6%
Not reporting	1.4%

TABLE 20. *Father's and Mother's Occupation of Brooklyn College Italian-American Students, Spring 1975*

OCCUPATION	FATHER	MOTHER
Professional, technical, and kindred	18.6%	15.5%
Managers, proprietors, and official	19.9%	11.1%
Clerical and kindred	5.3%	37.2%
Sales	6.1%	6.6%
Crafts and kindred	27.0%	15.5%
Operatives	6.5%	3.7%
Private household	2.0%	3.0%
Service	5.7%	3.0%
Labor	8.9%	4.4%

TABLE 21. *Father's and Mother's Education of Brooklyn College Italian-American Students, Spring 1975*

NUMBER OF YEARS COMPLETED	FATHER	MOTHER
8 or less	17.9%	13.8%
9–11	21.7%	17.2%
12	37.9%	52.1%
13–15	10.3%	8.6%
16	3.8%	1.7%
17+	1.4%	.7%
Graduate degree	2.8%	1.4%
Did not report	4.1%	5.2%

TABLE 22. *Principal Means of Financial Support for Brooklyn College Italian-American Students, Spring 1975*

MEANS OF SUPPORT	PROPORTION OF SAMPLE
Parents	60.1%
Self-employment	31.0%
Scholarship	1.7%
Veteran's benefits	1.4%
Other	5.8%

TABLE 23. *Attitudes Toward Job Placement and Advice of Brooklyn College Italian-American Students, Spring 1975*

THE COLLEGE SHOULD PROVIDE	PROPORTION OF SAMPLE
Actual job placement	9.3%
Advice and interviewing facilities	6.2%
Both of the above	81.4%
Neither of the above	1.7%
No response	1.4%

TABLE 24. *Best Sources for Advice on Personal Problems as Perceived by Brooklyn College Italian-American Students, Spring 1975*

SOURCE	PROPORTION OF SAMPLE
Faculty members	7. 9%
Friends	17.9%
Administration	11.0%
Counseling services	8.6%
Student associations	.3%
Other	3.4%
No response	60.7%

TABLE 25. *Best Sources for Advice on Academic Problems as Perceived by Brooklyn College Italian-American Students, Spring 1975*

SOURCE	PROPORTION OF SAMPLE
Faculty members	24.1%
Friends	6.9%
Administration	6.9%
Counseling services	36.9%
Office of student affairs	.3%
Student associations	.3%
Other	1.4%
No response	23.1%

TABLE 26. *Ranking of Types of Classroom Experiences Preferred by Brooklyn College Italian-American Students, Spring 1975*

TYPE	PROPORTION OF FIRST CHOICES
Small discussion	34.5%
Small lecture	31.4%
Field work	7.9%
Large lecture	7.6%
Laboratory	6.9%
Small seminar	5.5%
Other	6.2%

TABLE 27. *Rating of Instructors by Brooklyn College Italian-American Students, Spring 1975*

	PROPORTION WHO ARE SUPERIOR TEACHERS
Almost all	9.6%
More than half	29.7%
Less than half	34.5%
Very few	23.1%
None at all	1.7%
No response	1.4%

TABLE 28. *Perceived Satisfaction with College Experiences of Brooklyn College Italian-American Students, Spring 1975**

	UNSATISFIED			SATISFIED			
	EXTREMELY	VERY	MODERATELY	MODERATELY	VERY	EXTREMELY	NO RESPONSE
Personal counseling services	20.7	9.7	9.7	17.7	5.5	4.1	32.4
Tutoring services	4.1	3.4	7.6	14.5	4.8	1.7	63.8
Academic counseling	20.3	12.4	11.4	21.0	6.9	6.2	21.7
Secretarial and service staff	20.0	10.3	18.3	27.2	8.6	3.4	12.1
Administrators	15.9	9.3	12.4	23.4	7.2	2.4	29.3
Registration services	29.7	9.0	16.6	26.2	7.2	3.1	8.3
Library staff	2.4	1.7	7.2	33.8	27.6	13.4	13.8
Library facilities	5.2	2.4	10.7	29.0	27.2	16.9	8.6
Friendliness of students	9.3	7.9	16.9	31.4	19.7	11.0	3.8
Campus food service	15.9	9.3	17.2	30.0	11.4	2.8	13.4
College bookstore	13.8	8.3	16.2	36.2	16.9	3.8	4.8
Non-college bookstore	7.6	7.6	14.5	37.6	22.8	4.1	5.9
Amount gained from courses	4.5	3.4	9.7	39.7	28.3	11.0	3.4
Relevance of courses	7.9	5.5	15.9	33.1	22.8	11.0	3.8
Major department	6.6	6.2	11.7	25.9	30.7	6.2	12.8
Location of buildings	9.0	10.0	21.7	35.2	19.3	2.4	2.4
Classroom comfort	1.7	1.4	7.9	35.5	36.2	11.0	6.2
Internal structure of building	4.8	4.1	17.6	38.6	23.1	5.5	6.2
Extracurricular recreational facilities	2.1	2.8	11.0	19.3	20.7	9.3	34.8
Learning centers	1.7	1.7	4.5	17.6	11.4	2.8	60.3
Remedial courses	3.4	1.0	2.1	9.3	4.5	1.7	77.9
Student union facilities	3.1	2.4	6.9	21.0	29.3	20.0	17.2
Study space at college	10.3	8.3	14.8	29.0	19.0	9.3	9.3

*All figures given represent sample proportions.

TABLE 29. *Opinions Regarding College Experience Brooklyn College Italian-American Students, Spring 1975**

	DISAGREE			NO OPINION	AGREE		
	TOTALLY	GREATLY	MILDLY	NO OPINION	MILDLY	GREATLY	TOTALLY
I feel comfortable or "at home" at Brooklyn College	11.4	8.6	17.6	2.8	34.5	15.2	9.0
If I had a choice now I would attend BC	16.9	10.0	12.4	5.9	20.3	18.3	15.0
I come to BC in my free time	50.7	11.7	8.6	9.3	10.7	4.1	4.0
School work is easy for me	8.3	8.6	29.7	5.2	35.2	9.7	2.0
If I get a good job I wouldn't go to college	43.8	15.2	10.3	6.2	11.0	4.5	9.0
My employment interferes with school work	34.1	10.3	12.1	16.2	14.1	7.9	5.0
Courses here have little relevance to my life experience	18.6	11.7	29.3	7.2	20.7	5.9	6.0
The college should prepare students for jobs	5.2	2.8	6.2	7.2	22.4	21.4	33.0
Requirements for degrees make good sense	9.3	9.3	17.9	6.2	29.7	13.4	13.0
College should be stricter about student discipline	29.3	22.1	11.0	17.2	12.4	4.1	3.0
Grades are given out fairly by teachers	14.5	11.4	24.1	6.6	28.3	9.7	4.0
There is no favoritism shown by BC administrators	33.4	18.6	12.8	24.1	6.9	2.1	1.0
I feel that I am part of a Brooklyn College community	31.4	9.3	17.6	13.8	18.3	5.9	3.0
Many of my neighborhood friends go to Brooklyn College	31.0	9.3	12.4	4.8	20.7	11.0	10.0
Many of my high school friends go to Brooklyn College	24.8	11.7	11.4	3.8	26.9	10.1	11.0
Students who need help have no trouble getting it	21.7	19.0	16.2	22.4	10.0	4.5	5.9
My college education is important to me	3.8	0.7	1.4	2.1	9.0	24.1	56.2
My college education is important to my father	6.2	1.4	4.8	9.3	16.6	17.6	42.4
My college education is important to my mother	4.1	1.4	4.5	8.3	16.9	20.7	42.4
Most students at Brooklyn College are different from me	9.3	10.3	17.2	15.2	23.8	11.4	12.8
Most students at BC have the same likes and dislikes I have	12.4	12.1	20.0	17.9	22.1	10.0	5.5
I would prefer a college where students are more like me	18.3	9.3	12.8	24.1	16.2	7.6	11.7

*All figures given represent sample proportions.

TABLE 30. *Adequacy of Preparation for College Work, Brooklyn College Italian-American Students, Spring, 1975**

	VERY POORLY	POORLY	NOT FAIRLY WELL	FAIRLY WELL	VERY WELL	NO RESPONSE
Reading	2.4	2.4	10.3	29.3	52.4	2.8
Writing	4.8	7.9	17.2	36.2	31.4	2.4
Mathematics	6.6	7.9	19.0	26.9	34.5	5.2
Class discussion	4.8	7.2	9.7	36.6	38.3	3.4
Taking exams	1.7	4.1	12.8	43.8	34.8	2.8
Using library	7.2	6.2	13.1	34.5	35.5	3.4

*All figures given represent sample proportions.

TABLE 31. *Perceived Importance of General Student Objectives in College, Brooklyn College Italian-American Students, Spring 1975**

	NO RESPONSE	UNIMPORTANT	NOT VERY IMPORTANT	FAIRLY IMPORTANT	VERY IMPORTANT
Social activities	2.4	17.6	31.0	27.6	20.7
Student government	2.8	31.7	38.3	19.7	7.6
Cultural activities	3.8	13.4	30.3	36.2	16.2
Course work	5.2	1.7	8.3	33.1	51.7
Sports	2.8	21.7	23.8	24.5	27.2
Earning money	2.8	3.4	13.1	37.2	43.1
Grades	3.4	3.8	5.2	27.2	60.3
Intellectual pursuits	3.4	3.1	4.8	31.7	56.9
Specific job training	3.1	3.4	12.8	28.6	52.1
Learning how to solve problems	6.2	9.7	14.8	30.3	38.6

*All figures given represent sample proportions.

OUTLINE OF THE RESEARCH

The preliminary results of the Italian-American student survey, presented in this volume in the form of tables and brief summaries, were the product of a multi-staged process.

I. THE PILOT SURVEY

During the fall semester of 1974, we surveyed a small number of members of the Italian American Student Union (IASU) at the college. Questionnaires were distributed to students attending IASU functions and they were asked to return them to the Center for Italian American

Studies or the IASU. The aims of the small-scale study were:

1. To assess the receptiveness of students to a later, larger scale re-search project. The prior experiences of other researchers at the school had taught us that students on the campus were reluctant to participate in college-wide surveys. The results of our pilot project convinced us that our own survey had to be more than just another questionnaire if we were to gain the cooperation of the students.

2. To obtain a general picture of the concerns and problems the stu-dents themselves were concerned with, before surveying those aspects of their lives. In the pilot survey, most of the questions were open-ended. Reviews of the completed questionnaires, and discussions with students who had, and had not, filled out one, provided us with greater insight into the kinds of things the students were interested in and concerned about, these meetings also gave us ideas about how best to enlist their maximum cooperation and support.

Because the center staff was deeply concerned with the needs and as-pirations of our research subjects, we wished to draw from among them qualified students and student representatives to assist us in all phases of the project. In other words, we tried to establish a good working relation-ship between subjects and researchers for their mutual benefit. The pilot survey brought us to the attention of the students and also brought to our attention students who would later be of valuable assistance to us as re-search assistants and student-staff liaisons.

Although the number of returned questionnaires was low (28), they contributed greatly to the success of the later large-scale project. A gen-eral benefit was that it brought us closer to the population we wished to study, and we were able to make informed judgments as to the content of the final questionnaire, and the procedures to be followed in its distribu-tion, collection and analysis.

II. DRAWING THE SAMPLE

Drawing the sample for the study was the most difficult and sensitive part of the entire project. To begin with, for various reasons, there exists no reliable breakdown of students at the college by ethnic group. There are also no master lists of students organized by ethnicity. Therefore, our first problem was to assemble on our own, a list of Italian-American stu-dents at Brooklyn College. This became our survey population.

THE POPULATION

In assembling the population the trust and cooperation of Italian-American students was invaluable. The college provided the center with a master list of all the students; some 30,000 names and addresses. Knowledgeable students and faculty members reviewed the list and noted those persons who were definitely Italian American. We also were able to add to the selected list the names of those persons who were members of the IASU or who had signed rosters we had circulated at Italian-American student activities. These names of course were insufficient, but they did help us to make a good start in assembling our population. We were also able to obtain at this point students who might have been overlooked in the later stages of population selection, the methods of which concentrated on the "Italian-ness" of the students' names.

GENERAL (NON-INFORMED) SELECTION

The general selection procedure for the Italian-American student population involved three more or less valid and reliable criteria. How were validity and reliability established?

1. Last name was the first and most important criterion for population selection. We did not employ a simple process of choosing stereotypical Italian names (such as those ending with a vowel). The judges in the selection process were Italian-American students or faculty with some familiarity with Italian language and customs. Therefore, the entire surname and not merely the final vowel was the focus of their determination. Each name was also reviewed by at least two different judges.

2. The individual's first name was also considered, especially in those cases in which the last name left some doubt as to the appropriateness of inclusion in the population. Again, the familiarity of the judges with Italian language and customs was a valuable asset.

3. Finally, in dealing with names that were the most marginal, the residence (address) of the individual was included as a factor in the selection process. The fact that an individual with a possibly Italian name lived in a definable Italian-American neighborhood added to the likelihood that they would be added to the population. The locations of Italian-American neighborhoods were gathered from a recent study by the Congress of Italian-American Organizations.

As a result of this selection process 3,186 individuals were chosen as comprising the Italian-American student population at Brooklyn College or 11% of the total college population estimated at 30,000 at the Flatbush campus in all divisions. A breakdown of the population by sex and residence (zip code number) was accomplished at this point in order to provide some reference points to establish some degree of representativeness of the later sample to be drawn randomly from this population (see Tables A and B on pages 42–43).

THE SAMPLES

We in effect, have two samples to be considered in our study. The mailing sample of 981 randomly selected students sent questionnaires and the working sample of 290 returned by Italian-American students early enough to be included in this report. The mailing sample was drawn with a random sample method utilizing a random digit technique. All of those selections were mailed a questionnaire. Of those mailed out 339 were returned.

Of these, 31 were returned by the post office as undeliverable and 308 were completed returns. Of these, 290 could be defined as Italian-American respondents and 18 as non-Italian-American respondents. There are also 13 Italian-American returns that have not been coded and are not included in our present working sample.

Therefore, the response rate for the mailed questionnaire was 32.4% based on 308 completed returns and 950 valid addresses. This could be considered a better than average performance for mailed surveys and exceptional if we consider the following factors:

1. The lack of success of other student surveys.

2. The extreme length of the research instrument.

3. The sensitivity of many of the questions.

4. The traditional attitudes of Italian Americans and other ethnics toward protecting their privacy.

5. The absence of effective follow-up procedures due to the small budget of the project and the emphasis we placed on protecting the privacy of our potential subjects.

CONFIDENCE IN THE SAMPLE

We have confidence in the representativeness, reliability and usefulness of our working sample as a good picture of the Italian-American student population at Brooklyn College for a number of reasons. In this study, our goal is to make general statements about: the characteristics of a basically unknown population; therefore, our findings at this point should be reasonable estimates of population characteristics. Normally, when drawing a sample some important characteristics of the population are known beforehand. Then it is a relatively simple process of selecting a sample size and to use other techniques of sampling to increase confidence in one's ability to draw inferences about the population from knowledge about the sample. We have available to us at present only two pieces of reliable information about the Italian-American student population at Brooklyn College — sex and residence. Comparing these known population characteristics (which we ourselves assembled) we see no significant difference between our sample and the population. This increases our confidence in the representativeness of our sample and the reliability of our findings (see Tables A and B).

Another method to establish a high level of confidence in our sample data, i.e., that our sample results are good estimates of the characteristics of our population, is to consider whether the size is large enough to produce a distribution of values for each table that would be similar to a distribution of values had we in fact surveyed the entire population.

We have followed this procedure for our data using statistical techniques that give us an estimate of the possible range of error between our sample results and hypothetical population values.

Our tables of raw data, which are not presented in this volume, give the estimates of standard error for means. We have independently computed the most conservative standard error for means proportions.[1] Essentially we choose a 95% confidence level as a reasonable degree of trust in our sample results. This means that we are at least 95% sure that our sample data is an accurate estimate of our population characteristics within a narrow range (or interval) of possible variations. The tables and preliminary findings presented and discussed in this report have been

---

[1] The formulas used for establishing 95% confidence intervals for the data presented in this report are:

For sample Means: $X \pm 1.96 \frac{\sigma}{\sqrt{N}}$

For sample Proportions: $P_s \pm 1.96 \sqrt{\frac{PuQu}{N}}$

The Standard error of the mean $(\frac{\sigma}{\sqrt{N}})$ was computed for each table separately.

The Standard error of proportions $\sqrt{\frac{PuQu}{N}}$ was computed employing the most conservative method,

i.e., Pu = .50.

conservatively selected from our raw tables and modified to reduce statistical errors.

TABLE A. *Difference of Proportions: Italian-American Student Population and Sample by Sex**

	POPULATION		SAMPLE	
	NUMBER	PROPORTION	NUMBER	PROPORTION
Male	1703	53.5%	143	50.9%
Female	1483	46.5%	141	49.1%
Total	3186	100.0%	287*	100.0%

Note: Using the formula, $Z = \dfrac{Ps - Pu}{\sqrt{Pu \; Qu/N}}$ to compare the sex distributions (proportions) of population and sample we find the difference not to be statistically significant.

   $Z = -1.15$ $P = .246$

*The total number of students in the Italian-American sample is 290, but three "no response" answers to the sex questions were recorded.

TABLE B. *Comparison of Italian-American Student Population and Sample by Zip Code (residence)*

ZIP CODE	POPULATION		SAMPLE	
	NUMBER	PROPORTION	NUMBER	PROPORTION
11201	22	.69%	3	1.03%
11203	68	2.13%	11	3.79%
11204	247	7.76%	24	8.29%
11205	17	.53%	3	1.03%
11206	23	.72%	6	2.07%
11207	20	.63%	0	0.00%
11208	26	.82%	4	1.38%
11209	61	1.91%	12	4.14%
11210	106	3.33%	13	4.48%
11211	32	1.00%	4	1.38%
11212	12	.38%	0	0.00%
11213	12	.38%	1	.34%
11214	282	8.85%	32	11.04%
11215	82	2.57%	6	2.07%
11216	6	.19%	1	.34%
11217	15	.47%	1	.34%
11218	122	3.83%	9	3.10%
11219	153	4.80%	15	5.17%
11220	66	2.07%	5	1.72%
11221	19	.59%	0	0.00%
11222	5	.16%	2	.69%
11223	295	9.27%	26	8.98%
11224	24	.75%	2	.69%
11225	20	.63%	3	1.03%
11226	51	1.60%	4	1.38%
(continued on next page)				

(continued from previous page)				
11227	17	.53%	2	.69%
11228	183	5.74%	21	7.25%
11229	143	4.49%	14	4.83%
11230	115	3.61%	8	2.76%
11231	54	1.69%	7	2.41%
11232	19	.60%	1	.34%
11233	3	.09%	0	0.00%
11234	247	7.76%	17	5.86%
11235	61	1.91%	3	1.03%
11236	166	5.21%	12	4.14%
11237	14	.44%	2	.69%
11238	18	.56%	0	0.00%
Brooklyn, no zip	23	.72%	0	0.00%
Non-Brooklyn	337	10.58%	16	5.52
Total	3186	100.00%	290	100.00%

Note: Using a chi-square test to test the independence of the population and sample distribution by zip codes, we find the difference between the two distributions not to be statistically significant.

$x^2 = 1.65$ d.f.=17   p=.99

For the purpose of using the chi-square test, zip codes 1, 15, 17, and 31, 5, 6, 11, 16, 22, 37, and 38, 24, 29, and 35, 7, 8, 12, 13, 25, 27, and 33, 9, 20, and 32, 3, and 26 were combined to give expected frequencies greater than 10. To preserve geographic meaning of the areas the zip codes combined were contiguous zones.

III: THE QUESTIONNAIRE

In constructing the research instrument a number of factors were considered in order to maximize its effectiveness. Before constructing our own questionnaire we consulted with others at the college who had conducted student surveys in the past. We reviewed their instruments in reference to structure length, types of questions, etc., and noted strengths and weaknesses. For example, we found that student responses decreased as the questions became more personal, or asked for sensitive disclosure such as income. We learned from speaking with other researchers that students in general were hostile to institutional surveys and that most researchers experienced very low response rates to mailed questionnaires. Even student evaluations of faculty, when done on a voluntary basis, were by and large avoided by the students.

We intended to deal with many possibly sensitive issues and to use a mailing distribution and return procedure. Therefore we decided to take a somewhat radical approach in order to insure the achievement of our research goals. We learned by speaking with students and faculty that students felt that surveys were intrusions into their privacy and that they were tools of the college and not of benefit to them. They viewed questionnaires, particularly very structured ones, as coercive and not attuned to their interests. They seemed to want to express themselves with a minimum number of restrictions. Therefore, the structure of our instrument was made looser than we would have liked. We provided many opportunities for our subjects to express themselves in open-ended questions. We had also previously determined what kind of things the students themselves were interested in and included these kinds of issues along with questions representing our own interests.

The identity of the subject, who would answer questions openly, became a major problem. We decided to make it actually impossible for the returned questionnaire to be connected with any particular student. Therefore, no identification number was placed on the instruments. (This resulted in later problems in follow-up procedures.) The cover letter promised complete anonymity and the staff communicated that pledge to Italian-American students and student representatives during formal and informal encounters. In other words, we tried to gain the confidence of our subjects by demonstrating our respect and concern for them. We would recommend this extra effort to all others who wish to conduct research at the college level.

The questionnaire was constructed in such a manner to make it interesting and simple for the students to understand. Common language was used wherever possible and a minimum of survey or social science jargon was employed. The instrument covered a wide variety of issues and aspects of the students' home and college life that we were certain they would be willing to talk about. Some questions were included and some worded in such a way as to amuse the respondent, who was in effect, burdened with a rather long questionnaire.

The questionnaire was long because we had determined that the students who would be willing to fill it out would do so almost regardless of its length. Alternately, those who resented it, or who simply didn't fill out questionnaires as a matter of individual preference or principle, would reject one of any length.

Also, the results of a short questionnaire would ultimately be insufficient to meet our research goal of establishing a solid base of information from which to work. A number of questions from a survey by the Brooklyn College Division of Institutional Research were included in our survey in order to allow us to make some comparisons between our own population and the general college student body.

IV. MAILING AND FOLLOW-UP PROCEDURES

The questionnaire was mailed to the 981 members of the simple random sample. Included in the package were a cover letter and a self-addressed, stamped envelope. The cover letter, on Center for Italian American Studies stationary and signed by the center director and project director, explained the general goals of the survey, promised complete confidentiality and requested the cooperation of all those who received the questionnaire. The mailing commenced on April 9, 1975 and took two weeks to complete. Very shortly afterward, completed questionnaires began arriving at about 50 per week. The returns slowly declined and a follow-up letter was then mailed to all in the sample on May 30. It was necessary to send the letter to all in the sample due to our commitment to preserve the anonymity of the subjects. The questionnaire and subjects had not been given identification codes until after they were anonymously returned. We realize that this extra precaution was not necessary and that we could rely on our integrity, but because we were working closely with our student subjects, our promises had to be concretized. The follow-up letter resulted in a few more returns but by the middle of June 1975, they had virtually stopped coming in.

Other factors that decreased the response rate, besides general student reluctance and the size and scope of our instrument, were:

1. The research took place at the end of spring semester and continued through the summer vacation. Concern about examinations, graduation and the vacation mentality undoubtedly held the response rate down.

2. There is, however, a more important and salient factor involved. Students at commuter colleges such as Brooklyn College do not see themselves as members of a college campus community. Therefore, extracurricular activities, surveys being one type, are not very important to students and they tend not to participate in extra events and projects.

V. CODING

Most of the responses were fairly easy to code and some had been pre-coded, such as those taken from prior surveys. Many questions called for simple yes-no answers, or asked for numerical responses that were either entered as is or were later fitted into pre-coded numerical frames. There were several questions that provided the subject with an option to choose from pre-ordered categories. A battery of questions dealing with student satisfaction with and evaluation of the college were pre-scaled and simply called for them to enter a number corresponding to the scale. All these types of questions were easily coded.

The open-ended questions, of which there were a large number, were of course much more difficult to code. These were reserved until after a majority of the simple questions of the completed questionnaires were coded. Coders were instructed to take lists of responses that were developed into categories and assigned values.

Many of the most open of the open-ended questions remain to be analyzed, perhaps in a content analysis framework. There is also a great deal of potential information in the completed questionnaires that has not been coded due to lack of available resources. The data presented in this volume are of the most general and simple kinds. Perhaps 50% of the available information has presently been coded and subject to analysis.

The coded responses were entered onto "Opscan" sheets. Each questionnaire was given an identification number to facilitate later cross-tabulations and the sheets were converted mechanically to data processing cards that eliminated the need for card punching staff. This partially made up the time for the extra processing due to the fact that the instrument was not completely pre-coded.

For each subject there exists at present three cards, or decks. The data is composed of 870 cards and 188 variables. The variables range in value from 0–9. Due to the lack of multiple punching, some variables are collapsed decreasing at present the range of available information. It is suggested that the center at some future date (given the opportunity) recode these responses by creating two or more character field widths. The recoding would also allow the insertion and analysis of reserved data and in general a more informed and efficient organization of the data would result.

The original raw data is kept in storage at the center office for future coding revision and analysis, particularly the content analysis of extended student comments.

VI. MACHINE ANALYSIS

The coded data cards are organized in such a way as to make extensive use of the Statistical Package for the Social Sciences (SPSS), a canned program that is available at the Brooklyn College computer center. This makes possible the utilization of the computer center machine and staff capabilities. The center staff is also familiar with the program and machine processing techniques available. The descriptive tables, data and simple analysis we provided are the result of the use of the Brooklyn College computer center staff and facilities. Later more complicated and specific analysis can be easily performed. The data therefore has a great potential for use by a wide variety of faculty and students interested in studying the Italian-American students at Brooklyn College. The Center for Italian American Studies, at present, plans to do a series of more specific reports utilizing the college computer center if funds and time become available.

VII. FUTURE RESEARCH

Besides the necessity to revise the materials already collected in order to maximize the usefulness of our data, the center staff believes that a modest program of future research activities be undertaken. At first these will be focused primarily on Brooklyn College's Italian-American student population. However, we believe that with the knowledge and experience gained from this basically exploratory survey, we should widen our focus to include Italian-American students at other CUNY colleges, and ultimately studies of other ethnic student populations in CUNY and outside of it, in order to provide us and other interested parties with the capability to make interethnic comparisons.

We also believe that our research should take a longitudinal or panel direction, repeating the survey at two to four year intervals in order to note changes within our various populations. Our present modest project and report has much to offer despite its limitations and we are certain that a larger scale, or better institutionalized project, would be an invaluable source of information to make the best judgments about decisions which affect all of our students.

Acknowledgements

In arranging for needed typing and secretarial assistance, we would like to take this opportunity to thank the Congress of Italian-American Organizations and its director, Mary Sansone. A special thank you goes to Jo Anne Guistino, Linda Savasta, Sandy Talerico, Norma Genco, Anne Brancato, Venice Maniscola and Francis Ciatta for their work in typing a number of versions of this report. We are also grateful to Professor Tom Birkenhead for his support during the early stages of this project.

Italian-American Female College Students: A New Generation Connected To the Old

JEROME KRASE

As so well documented and analyzed by Judith E. Smith, Sharon Hartman Strom, and Colleen L. Johnson, Italian-American women have traveled a great distance over three generations and thousands of miles to arrive at their present station. The young Italian-American women students at Brooklyn College in New York City about whom I report are in many respects representative products of past generations of the slowly Americanized and modernized Italian immigrant woman.

Although it can be argued (for example, Kessner, 1977, pp. 83–87, and many others) that Italian women have not moved upward as rapidly as their counterparts among other immigrant groups, a more intriguing and valid evaluation of their progress, I suggest, could be made if we compare them to Italian-American men. The movement toward sexual equality is as important for female social mobility as the broader assimilation process. I offer the idea that sexual equality is, in fact, part of the American assimilation process itself. I also firmly believe that from the current generation of Italian-American women will emerge the significant influence that will carry Italian-Americans, in general, to a position of parity with those groups to which they have historically been less than positively compared.

My own findings, based on a limited study of a small population of Italian-American women, will be expanded to include national, and perhaps international, samples of descendants of Italian immigrants to the new world. In my research a sample of 291 (146 female and 141 male students answered the sex identification question) Italian-American students of the estimated 3,000 at Brooklyn College in the spring of 1974, returned an extensive mailed questionnaire. The instrument concerned, among many other issues, their family backgrounds, college experiences, and their future plans. From this data a profile of the Italian-American students at the college was complied and a report produced (Krase and Fuccillo, 1975).

This paper is based on cross tabulations and simple statistical analyses of the Italian-American students, by sex, for over 180 variables. The general results of these comparison show that the two subsamples differ significantly (for chi-squares p. 05) on only a few items. In particular the study may undermine a number of myths — both stated and unstated — about Italian-American mothers and the Italian-American family in general. Myth 1: Italian-American women are essentially housewives, and those who do work are employed in low status jobs. My own sample of 291 mothers shows that 47.6% are employed and of these 70% had white-collar jobs; 15.1% were in professional, technical, and related occupations. This becomes even more pronounced it we note that Italian-American fathers in the sample were represented in this professional, etc., occupational category at only 15.9%. Myth 2: Italian-American women are not well educated, and not as well educated as Italian-American men. In my sample of Italian-American mothers only 30% had less than a completed high school education and 11.8% had some college training. Although this situation may not be laudable, it is significant if we consider that of the fathers, 37.9% had less than a high school education, and 19.1% had some college experience. It appears that the previous generation of Italian-American women may have realized their higher education aspirations via their children.

Both the present college experience and the future plans of the female Italian-American students confirm the aspirations of past generations. The female students do much better in their college performance than the males: 51.1% of the women and only 31.1% of the men report grade averages of 3.0 or higher (in a 4.0 system). Also the female students take more credits per semester than their male Italian-American counterparts: 52.2% of the women and 35.6% of the men register for more than 16 credits per semester.

Table 1 suggests that females do better because they are less likely to be employed while attending college. The differences between the male and female students, however, as to employment, hours worked per week, weeks worked per year, and their respective "primary means of support" are not great at all.

The attitudes of the Italian-American young women toward college are probably a better explanation for their better performance in schoolwork. For example, in reference to the question: "My college education is important to me," 90.1% of the females and 88.3% of the males agreed with the statement, 58.5% of the females and 53.4% of the males totally agreeing, 4.8% of the males totally disagreed versus 2.8% of the females.

TABLE 1. *Employment Status of Italian-American Students*

	FEMALE	MALE
Employed	54.6%	60.3%
21 hours per week or more	15.5%	21.8%
31 hours per week or more	43.2%	50.0%
Parents as primary means of support	62.4%	57.5%

As to psychological support from parents for pursing a college degree, some slight differences were also apparent. In answer to the question: "My college education is important to my father," female students agreed more with the statement than male students: 77.4% versus 75.4% respectively. In answer to the question, "My college education is important to my mother," 79.1% of the female students and 70.1% of the males agreed with the statement. In general, it appears that Italian-American female college students receive greater support for their pursuit of higher education at home. This may be due, in part, to the finding that 48.9% of female students have another female family member presently attending college, in contrast to 32.2% of the male students. In female student households females are also more likely to have already attained a college degree: 32.2% of female and 25.3% of male households, respectively.

The commitment of Italian-American female students to their college education is also demonstrated in their response to the question: "if I could get a job I would not go to college." While 74.4% of the females disagreed with this statement, only 63.1% of the males disagreed with it. Italian-American female students also tended to feel that they were better prepared for college work than the males (see Table 2). In general, Italian-American female students seemed more disposed toward college work itself, giving greater importance to "coursework," "grades," and "intellectual pursuits" than males.

TABLE 2. *Preparedness of Italian-American Students for College Work*

	FEMALE	MALE
Reading	56.7%	48.6%
Writing	42.6%	21.2%
Mathematics	39.7%	29.5%

Both male and female Italian-American students demonstrate pragmatic orientations toward a college education and are relatively uninter-
ested in such things as cultural activities, social activities, student government, sports, and "learning to solve social problems." According to
Yankelovich (1974), such a practical and conservative attitude in college
students is typical of the changing youth values in the 70s.

To 92.2% of the female students and 89.1% of the males, "Italian" is a
major component of their ethnic identity. Both Italian-American females
and males are unlikely to involve themselves in school or non-school extracurricular activities, continuing an Italian-American tradition of non-
involvement in issues wider than the family or neighborhood. Female
Italian-American students are generally more "religious" (as gauged by
church attendance) than the males: 44.7% of the females and 25.4% of the
males attend Catholic services on a weekly basis. However, if we look at
participation on a "greater than monthly" basis it is noticed that although
the females continue to lead in attendance, we find that almost half
(46.1% versus 32.2% of the males) of the females do not attend church
services on at least a monthly basis, 9.9% of the young women and 13.0%
of the young men "never" attend religious services at all.

There is a difference in the frequency of the use of the Italian language
in the households of male and female Italian-American students. In female student households the language is more likely to be used "regularly" or "frequently": 14.9% in female and 9.6% in male student households. Although more likely to hear the language used at home, females
are not very different from males in their own use of the language, at
least nominally: 39.7% of the male and 38.3% of the females report Italian
as their second language. Females are, however, significantly different in
their expressed competence in the language itself. The female students
express greater confidence in their abilities to speak, read, and write in
Italian. Another traditional variable should be noted before going further,
that is, family size. The median family size for both male and female students is approximately 4.3. Females are, however, more likely to come
from unusually large Italian families, with 19.1% of the females and 17.2%
of the males coming from families with six or more members.

Generational distance from Italian traditions is another important
variable. Italian-American female students are only slightly less likely
than males to have mothers who were born in Italy: 29.1% versus 32.2%.
But there is a greater difference in the same direction on the origins of

their maternal grandmothers: 17.7% of the grandmothers of female students were Italian born versus 23.3% of the male students' grandmothers. All grandparents of the female students are in general more likely to be American born, particularly on the maternal side of the family. This connects them firmly, in an historical perspective, to the Italian immigrant and American born women who were the focus of Smith and Strom's papers. Although differences in generation of the Italian male and female students exist, they are not statistically significant.

We should move now to the career and other aspirations of the Italian-American college students. Italian-American female students appear to have slightly higher career aspirations than their male counterparts. They are more likely to plan on attending a graduate school, although not immediately upon college graduation: 35.4% of the females and 27.4% of the males intend to go to graduate school, but, as to immediate plans after graduation, 22.7% of the females and 30.1% of the males intend to go, whereas 47.5% of the females and 38.4% of the males intend to go to work. As an aside, 4.2% of the females and 2.1% of the males have marriage as an immediate plan after graduation. We might say that marriage is no longer the significant vocation of the contemporary Italian-American college-educated generation.

One might be tempted to argue that major differences in the general family backgrounds of the female Italian-American college students would account for their better college performance and attitudes as well as their higher aspirations; however, the differences between the students' families are not greater. Still, there is a distinguishable pattern that offers some explanations for performance and attitude variations. The female Italian-American student is generally preceded by a mother who is more successful in the individual sense than the mothers of the male students. For example, the mothers of the female students are more likely to have completed high school (54.6% versus 50.0%), more likely to have attended college (13.0% versus 11.0%), and to be employed outside the household (51.1% versus 42.5%). These differences between mothers become more important when one considers that although the fathers of the female students are also more likely than those of male students to have attended college (20.5% versus 16.4%), in general, they are not as likely as a group to have white-collar occupations (48.2% versus 55.0% respectively for female and male students' fathers).

It seems reasonable to assume that the mothers of female Italian-

American college students continue to live, as they have been in the past, through their daughters. Those mothers that have gone as far as they could in school and are employed outside the family, as well as those who because of family or economic pressure were not able to fulfill their aspirations, are going further via their daughters.

Finally, there are some social-psychological areas in which Italian-American male and female students do differ significantly that may relate to the assimilation process. Students were asked to rank the "greatest disadvantages to your attaining your career or occupational goals." Female students ranked their sex as their greatest disadvantage (27.0% versus 1.4% for male students), while male students ranked ethnicity or nationality as their greatest disadvantage (23.3% versus 8.5% for female students). In the second and subsequent "greatest disadvantages," the differences between male and female Italian-American students diminished sharply. It should also be noted here that in terms of confidence in their futures, 41.1% of the female and 37.7% of the males offered no response to this question of disadvantage at all.

Based on this and other data from the Italian-American student survey, I would conclude that when provided with the opportunity for higher education and occupational mobility through the sacrifice and hard work of their immigrant forebears, the present generation of Italian-American women are willing, and extremely able, to take the position of equality and leadership within the Italian-American community to which they are entitled. I would also like to suggest my own observation that perhaps the greatest handicap for Italian-American women in this generation is not the traditions which were brought to the new world from Italy, but the economic situations which have kept Italian-American families for too long in lower-status, and generally blue-collar, occupations. The importance of parents as role models in traditional Italian families insures that if mothers and fathers, by their own image, offer no opportunity or inspiration for female or male achievement, little such upward mobility will be forthcoming.

Bibliography

Kessner, T. (1977). *The Golden Door: Italian and Jewish Immigrant Mobility in New York City 1880–1915.* New York: Oxford University Press.

Krase, J. and Fuccillo, V. J. (1975). "Italian Americans and College Life: A Survey of Student Experiences at Brooklyn College." Unpublished manuscript, Brooklyn College, City University of New York, Department of Sociology and Center for Italian American Studies.

Yankelovich, D. (1974). "Changing Youth Values in the 70s: A Study of American Youth." New York: The John D. Rockefeller III Fund, Inc.

A Demographic Study of Italian-American College Students Attending the City University of New York

LAWRENCE V. CASTIGLIONE

INTRODUCTION

This survey was conducted under the auspices of the Italian American Institute to Foster Higher Education (Institute). The central focus of the investigation was to obtain basic descriptive and demographic information on Italian-American students at the City University of New York. The survey grew out of a need for improving our knowledge of Italian-American students. Statistics on various aspects of student life at CUNY colleges are collected, but rarely is data on Italian-American students published. These students are typically categorized within the group of "white students" or grouped in a residual "others" category.

Clearly, it is impossible to derive any useful data about Italian-American students from statistics on "others" or "whites." A sample of Italian-American college students attending the various branches of the City University of New York was surveyed in the spring semester of 1982. The report which follows provides a general composite portrait of the Italian-American students at the following colleges: Brooklyn, Baruch, College of Staten Island, Lehman, Hunter, York, John Jay College of Criminal Justice, City College, Queens, Kingsborough Community and New York Technical College. It offers demographic, occupational and academic data of various types.

MAILING AND FOLLOW-UP PROCEDURES

The Institute provided a list of student club presidents, campus coordinators, CUNY counselors and faculty. Principal contacts were made throughout the City University using the information provided. Individuals were contacted by telephone and introduced to the survey.

Subsequently, packages ranging from 10–100 questionnaires were mailed or hand delivered to them. These contacts distributed the questionnaires to Italian-American students on their respective campuses. In total, 910 questionnaires were mailed or delivered. A package was delivered if the contact was either at a convenient location, or had attended the April 13, 1982 institute meeting. Included in the package were a cover letter and a self-addressed, stamped envelope. The cover letter, on Queens College letterhead, signed by the project director and the assistant, explained the general goals of the survey, suggested the procedure of distribution, and impressed upon the contact the importance of their efforts. A letter was sent to the contacts that were unreachable by telephone, mentioning the suggestion of the Institute's director, Mr. Louis Cenci, to contact them. The College of Staten Island was an exception to this procedure. The college was visited on July 19, 1982 and a minimum sample was obtained by one of the research assistants. The mailing commenced on April 8, 1982 and took 2 to 3 weeks to complete, with the bulk of packets mailed on April 13, 1982. Hand deliveries were also made during this period. Not until three weeks afterward, did complete questionnaires begin arriving at a rate of about 40 per week. The return then slowly declined, and repeated follow-up calls were made at regular intervals to all of the contacts. After these follow-up calls, additional questionnaires were returned. By the middle of June 1982, returns had virtually stopped coming in. At that time, a telephone survey of college contacts revealed that no more questionnaires could be expected to be returned. At this point data processing was begun, using the 320 usable questionnaires that had been returned.

TABLES AND DISCUSSION OF THE DATA

Table 1 reveals that 44.8% of the respondents were male and 55.2% were female.

TABLE 1. *Gender of Respondents*

	NUMBER	PERCENTAGE
Male	145	44.8
Female	179	55.2

TABLE 2. *Age of Respondents*

NUMBER	MEAN	MEDIAN	STANDARD DEVIATION
320	21.16	20.41	3.89

The respondents to this survey were, on average, approximately 21 years old with ages 17 through 21 accounting for 71.3% of the group. The remaining 28.7% of the respondents are 22 years old or older. The range of age is 33 years, from age 17 to age 50.

TABLE 3. *Martial Status of Respondents*

STATUS	NUMBER	RELATIVE FREQUENCY
Single	306	94.4%
Married	11	3.4%
Divorced	4	1.2%
No response	3	.9%

Table 3 reveals that 94.4% of the respondents are single and have never been married. Approximately 3.4% are currently married, and 1.2% are divorced. Only .9% did not respond to this item.

TABLE 4. *Borough of Birth of NYC Born Respondents*

BOROUGH	NUMBER	PERCENTAGE
Manhattan	17	8%
Brooklyn	103	47%
Queens	41	19%
Bronx	48	22%
Richmond	8	4%

Nearly half of the respondents who were born in New York City were born in Brooklyn. This percentage may reflect the sampling bias, since the sampling was not strictly random but rather depended upon the cooperation of contacts at the various colleges within the City University system.

TABLE 5. *Respondents' State of Birth*

STATE	NUMBER	PERCENTAGE
New York	229	98.3%
Texas	1	.4%
Virginia	1	.4%
California	2	.8%

New York State was the birthplace of over 98% of the total sample of respondents. Approximately 27% of the total sample was born outside of the United States. Table 6 shows the distribution of respondents with respect to country of birth.

TABLE 6. *Respondents' Country of Birth*

COUNTRY	NUMBER	PERCENTAGE
United States	236	72.8%
Italy	78	24.1%
Spain	1	.3%
Switzerland	1	.3%
Canada	1	.3%
France	1	.3%
Dominican Republic	1	.3%
Australia	1	.3%
Yugoslavia	1	.3%
Argentina	1	.3%
Venezuela	1	.3%
Panama	1	.3%

The preponderance (72.8%) of respondents were born within the United States. Approximately 24.1% were born in Italy. The remainder, 3.4%, were born in 10 foreign countries other than Italy. These data were verified in order to make sure that at least one parent was of Italian heritage.

TABLE 7. *Citizenship of Respondents*

	NUMBER	PERCENTAGE
US citizen	266	82.1%
Not a US citizen	57	17.6%
No response	1	.3%

Most of the respondents hold United States citizenship, as might be expected. Combining the data of Tables 6 and 7 shows that 65% (57 of 88) of the respondents who were born outside of the United States do not now hold citizenship in this country. The remaining 35% (N=31) have obtained citizenship.

TABLE 8. *Composition of Respondents' Households*

MEMBER OF FAMILY IN HOUSEHOLD	NUMBER	PERCENTAGE
Self	20	6.2%
Mother	287	88.6%
Father	266	82.1%
NUMBER OF BROTHERS		
1	120	68.0%
2	45	25.6%
3	8	4.5%
4	2	1.1%
5	1	.6%
NUMBER OF SISTERS		
1	128	39.5%
2	31	9.6%
3	7	2.2%
4	2	.6%
SPOUSE		
Wife	2	.6%
Husband	9	2.8%
Other (grandparents, cousins, aunts, uncles, etc.)	36	11.1%

TABLE 9. *Estimated Average Size of Respondents' Households*

NUMBER	MEAN	STANDARD DEVIATION	MEDIAN	RANGE
313	4.21	1.55	4.2	1–9
No response = 11				

This estimate of respondents' average household size was developed in order to help gauge the extent to which family resources were likely to be stretched. This variable was also used in additional statistical analyses where the influence of family size was hypothesized to affect selected dependent variables.

TABLE 10. *Parents' Ages*

	NUMBER	MEAN	STANDARD DEVIATION	MEDIAN	RANGE
Father	227	53.74	7.19	53.80	35–79
No response	47				
Mother	300	49.97	7.13	49.75	36–78
No response	24				

Inspection of the distribution of respondents' parents' ages shows that 73% of the fathers are between 47 and 61 years of age. Among the mothers, 65% fall between the ages of 45 and 56.

TABLE 11. *Fathers' Countries of Birth*

	NUMBER	PERCENTAGE
United States	120	37.0%
Italy	161	49.7%
Greece	1	.3%
Dominican Republic	1	.3%
Yugoslavia	1	.3%
No response	40	12.3%

A majority of respondents' fathers were born outside of the United States. Approximately 58% of all those who responded to this item have foreign born fathers.

TABLE 12. *Mothers' Countries of Birth*

	NUMBER	PERCENTAGE
United States	139	42.9%
Italy	154	47.5%
Puerto Rico	4	1.2%
Panama	2	.6%
Germany	2	.6%
Greece	1	.3%
Canada	1	.3%
France	1	.3%
Dominican Republic	1	.3%
Spain	1	.3%
No response	18	6.0%

A majority of the respondents' mothers were born outside the borders of the United States. Approximately 54% of those who responded have foreign born mothers.

TABLE 13. *Highest Grade Completed by Respondents' Fathers*

LEVEL OF EDUCATION	NUMBER	PERCENTAGE
Less than 12th grade	151	46.6%
High school graduate	123	38.0%
Bachelor degree	5	1.5%
Master degree	1	.3%
Doctoral degree	1	.3%
No response	43	13.3%

Inspection of Table 13 reveals that the majority of the respondents' fathers have not had any exposure to higher education. This finding confirms the results of our preliminary survey. Taken with the data of Table 14, these data indicate the respondents come from significantly under-educated backgrounds.

TABLE 14. *Highest Grade Completed by Respondents' Mothers*

LEVEL OF EDUCATION	NUMBER	PERCENTAGE
Less than 12th grade	157	48.5%
High school graduate	138	42.6%
Bachelor degree	10	3.1%
No response	19	5.9%

One hypothesis that is suggested by these data is that better educated Italian Americans do not send their children to the City University of New York. Another hypothesis is that Italian-American parents are less well educated than might be expected. A wider survey of parents with college-age children would be needed to test this hypothesis.

TABLE 15. *Respondents' Fathers' Occupations*

LEVEL	NUMBER	PERCENTAGE
Structural	26	8.0%
Bench work	8	2.5%
Machine trade	39	12.0%
Processing	1	.3%
Agriculture	4	1.2%
Service	23	7.1%
Clerical	15	4.6%
Professional	76	23.5%
Other and missing	132	40.7%

Inspection of Table 15 reveals the socioeconomic standing of the respondents' fathers' occupations. The median occupation is at the level of "service," a socioeconomic standing that is higher than the educational level reported by respondents; in addition, 76 respondents marked the category professional even though only 6 respondents report that their fathers hold college degrees. These findings appear to indicate that the term "professional" may have substantially different meaning for the respondents than it does for social scientists (e.g., a professional dry cleaner is not a professional in the view of social scientists.)

TABLE 16. *Respondents' Mothers' Occupations*

LEVEL	NUMBER	PERCENTAGE
Structural	2	.6%
Bench work	2	.6%
Machine trade	27	8.3%
Processing	1	.6%
Service	12	3.7%
Clerical	53	16.4%
Professional	33	10.2%
Other and missing	194	60.0%

Table 16 reveals the same pattern as did the data for fathers' occupations. Further, 60% of the respondents did not complete this item or used the "other" response. The systematic misinterpretation of occupational categories by respondents has serious effects upon our efforts to assess the extent to which socioeconomic factors influence the achievement of Italian-American college students. It may be advisable to return to using the questions on occupation and income that were developed for the long form of the questionnaire used in 1981.

TABLE 17. *Type of High School Attended by Respondents*

CATEGORY	NUMBER	PERCENTAGE
Public	229	70.7%
Parochial	79	24.4%
Private	12	3.7%
Vocational	2	.6%
No response	2	.6%

Table 17 reveals that more than 70% of the respondents attended a public high school. The City University of New York does not draw a substantial percentage of its' Italian-American students from the ranks of those who have attended private schools. Less than one-quarter of the respondents attended parochial high schools.

TABLE 18. *Languages Spoken at Home by Respondents*

LANGUAGE	NUMBER	RELATIVE FREQUENCY
English	142	43.8%
Italian	36	11.1%
English and Italian	131	40.4%
English, Italian and Spanish	8	2.5%
Italian and Croatian	3	.9%
English, Italian and Greek	1	.3%
English and Greek	1	.3%
English and Polish	1	.3%
English and Spanish	1	.3%

Table 18 reveals that 43.8% of the respondents speak English at home, 40.4% speak English and Italian, and 11.1% speak only Italian. 2.8% speak English, Italian and another language, and .9% speak Italian and Croatian. The remaining .9% speak English and another language.

TABLE 19. *Languages Spoken at Home by Respondents' Fathers*

LANGUAGE	NUMBER	PERCENTAGE
English	94	29.0%
Italian	95	29.3%
English and Italian	85	26.2%
English and other than Italian	8	2.5%
No response	42	13.0%

Only 29% of the respondents' fathers speak only English at home. Approximately 56% speak Italian and English, or only Italian.

TABLE 20. *Languages Spoken at Home by Respondents' Mothers*

LANGUAGE	NUMBER	PERCENTAGE
English	94	29.0%
Italian	97	29.9%
English and Italian	98	30.2%
English and other than Italian	15	5.0%
No response	20	6.2%

As was the case with fathers' language used at home, only 29% of the respondents reported that English was the only language used at home by their mothers.

TABLE 21. *Sources of Guidance Given Respondents in High School*

SOURCE	NUMBER	PERCENTAGE
Parents	175	54.0%
Siblings	95	29.3%
Friends	92	28.4%
Guidance counselor	122	37.7%
Clergy	14	4.3%
Teacher	14	4.3%
Others	128	39.5%
None	52	16.0%

The questionnaire included a series of items concerning sources of guidance in high school and in college. Table 21 reveals the paucity of educational guidance offered to Italian-American students. Even guidance counselors in high school were available to fewer than 40% of the respondents. Teacher guidance was nearly non-existent. The absence of appropriate educational guidance may have serious effects upon educational decision-making. The Institute's efforts directed toward providing guidance appear to be sorely needed.

TABLE 22. *Sources of Guidance Given Respondents in College*

SOURCE	NUMBER	PERCENTAGE
Parents	112	34.6%
Siblings	80	24.7%
Friends	128	39.5%
Guidance counselor	105	32.4%
Clergy	7	2.2%
Teacher	16	2.2%
Others	90	27.8%
None	80	24.7%

The guidance given Italian-American students is equally meager at the college level. Table 22 reveals that approximately one quarter of the sample received no guidance whatsoever and only 32.4% received guidance from a professional. One might expect that these figures are actually inflated by the common misperception among students that any interaction with another person concerning their educational plans constitutes "guidance." A more stringent and accurate definition of educational guidance would probably lead to a sharp drop in the percentages reported.

TABLE 23. *Respondents' Choice of College*

COLLEGE	NUMBER	PERCENTAGE
Brooklyn	80	24.7%
Queens	51	15.7%
Baruch	51	15.7%
Lehman	35	10.8%
Hunter	33	10.2%
College of Staten Island	22	6.8%
John Jay College of Criminal Justice	18	5.6%
City College of New York	9	2.8%
NYC College of Technology	9	2.8%
Kingsborough Community	8	2.5%
York	6	1.9%
Borough of Manhattan Community	1	.3%
Brooklyn Polytechnic	1	.3%

Table 23 shows the respondents' current college. These data suggest that there was significant under representation from the College of Staten Island. What is learned in the process of collecting data is often as informative as the data analyses of a study. Affable cooperation at a purely verbal level was not difficult to obtain, but actual effort and productivity were very difficult to elicit at some colleges.

TABLE 24. *Respondents' Chosen Major*

MAJOR	NUMBER	PERCENTAGE
Accounting	24	9.1%
Anthropology	2	.8%
Art/Art history	6	2.3%
Biology/Pre-medical	10	3.8%
Business administration/Management/Marketing	36	13.6%
Chemistry	2	.8%
Computer science	16	6.0%
Criminal justice	6	2.3%
Economics	14	5.3%
Education	9	3.4%
Engineering	8	3.0%
English	7	2.6%
Geography	2	.8%
Government/Political science	17	6.4%
Health/Physical education	5	1.9%
Home economics	3	1.1%
Humanities/Liberal arts	3	1.1%
Linguistics/Speech	3	1.1%
Mathematics	1	.4%
Mass communications/Film/TV/Radio	17	6.4%
Music	1	.4%
Nursing	2	.8%
Ophthalmology	9	3.4%
Philosophy	1	.4%
Psychology	16	6.0%
Romance/Modern language	42	15.8%
Sociology	1	.4%
Theatre	2	.8%

Approximately 82.7% (N=268) of the sample have chosen a major; Table 24 shows the respondents' choice of major. These data are highly reactive to sampling procedures. Frequently, the choice of a respondent's college is involved with the choice of major. A respondent who elects to attend John Jay College of Criminal Justice may very well do so in order to be able to major in criminal justice, a major that is not available elsewhere in the CUNY system. A more systematic and representative sampling procedure must be used if we wish to obtain data that is accurate and representative.

TABLE 25. *Other Colleges Attended*

UNIVERSITY	NUMBER	PERCENTAGE
CUNY senior college	12	17.9%
CUNY community college	26	38.8%
SUNY senior college	4	6.0%
SUNY community college	3	4.5%
Out of NY public university	2	3.0%
Catholic university	7	10.4%
Private university	7	10.4%
Italian university	1	1.5%
Out of US university	1	1.5%
Other	4	6.0%

Respondents reported that they attended colleges other than their current one, as 20.7% of the sample (N=67) transferred or graduated from other institutions. Only 25 respondents, 7.7% of the sample, received a degree from another institution of higher learning. The community colleges appear to function as a system of feeder schools into the CUNY system for Italian-American students.

TABLE 26. *Type of Degree Received from Other College*

TYPE	NUMBER	PERCENTAGE
Associate	24	7.4%
Bachelor	7	2.2%
Master	2	.6%
No response	291	89.8%

The distribution of respondents with prior degrees by type of degree (Table 26) is about what might be expected. More associate degrees will occur as the community colleges design their programs so as to mesh with the four year schools within the system.

TABLE 27. *Type of College Respondents Now Attend*

TYPE	NUMBER	PERCENTAGE
Public two year or technical	17	5.2%
Public four year or university	307	94.8%

The greatest preponderance of the sample was drawn from the four year colleges within the CUNY system. When data on Italian-American enrollment in the CUNY system becomes available, we will be able to assess the representativeness of our sampling procedures.

TABLE 28. *Current Class of Respondents*

CLASS	NUMBER	PERCENTAGE
Freshman	78	24.1%
Sophomore	72	22.2%
Junior	87	26.9%
Senior	81	25.0%
Graduate	6	1.9%

Table 28 reveals the fall 1982 standing of the respondents in college. Approximately 24.1% were freshmen, 22.2% were sophomores, 26.9% were juniors, and 25% were seniors. Our sample of graduate students was quite small; only 1.9% were graduate students. The majority of respondents are full time students; 7.4%, or 24 out of 324, are attending college on a part time basis.

TABLE 29. *Percentage of Respondents Receiving Financial Aid from Other Sources*

SOURCE	NUMBER	PERCENTAGE
Scholarship	40	12.3%
Research assistantship	2	.6%
Teaching assistantship	2	.6%
Loans	56	17.3%
Savings	89	27.5%
Parents	154	47.5%
Own earnings	168	51.9%
Grants	175	54.0%
Special programs	9	2.8%
Other	2	.6%

Grants, such as BEOG, TAP, etc. are the most frequently mentioned sources of financial aid. However, because many types of grants are available, the percentage of recipients of some sort of grant might be expected to be considerably higher. Respondents' parents' and respondents' own earnings are significant sources of support. Special programs (e.g., SEEK, College Discovery, etc.) seem closed to Italian-American students. Scholarships, research and teaching assistantships account for only 13.5% of the sample. This seems to be disproportionately low relative to the size of the Italian-American population within CUNY.

TABLE 30. *Percentage Indicating Most Important Source of Financial Support Among Respondents*

SOURCE	NUMBER	PERCENTAGE
Scholarship	9	2.8%
Loan	13	4.0%
Savings	11	3.4%
Parental aid	69	21.3%
Own earnings	45	13.9%
Grant	126	38.9%
No response	51	15.7%

Grants are clearly perceived as the single most important source of income for college by the respondents. Compared with Table 29, Table 30 shows that parental aid is perceived as a less important source of support, even though 47.5% of respondents indicated that they receive parental financial aid. Any reduction in grant funding will markedly increase the importance of other aid categories, parental support included.

TABLE 31. *Employment Status of Respondents*

STATUS	NUMBER	PERCENTAGE
Employed	213	65.7%
Not currently employed	109	33.6%
No response	2	.6%

The majority of respondents, approximately 66%, are employed. The average number of hours worked per week is 23.44 and the standard deviation is 8.75. The range is 46 hours, from 4 hours per week to 50 hours per week. These data indicate a substantial level of effort directed toward non-academic goals by this group of college students. Further investigation is recommended. The type of employment (whether it permits reading on the job, or direct application of skills learned in schools, for example) as well as the pattern of working hours is not known. When data is collected on these variables, we may be able to reach a clearer idea of the relation of employment to achievement for these students.

TABLE 32. *Involvement of Respondents in Italian Language Instruction*

LANGUAGE INSTRUCTION	NUMBER	PERCENTAGE
Taking Italian courses	224	69.1%
Not taking Italian courses	99	30.6%
No response	1	.3%

The data of Table 32 reflects the fact that questionnaire distribution frequently took place in Italian language courses. Caution is therefore recommended in the interpretation of these data.

TABLE 33. *Respondents' Knowledge of Italian-American Programs on Their Campus*

PROGRAM KNOWLEDGE	NUMBER	PERCENTAGE
Know of programs	225	69.4%
Uncertain	29	21.3%
Do not know of programs	29	9.0%
No response	1	.3%

Table 33 reveals that more than 21% of the respondents are uncertain whether there is an Italian-American program on their campus. Clearly, there is a substantial need for the Institute to reach out to this segment of the population. Better communications ought to be established between faculty and students. Faculty should be actively encouraged to inform students of the programs that are available to them.

TABLE 34. *Respondents' Involvement in Courses Offered by Italian American Studies Programs*

IA STUDIES PROGRAM	NUMBER	PERCENTAGE
Have taken courses	98	30.2%
Have not taken courses	171	52.8%
No response	55	17.0%

Most respondents have not taken courses offered by the Italian American Studies program on their campus. According to program directors, a limiting factor may be the number of electives available to the students and/or the scheduling of Italian American courses offered by the programs. Others have argued that Italian-American students are simply not interested in the courses offered by the Italian American Studies programs. This issue might be considered as a focus of future studies.

TABLE 35. *Degrees Sought by Respondents*

DEGREE	NUMBER	PERCENTAGE
Associate	22	6.8%
Bachelor	288	88.9%
Other (Master-Doctoral)	6	1.8%
No response	8	2.5%

Table 35 shows the degree that respondents expect to obtain in their current course of study. Approximately 98.1% (N=318) of the sample expect that they will graduate. The bachelor's degree accounts for about 88.9% (N=288) of the sample's expectations.

TABLE 36. *Respondents' Plans to Enter Graduate School*

PLAN	NUMBER	PERCENTAGE
Enter graduate school	123	38.0%
Not enter graduate school	54	16.7%
Uncertain	139	42.9%
No response	8	2.5%

Table 36 reveals that only 16.7% of the respondents do not plan to further their education to the graduate level. A rather large proportion, 42.9%, are uncertain. At this writing, we do not have information that would inform us of the nature of their expressed uncertainty. It could stem from a variety of sources: personal, financial, etc.

TABLE 37. *Type of Graduate Program Respondents Expect to Enter*

TYPE	NUMBER	PERCENTAGE
Master	137	42.3%
Doctoral	12	3.7%
Professional (law, medicine, etc.)	36	11.1%
Other	1	0.3%
No response	138	42.6%

Note that Table 37 shows that 185 respondents expect to enter some program of graduate education, 62 more than those who state that they expect to go on to a graduate program (Table 36). These results may have been obtained because some of those who are uncertain about their plans are sure of their interests. Only seven students report that they have been accepted into a graduate school. The survey was completed prior to the time seniors would have been notified by the college to which they had applied, so the number of acceptances to date are not reflective of the true proportion of students who will be accepted into a graduate program.

Table 38 lists the type of employment that respondents expect to be engaged in five years after graduation. These data indicate the respondents' level of aspiration for the near future. The single highest category is "teacher," accounting for 11.4% of the sample. Only four students plan to enter medicine. Others have listed occupations for which college, per se, is not needed (e.g., bank teller, artist). Inspection of these occupations suggests a relatively modest level of aspiration.

TABLE 38. *Respondents' Anticipated Employment Five Years After Graduation*

OCCUPATION	NUMBER	PERCENTAGE
Teaching	37	11.4%
High school counselor	4	1.2%
FBI agency	1	.3%
Bank teller	1	.3%
Psychologist	5	1.5%
Legal system	1	.3%
Congressman	1	.3%
Doctor	4	1.2%
Lawyer	15	4.6%
TV-Radio reporter	2	.6%
Accountant	23	7.1%
Executive	24	7.4%
Film critic	1	.3%
Paralegal	1	.3%
Computer programmer	10	3.1%
Social worker	2	.6%
Translator	12	3.7%
Journalist	4	1.2%
Travel agent	1	.3%
Systems analyst	5	1.5%
Urban planner	1	.3%
Nurse	4	1.2%
Self-employed	9	2.8%
Civil service	1	.3%
Public relations	3	.9%
Advertising	1	.3%
Financial management	3	.9%
Artist	2	.6%
TV producer	2	.6%
Engineer	5	1.5%
Hospital administration	1	.3%
Fashion industry	1	.3%
International business	2	.6%
Speech therapist	2	.6%
Media industry	2	.6%
Industrial sales representative	1	.3%
Medical research	1	.3%
College professor	3	.9%

(continued on next page)

(continued from previous page)		
Legislative aide	1	.3%
Optometrist	2	.6%
Opthalmic dispenser	2	.6%
Italian state department	1	.3%
TV director	1	.3%
Cable producer	1	.3%
Priest	2	.6%
Psychoanalyst	1	.3%
Stock broker	1	.3%
Product planner	1	.3%
Pharmacist	1	.3%
Food service manager	1	.3%
Airlines	1	.3%
Forensic anthropologist	1	.3%
Marketing research director	2	.6%
Musician	1	.3%
Construction engineer	1	.3%
High school principal	1	.3%
No response	104	32.1%

TABLE 39. *Type of Extracurricular Activities Participated in by Respondents*

TYPE	NUMBER	PERCENTAGE
Academic	77	23.8%
Athletic	84	25.9%
Religious	25	7.7%
Career	52	16.0%
Hobby	51	15.7%
Political	36	11.1%
Service	29	9.0%
Other	44	13.62%
None	88	27.2%

Table 39 shows percentages of the total sample for each type of extra-curricular activity. Approximately 27.2% of the respondents never participated in any type of extracurricular activity. Some individuals participated in several sorts of activities.

TABLE 40. *Frequency of Participation in Extracurricular Activities*

FREQUENCY	NUMBER	PERCENTAGE
Rarely	78	24.1%
Sometimes	45	13.9%
Often	75	23.1%
Very often	77	23.8%
No response	49	15.1%

The distribution of participation is nearly rectangular. These data are of interest in relation to the extent to which students are employed. (See cross tabulations.)

TABLE 41. *Source of Information Concerning Italian American Institute to Foster Higher Education*

SOURCE	NUMBER	PERCENTAGE
Media	11	3.4%
Institute publicity	27	8.3%
Friend	42	13.0%
Parent	1	.3%
Teacher	14	4.3%
Advisor	2	.6%
Counselor	18	5.6%
Administrator	2	.6%
Institute speaker	1	.3%
Brooklyn College Center for Italian American Studies	1	.3%
Flyers	1	.3%
Institute employee	1	.3%
Fiao club	2	.6%
Italian-American student society	1	.3%
School paper	1	.3%
No response	199	61.4%

Word of mouth is the most frequently listed source of information about the Institute. Counselors reached only 5.6% of the sample; this is less than Institute publicity, which reached 8.3%. "Media" as a category was not specific enough to precisely describe what medium was employed.

TABLE 42. *Respondents' Awareness of the Italian American Institute to Foster Higher Education*

AWARENESS	NUMBER	PERCENTAGE
Aware of the Institute	126	38.9%
Did not know of the Institute	197	60.8%
Missing	1	.3%

Most students are unaware of the Institute's existence. A more comprehensive communication needs to be done in this area. A mailing to the parents and students of Italian-American origin in each entering class might be useful in increasing student awareness of the Institute and its activities.

TABLE 43. *Relationship of the Source of Guidance to the Choice of Two or Four Year College*

VARIABLE	CHI-SQUARE	SIGNIFICANCE
Parents	.10669	N.S.
Siblings	.16244	N.S.
Friends	.01213	N.S.
Counselor	.00002	N.S.
Clergy	.05173	N.S.
Teacher	.15243	N.S.
Others	.01528	N.S.
None	.03054	N.S.

A chi-square test was applied to the variables of source of guidance and choice of two or four year college in order to determine if there was any significant association between them. The data shown above reveal that there is no influence of a systematic sort exerted by a particular source of guidance upon the respondent's decision to attend a two or four year college. These results may be interpreted to mean that there is no evidence of steering Italian-American students to two year rather than four year colleges in the sample we have studied.

TABLE 44. *Relationship of Parental Guidance to Sources of Financial Support in College*

VARIABLE	CHI-SQUARE	SIGNIFICANCE
PARENTS AND:		
Scholarship research assistantship	.07064	N.S.
Teaching assistantship	.07064	N.S.
Loan	.20837	N.S.
Savings	2.01352	N.S.
Parents' assistance	10.73640	.05
Own earnings	.11157	N.S.
Grant	.00319	N.S.
Special programs	.09978	N.S.
Others	.50000	N.S.

Table 44 reveals that the only significant association that was obtained between parental guidance and the various sources of financial support in college involved the parents own assistance to their child. One might conclude that these parents are financially supportive of their children to the extent that they are also involved and concerned in a less tangible, more advice-giving role.

TABLE 45. *Relationship of Counselor Guidance to Sources of Financial Support in College*

VARIABLE	CHI-SQUARE	SIGNIFICANCE
COUNSELOR AND:		
Scholarship	2.28468	N.S.
Research assistantship	.04091	N.S.
Teaching assistantship	.04091	N.S.
Loan	.06237	N.S.
Savings	2.92733	N.S.
Parents' assistance	.07576	N.S.
Own earnings	1.13084	N.S.
Grant	3.97950	.05
Special programs	.05676	N.S.
Other (N's too small to test)	-	-

Table 45 is of special interest in the present investigation, for it shows a significant association between guidance given by a professional counselor and students obtaining financial grants. This finding should not be interpreted as a cause and effect relationship but rather as an important point of departure for further investigation. The questions to be answered now are: (1) Why do students who have seen professional counselors receive more grants than those who have not been professionally counseled? (2) Will increasing the frequency by which students are seen by counselors also increase the frequency with which those students receive grants? Considerably more research needs to be done in order to adequately answer these questions.

TABLE 46. *Relationship of Sibling Guidance to Sources of Financial Support in College*

VARIABLE	CHI-SQUARE	SIGNIFICANCE
SIBLINGS AND:		
Scholarship	.42569	N.S.
Research assistantship	2.75645	N.S.
Loan	.00017	N.S.
Savings	.21816	N.S.
Parents' assistance	6.21710	.01
Own earnings	.00202	N.S.
Grant	.16811	N.S.
Special programs	1.77833	N.S.
Other (N's too small to test)	.50000	N.S.

Table 46 reveals that the decision to tap parental resources for our siblings college education is a family affair. There is a significant association between siblings guidance and parents assistance as a source of financial support.

TABLE 47. *Relationship of Friends Guidance to Sources of Financial Support in College*

VARIABLE	CHI-SQUARE	SIGNIFICANCE
FRIENDS AND:		
Scholarship	.23284	N.S.
Research assistantship	1.01032	N.S.
Teaching assistantship	.19478	N.S.
Loan	.00017	N.S.
Savings	2.90645	N.S.
Parents' assistance	4.13643	.05
Own earnings	3.30948	N.S.
Grant	.00015	N.S.
Special programs	.00861	N.S.
Other (N's too small to test)	-	-

Table 47 shows that there was a significant association between obtaining college guidance from friends and receiving financial support for college from one's parents. It seems unlikely that friends were consulted relative to any question concerning financial support from a students' parents. Rather, it seems more likely that a coincidental relationship has occurred due to the high frequency with which students both consult their friends and receive aid from their parents.

TABLE 48. *Relationship of Teachers Guidance to Sources of Financial Support in College*

VARIABLE	CHI-SQUARE	SIGNIFICANCE
TEACHERS AND:		
Scholarship	.17535	N.S.
Research assistantship	1.64141	N.S.
Teaching assistantship	1.64141	N.S.
Loan	.83250	N.S.
Savings	1.23141	N.S.
Parents' assistance	.04163	N.S.
Own earnings	1.15473	N.S.
Grant	.08210	N.S.
Special programs	.00343	N.S.
Other (N's too small to test)	-	-

The data of Table 48 show that for this sample of respondents, teachers guidance was not associated with any of the various sources of financial support. One may raise the question: How knowledgeable are teachers about financial support for college, and, further: How strong is their desire to involve themselves in the difficult problems of college financial aid? Although the present survey cannot answer these questions, the information we have obtained clearly suggests that these should be questions of interest for further study.

TABLE 49. *Relationship of Clergy Guidance to Sources of Financial Support in College*

VARIABLE	CHI-SQUARE	SIGNIFICANCE
CLERGY AND:		
Scholarship	.10849	N.S.
Research assistantship	5.70427	.01
Teaching assistantship	5.70427	.01
Loan	.21042	N.S.
Savings	2.68730	N.S.
Parents' assistance	.19712	N.S.
Own earnings	.05341	N.S.
Grant	.01457	N.S.
Special programs	.64833	N.S.
Other (N's too small to test)	-	-

One of the more unexpected findings of the present investigation is revealed in Table 49. There is a significant association between guidance received from the clergy and a respondent's obtaining financial support in the form of research and teaching assistantships. Although it is true that the number of students receiving such awards is small, this does not present a substantial problem in interpretation since the total number of such awards has been rather small. It might be of value to interview clergy with a view toward finding out what approaches are used to obtain the evident results.

TABLE 50. *Relationship of "Others" Guidance to Sources of Financial Support in College*

VARIABLE	CHI-SQUARE	SIGNIFICANCE
OTHERS AND:		
Scholarship	.04599	N.S.
Research assistantship	.00473	N.S.
Teaching assistantship	.00473	N.S.
Loan	4.35293	.05
Savings	.14053	N.S.
Parents' assistance	5.89361	.01
Own earnings	.04996	N.S.
Grant	.25583	N.S.
Special programs	.00344	N.S.
Other (N's too small to test)	-	-

The data of Table 50 may be interpreted to suggest that "other" family and friends are both consulted and contributors, in the form of loans, to the support of Italian-American students in CUNY.

TABLE 51. *Relationship of No Guidance to Sources of Support in College*

VARIABLE	CHI-SQUARE	SIGNIFICANCE
NO GUIDANCE AND:		
Scholarship	.06396	N.S.
Research assistantship	.00006	N.S.
Teaching assistantship	.00006	N.S.
Loan	.04636	N.S.
Savings	1.30694	N.S.
Parents' assistance	8.95806	.003
Own earnings	.00065	N.S.
Grant	.00751	N.S.
Special programs	.02959	N.S.
Other (N's too small to test)	-	-

Table 51 reveals a significant association between the absence of guidance and the receipt of parental assistance. This most likely means that students who do not receive guidance are more likely to have to depend upon family resources for support than those students with support from sources outside their families.

TABLE 52. *Multiple Regression Analysis of All Respondents With Complete Data: Relation of Hours Worked, Family Size, and Socioeconomic Status Upon Grade Point Average*

VARIABLE	MULTIPLE R	R^2	BETA
Hours worked per week	.2076	.0431	−.2092
Total persons in household	.3057	.0935	.2205
Father's occupation	.3123	.0975	−.1044
Mother's occupation	.3174	.1008	.0699

Table 52 reveals that the combination of hours worked per week, total size of household and the socioeconomic status of the students' parents accounts for only 10% of the total variance in cumulative grade point average. This should not be interpreted to mean that these variables have little influence upon academic achievement, even though they do appear at first blush to be minor contributors to the overall variability. Grade point averages are considered reactive in that an individual can change behavior in order to influence the variable. Consider the following examples: (1) A student who has been working 35 hours a week becomes aware that his school work is suffering because of his inability to devote sufficient time in study or preparation. As a consequence, the student takes less demanding courses the next semester. This action results in an upturn in the students GPA even though the number of hours worked has not changed. The student has compensated for the diminution in study time by taking courses that do not require very much study time. (2) Another student quits a part time job in order to take several difficult required courses. His/her average for the semester is B-. Both the illustrations have in common one very important element that effects the present investigation; in each, the effect of work on grade point average is masked by the student's efforts to cope with the situation. If we are to attempt to study the influence of work on academic achievement, we shall have to control for such factors as course difficulty, the cyclic nature of work (some kinds of work have a more pronounced fatiguing and interfering effect upon study time than other types), the *kind* of work (some work well may constitute applied practice in one's chosen field and indeed may actually contribute to higher achievement in college), and the subjective level of difficulty generated in individuals by a given course. As difficult as it may be to pursue such an investigation it promises to be worthwhile, in that the information it could develop would have immediate application in college guidance for Italian-American students.

TABLE 53. *Relationship of Grade Point Average to Employment*

	NOT EMPLOYED	EMPLOYED
BELOW MEDIAN GPA		
Number	54	95
Percentage	49.54	44.60
ON AND ABOVE MEDIAN GPA		
Number	55	118
Percentage	50.46	55.40
CHI-SQUARE=	.52308	N.S.

To test for the possibility that the relation between grade point average and employment might not be linear in nature and thus not appropriately tested by multiple linear regression analysis, a chi-square test was applied. The chi-square test does not rest upon an assumption that the relationship between two variables is linear. A median split was used to form two groups, one below the median GPA and the other on and above the median GPA. There was no significant association in these data between paid employment and student's grade point average. The same qualifications that were raised with respect to the multiple regression analysis of these data apply here also.

TABLE 54. *Relationship of Plans to Enter Graduate School to Language Used at Home*

	ENGLISH	ENGLISH AND ITALIAN	ITALIAN
BELOW MEDIAN GPA			
Number	26	19	7
Percentage	33.77	36.84	27.14
ON AND ABOVE MEDIAN GPA			
Number	51	51	12
Percentage	66.23	63.16	72.86
CHI-SQUARE=	1.05127	N.S.	

The data of Table 54 show that there is no significant association between the languages that a student uses at home and an indicant of their academic aspirations: plans to enter graduate school.

TABLE 55. *Relationship of Grade Point Average to Language Used at Home*

	ENGLISH	ENGLISH AND ITALIAN	ITALIAN
BELOW MEDIAN GPA			
Number	61	59	22
Percentage	42.96	45.04	61.11
ON AND ABOVE MEDIAN GPA			
Number	81	72	14
Percentage	57.04	54.96	38.89
CHI-SQUARE=	3.88754	N.S.	

Although there is no significant association between grade average and the language used at home, there is some suggestion of a trend. Note that the column percentages reported above change from a majority of English-speaking-at-home students falling into the higher GPA group to a majority of Italian-spoken-at-home falling into the lower GPA group. The absence of English language practice and reinforcement at home may be a latent problem for Italian-American students. Further research will be needed to confirm this hypothesis.

SUMMARY AND ANALYSIS OF RESULTS

The socioeconomic and demographic data of this investigation describes the Italian-American college student attending the City University of New York as coming from an economically vulnerable segment of American society; the lower middle and upper lower class. These students are achieving levels of education very significantly greater than those of their parents. But the data suggests that they and their families may be "on the edge" economically.

There are between four and five members in a typical student's household. Often, both mother and father are employed. Well over half of the students sampled work either full or part-time. This description fits an industrious but financially pressed family, an interpretation based upon the assumption that employment is at least as much a function of economic necessity as a means of self-fulfillment in contemporary society.

There does not seem to be a significant negative association between the extent of employment and academic achievement. The fact that no significant relationship was found was quite surprising, and the phenomenon deserves further study. It may well be that students either successfully compensate for the increased pressure upon their time that work typically brings with it, or they may dropout either from school or, temporarily, from work. Either of these situations would explain the low association between GPA and the number of hours worked. Further investigation would be needed to test these hypotheses.

Sources of financial aid apart from their own family and earnings do not appear to be utilized by these young people to the extent that might be expected. One might speculate that more extensive guidance would make financing options better known and, consequently, more frequently used. The data suggest that this is a real possibility, since a significant association was found between the frequency with which students obtained grants and the frequency with which they received professional guidance. Further investigation is suggested to determine the extent to which the lower-than-expected frequency of guidance obtained by this sample is attributable to its unavailability or to cultural factors among Italian-American students that mitigate against going to strangers for help with personal, educational, or financial problems.

A series of statistical tests were done to test the hypothesis that there is a relationship between the source of guidance that a student receives in high school and the student's subsequent choice of a two year or four year college. No statistically significant association was found. In brief, there is no evidence that any of the listed sources of guidance — parents, siblings, friends, counselors, clergy, teachers, or others — had any systematic relationship to the type of college students elected to attend.

There is no significant relationship between gender and employment or receiving aid from any of the sources of financial aid. Thus there is no obvious statistical evidence that would suggest sex discrimination in these data. Additional analysis showed that there is no statistical association between the respondents' plans to enter graduate school and the language spoken at home, thus suggesting that the use of the Italian language at home is not related to any diminution of the students' academic ambitions. There is, however, some tentative evidence that students' grades are associated with the language used at home. In particular, a trend, not truly statistically significant, is latent in the language data. It suggests that grade point average declines as the frequency of the use of Italian at home increases. Although this trend is suggested by the data, it is by no means persuasive. Once again, further study is warranted.

An analysis of the frequency with which respondents engaged in extracurricular activities and its relation to employment status showed that there is not a significant association between the two variables. Working students do engage in extracurricular activities about as often as do students who do not work during the school year. Further, there was no association between the pursuit of hobbies and employment status.

The data shows that there are a wide variety of interests among the group sampled, as is evidenced by the variety of their majors. However, especially noteworthy is the low incidence of students planning on a medical career. It may well be that those who plan on entering medicine have elected to attend private rather than public universities. A study of high school seniors applying for college and their future plans and aspirations would provide useful information for those interested in guiding and counseling Italian-American students. As for the present, we may only speculate that there is surely some reason for the unusually low percentage of public university students intending to enter medicine as a profession.

Acknowledgements

I would like to take this opportunity to thank the Italian American Institute to Foster Higher Education and especially its director, Mr. Louis Cenci, for his support and encouragement. Thanks are also due to my research assistants, Ms. Marie DeVito and Mr. Frank Sapienza. In addition, I should like to express my appreciation to those students and faculty who cooperated in the collection of the data. Without their reports this study would not have been successfully completed.

Educational Attainment and Educational Values: Italian-American Generations

JEROME KRASE, PH.D.

There are as many myths as there are realities regarding educational aspirations and achievements of Italian Americans. Often myth and realities are mixed together in such a way as to make differentiation between the two difficult, if not impossible. It seems that the major reason for the present day confusion between fact and fiction is the paucity of research on the social status of Italians in American society.

It is difficult enough for social scientists, educators and Italian-American community leaders to get a handle on the complex problem of educational mobility among the ten million or so persons of Italian descent in the United States without it being made more bewildering by the absence of a substantial body of easily accessible and relevant data. This situation is further aggravated by the lack of support for those persons or institutions willing and able to do what is necessary to fill the information void. At present the expert and non-expert alike are forced to rely on pat generalizations, historical stereotypes, personal observation and intuition when asked for comment on the situation. Such comment and insight, when put into practice, is frequently patronizing or otherwise destructive. One of these stereotypical burdens, and the substantive focus of this paper, is the view that Italian Americans do not take advantage of opportunities for higher education and that somehow, Italian cultural values (high or low culture) are responsible for this situation. Egelman (1982a), Greeley (1977), Alba (1981), and others have argued that the first of these preceding statements does not stand up to scrutiny. It then must follow that the second statement demands some close attention on as well. As noted by Egelman (1982b), analysis of data from the last few decennial US Census reports have shown that persons of Italian descent have scored at or above the national average for educational achievement. Perhaps Italian values are responsible for this fact. In any case, the theoretical focus of this paper is the relationship between cultural values, educational achievement and aspiration. This essay will not solve all the problems or correct all the misperceptions concerning Italians and education in American society, but I am certain that it will contribute some important points in the required reappraisal.

There are two main operating generalizations about Italian Americans and education, especially higher education, both of which are contrary to the limited evidence available. The first of these is the perception, almost accepted as a truism, that they are disinclined toward educational and professional career mobility. "Italian Americans do not have the high aspirations of other Americans" is the common phrase. The second generalization, related to the first, is that there has been little change regarding actual achievement and aspirations since the onset of mass immigration. Much of this is due to the stereotype of Italians and Italian Americans as only lower class, working class, or peasant, rural, backward collectivities who are still adapting (or maladapting) to the modern world. Put very simply, when people look to study the Italian-American community, they tend to identify those who have achieved the least and who are least like "normal" Americans. Needless to say, this last, generally positive stereotype of high achieving "normal Americans" is equally uninforming.

Certainly a significant segment of the Italian-American population might be educationally deficient but it is far from the majority and therefore much more stereotypical than typical. Egelman (1982a, 1982b), Gans (1962) and Dyer (1979) have commented on the variations and changes in educational achievement among Italian Americans. William F. Whyte (1943), in his classic study of Italian Americans in "Cornerville," pointed out that even in the worst time of the Great Depression a significant proportion of the Italian-American population aspired toward higher education and high status career mobility. Unfortunately, readers are more likely to remember the less mobile and motivated "corner boys," and the racketeers than the "college boys" whom Whyte described. Another related problem is the view of the Old World; that is, Italy and the Italian population have not changed much since the mass diaspora of the late nineteenth and early twentieth centuries. Italy in the minds of many people, including Italian Americans of later generations, is still educationally and technologically backward. The most common vision of Italy, aside from the tourist attractions, is that portrayed by Banfield (1958) and Levi (1947). Again, without a doubt, there are parts of modern Italy in which education is still difficult to obtain, or where because of circumstance or cultural values, discouraged but the majority of modern Italian immigrants to the United States are far from the mostly illiterate itinerants of almost a century ago. Related to this last point, some social scientists are beginning to argue that perhaps even the mass of early Italian immigrants were not as educationally, economically and socially backward as is currently believed. In sum, a great deal of research remains to be done on the early as well as contemporary Italian Americans.

Milton Gordon (1964) has provided us with the most frequently used model for discussing the adjustment of immigrant groups to American society. The widespread use of his model is based primarily on its simplicity and therefore it's utility in studying many different ethnic groups in our complex and diverse nation. He notes that the overall assimilation process by which new groups are absorbed into the dominant society can be neatly divided into two theoretically distinct but historically integrated phenomena. The first of these interrelated processes is cultural assimilation, or the adaptation of the immigrant culture to the dominant culture; sometimes called acculturation. The second of these processes is structural assimilation, or the more objective movement of the new people into the socioeconomic structure of the dominant society. Culture includes the norms, values, language, styles or ways of life of society, while structure refers to the statuses, positions, strata, and institutions of society. Gordon (1964), Child (1943), and others have argued that cultural assimilation is usually an easier and more rapid adjustment but that both processes occur simultaneously so that a lag between the two is common, i.e., most ethnic groups are more culturally than structurally assimilated. Different groups have different rates of adaptation or absorption that are influenced by such factors as the degree of difference between the dominant and minority societies and the relative receptivity of both to each other.

In this paper we are focusing on the adjustment of Italians to American society relating to cultural values regarding educational attainment and structural assimilation as well, as represented by achievement. Educational achievement and related movement into professional and white-collar careers by people of Italian descent in American society is most often seen as the result of the Americanization process by which Italian anti-educational values and attitude are slowly transformed over the generations, until they are replaced, in effect, with American pro-educational values and attitudes. This in turn results in the occupational mobility of Italian Americans. Italian values have been seen as impediments to higher educational achievement (Egelman and DeVito-Egelman, 1981). Let us turn now to a discussion of Italian culture and its real and presumed impact on educational and career mobility.

As noted by virtually all observers of Italian and Italian-American life, the central cultural and structural entity is the family (Tomasi, 1972). Educational and general socioeconomic mobility in American society is most accurately described however as a more individualistic phenomenon. At least at the level of mythology and folklore, achievement in America is primarily the result of individual effort, whereas for Italians, success of individuals must be tempered by concern and respect for the family and its demands. The classic examples of Italian immobility are frequently related by educators, researchers and ordinary people who cite the young man or woman who forgoes educational or career opportunities in order to stay closer to home.

"Closer to home" has both a geographical and sociocultural meaning. Often opportunities for advancement exist at locations at great distance from the locus of the family or its extension; the neighborhood. In some working-class Italian-American areas there appears to be some justification for this perception. Among Italian Americans who have already passed into the white-collar world, the reluctance is more frequently overcome or somehow accommodated. More intensive research would be needed to substantially document both extremes. It should be noted before continuing that the immobility of Italians is, prima facie, false at least as it relates to the historical record. The record shows that Italians have been one of the most voluntarily mobile groups as evidenced by their vast diasporic experience, seeking economic opportunities in places scattered across the world. Even this extraordinary movement is tempered by concern for family and kin.

In general, "closer to home" means family obligations. Another meaning of the term refers to specific values and relations within each family itself. For example Sennett and Cobb (1972) have noted in their studies of working class culture that some families, and individuals within families, see the educational or socioeconomic advancement of offspring and siblings as rejections of the family itself. Direct and indirect pressure may be placed on the younger generation not to succeed or to seek advancement if it is interpreted as a rejection of the family. Achievement is channeled to acceptable areas. One might see this as subconscious rather than conscious activity on the part of parents who might ridicule or otherwise demean the airs of their children. In any case, children sense even the unspoken fears of their parents that they might lose a child to the outside world. These children in turn become chronic underachievers.

The problems of the working class family are a worthwhile topic for investigation by themselves. Since a common stereotype of Italian Americans is as a working class group it deserves special attention here. It is this view of Italian Americans that spurs the concern for creating new and more American role models for Italian-American youngsters. There are, however, several ways in which the role of the Italian family in educational attainment can be interpreted, if in fact it is an accurate impression. The most direct route is to take this impression for granted and to try to effect not only changes in the family, but in the educational system itself so that they are both less of an impediment to achievement. Very simply put, one solution is to make it possible for opportunities for higher education to exist "closer to home" both geographically and culturally. In other words, making higher education less of a threat to the family by making the higher institution more a part of family neighborhood life. That segment of the Italian-American population, then, with the greatest resistance can be accommodated and be able to take advantage of opportunity, if so chosen. It should be noted that Stryker (1981), Abramson (1973) and others have noted the positive effect of Catholic private school experiences on Italian-American achievement. In this context; parochial schools may be more in conformity with Italian cultural and family values.

It is my firm belief, supported by impressions, personal experiences, interviews with educators, parents and students, and finally, real data such as that present here, that when real opportunity for higher education exists for Italian Americans of all socioeconomic and cultural backgrounds it will be taken advantage of with great gusto and success. This is true regardless of their misunderstood values and attitudes. What is needed at this point is a reinterpretation of Italian and Italian-American values vis-à-vis education. This examination does not reject prior notions but integrates them into a practical reality all too frequently avoided by scholars and practitioners.

Let us, for now, accept the fact that some, perhaps many, people of Italian descent do not take advantage of opportunities for higher education. Let us further accept the proposition that, above all, Italians are family-oriented and that the least they expect from educational institutions is respect for their traditions and concerns. Additionally, let us agree that some are not convinced of the value of educational achievement. What then could be done to take these factors into account and create a situation wherein even the hardcore will allow themselves and their children to pursue socioeconomic advancement via college education? When these questions are addressed, the reinterpretation of values becomes clearer.

Higher education must be made a part of Italian-American life. It must be made to complement rather than conflict with traditional values. A theoretical case in point: if higher education is a family value, then Italian Americans would become leaders in achievement. The reality is that for already successful Italian Americans, higher education has become a family value. For them education and achievement is "closer to home." This is true despite the common experiences of many Italian-American achievers of being unwelcome at many institutions of higher learning because of anti-Italian, anti-working class, and/or anti-Catholic biases, often acceptable in American intellectual and academic circles (Greeley, 1969).

Similar reception has been provided both in the past and at present for Jews, Blacks, Hispanics and other more or less visible minorities. Italians for the most part have employed the strategy of low visibility on college campuses to avoid conflict. At public colleges, such as the one that is the locus of this research, Italian-American students are unlikely to participate as Italian Americans in campus affairs. Militant ethnicity or ethno-nationalism is not yet part of the Italian-American scene. Except for the more recent immigrants from Italy, Italian-American students are not likely to perceive the vast contributions of Italy to the university curriculum as a part of their own heritage. Working class Italian Americans tend to see their own cultural heritage when presented to them in a college environment as alien to them and their experience. Conversely, professional staff at the colleges find it difficult to find a connection between the Italian-American students in their classes and the Italians who produced much of what they teach and study. This combination of misconception and misperception on the part of Italian-American students and their professors is part of the reason for the discomfort that the young feel when they are first in their family to enter college. In order to feel at home in the college environment it is important and necessary for students to find things there with which they are familiar and which they bring back and make part of their family and neighborhood life.

We shall now turn to consider some recent empirical evidence which can be used to support some of these preliminary arguments and which will bring some important points into clear focus about Italian Americans. First of all, as to overall Italian achievement in America, Greeley (1977) and Egelman (1982b) clearly showed that they have achieved at or above national averages for educational achievement, occupational status and income. Despite these facts, based on census and national survey data, the view of Italian Americans as underachievers still persists. When the facts are truly appreciated undoubtedly the explanation will be that they have therefore become Americanized, as the theory of assimilation predicts. Few will question the common perception of Italian values as perhaps being erroneous in the first instance. The remaining sections of this paper, hopefully, will increase the likelihood that such a re-evaluation might be undertaken.

Although the data to be presented here are far from sufficient to adequately test the general theory of assimilation, to which the author totally ascribes, it does provide some sociological food for thought regarding some of its assumptions about American life in general, and urban working-class Italian Americans specifically. In other words, the theory is adequate although the facts were not. The data, and other observations made by the author, seem to suggest that regarding the Italian-American experience in the areas of career and educational mobility, structural change has occurred without the hypothesized cultural change. This finding places emphasis on the structure of opportunity as being more crucial to socio-economic mobility, independent of attitudinal and value change. More directly, Italian Americans do not have to be less Italian in order to achieve.

The 1970s provided a great, perhaps even noble, experiment in higher education policy in New York City — open enrollment at the City University of New York, the city's public college system. During the open enrollment era, every high school graduate in New York City was guaranteed access to higher education. An added incentive was that for some years tuition was also free. In anticipation of the experiment's onset, educational policy experts predicted the major beneficiaries of the program would be blacks and other groups defined as deprived minorities. In fact, open enrollment was designed as a mechanism to compensate minorities for past discrimination in educational opportunity. Contrary to the expectation of planners and experts, the ethnic group that perhaps took great advantage of the opportunity was Italian Americans. Many experts, including those of Italian-American background, were surprised but they should not have been. The open enrollment-free tuition policy removed the most basic obstacles to higher education by even the most reluctant of Italian Americans. When resistance to higher education is translated into dollars, the free tuition made the point moot. Geographically, City University colleges were within easy commuting distance to most Italian-American neighborhoods and further, they offered many programs at the two and four-year levels which were clearly translatable into practical advantage: preparation for jobs. As noted in an earlier paper by this author, even Italian-American women in large numbers took advantage of the opportunity, upsetting convenient stereotypes.

At Brooklyn College, for example, almost half of the Italian-American students who attended were female. How much did Italian Americans change in a few months so that all of a sudden they were interested in higher education and social mobility? My own sense is that they did not change and that their behavior was consistent with their values. The data and discussion that follows, I believe, will show this, as well as bring to the fore some even more interesting aspects of educational values and experiences. The discussion should stimulate further research on Italian Americans as well as other ethnic groups whom, I believe, we understand less than we think. We shall pay special attention to the differences and similarities between generations of Italian-American students, as indicated by their parental backgrounds and their own experiences and attitudes regarding higher education and social mobility.

The primary data for this discussion was collected during 1975 at Brooklyn College and analyzed at subsequent times. Other observations related to the issue of Italian Americans and higher education, noted herein, were made during and after the collection of the data. A preliminary report was published in 1975 (Krase and Fuccillo) and another paper focusing on the differences between male and female students at Brooklyn College by this writer was published in 1978. In 1982, a grant from the Italian American Institute to Foster Higher Education made it possible to further analyze the data for this paper.

Based on a random sample of 290 cases, in 1975, we obtained this general profile of the Italian-American students who took advantage of the open enrollment opportunity. Greater detail is available in the 1975 report. None of the findings were inconsistent with common assumptions about urban Italian Americans. The surprising fact was that they were attending college. About 63% of the students' fathers held blue-collar jobs and 46% of their mothers were also employed outside the household. Despite the fact of free tuition and parental employment, at least half of the students worked an average of 15 hours per week, continuing the tradition of Italian youth employment and self-sufficiency. About 40% came from families of five or more persons and the vast majority had parents who never attended college themselves (only 8% of the fathers and 3.8% of the mothers had earned a college degree). These students were often the first in their families to pursue higher education. Almost a third of the students had at least one parent born in Italy. As expected, the study showed that the students were job-oriented and viewed their education from a career-based perspective. Also not surprising, the students spent little of their spare time at the college in extracurricular activities. The students were evenly divided between those graduating from public and parochial high schools.

More to the point of attitude and values, the study showed that the Italian-American students, although doing well at school, felt alienated and did not take advantage of on-campus opportunities because of the perceived coldness and lack of personal touches. In other words, the college did not operate in the Italian-American fashion of intimacy. The lack of other persons "like them" in the administration and on the faculty also left them feeling isolated at times and they either clustered in small groups or returned home to their easily identifiable Italian-American neighborhoods for primary relationships.

With this general picture of the Italian-American student in mind we shall turn now to the specific issues of differences and similarities between generations and how they relate to attitudes toward educational and career mobility. We will also use this data to discuss whether Italian values change and therefore make higher education possible or whether the change in the opportunity itself makes the difference. The assimilation model predicts that the longer any group is in America the more they will express American values. Therefore we should expect great differences between cases in which grandparents were born in the America versus those parents more recently emigrating from Italy. The data is presented below, both patri- and matrilineally, which may also suggest the relative impact of fathers' or mothers' nativity in value changes. Although the data collected and analyzed includes all grandparents, reported in these tables are only father's father and mother's mother. In each case a table, or several tables will be presented, followed by a discussion of relevant issues.

Because of the limitations of the sample, statistical analysis with any great degree of confidence is not possible and therefore not attempted here. The data presented here is exploratory and suggestive in nature. My intention is to provoke and stimulate further research into the issues raised about Italian Americans. For example, when we speak of differences between generations of students it should be noted that 63.4% of the students' fathers, 8.2% of their father's fathers, 72.2% of students' mothers and 19.0% of their mother's mothers were born in the United States.

The total sample size in this analysis is only 273 and therefore making absolute statements about differences between generations would be too ambitious. The number of fathers and mothers born in Italy is 73 and 46 respectively. The number of father's fathers and mother's mothers born in the United States is 24 and 52 respectively. The overall nativity for students' parent and grandparents is given below. It should be noted that the figures for grandparents born in Italy include students whose parents were born in Italy as well.

Nativity of students' parents and grandparents

	US	ITALY	OTHER	DON'T KNOW
Father	171	73	19	10
Mother	198	46	27	2
Father's father	24	230	18	1
Father's mother	40	210	22	1
Mother's father	38	188	45	2
Mother's mother	52	171	48	2
N = 273				

Tables 1–5 give an indication of the relative degrees of educational and occupational attainment of the families from which our Italian-American student sample came. The data shows that the more Americanized parents have to a much greater degree attained at least minimal levels of education, as compared to the less Americanized. The mothers and fathers, whose own mothers and fathers, were born in the United States are much more likely, for example to have completed at least eight years of education (primary school). Of those born in Italy 35% of fathers and 43% of mothers had only eight years or less education, versus 9% and 2% respectively for those whose own parents were born in America. Similarly, the more Americanized were more likely to have graduated from high school. This

advantage does not, however, hold true at the level of college education where the two groups are virtually equal in educational attainment.

Interestingly, the advantage that the more Americanized parents have in educational attainment seems not to have been translated into the same degree of occupational achievement. If we group occupational levels and look at the highest and lowest prestige strata we find that the fathers born in Italy are more likely to have high status jobs (professional, technical and administrative) than those fathers whose own fathers were born in the United States. The less Americanized are also more likely to hold low status positions as operatives, service workers and laborers. If we look at all those fathers born in America, including those whose fathers were born in Italy, we are further confounded. This group has attained more than either the least or most Americanized groups in high status positions but did worse in low status jobs. How can this be explained?

Although the data presented here is limited, some informed discussion is possible. It is suggested that these complex findings are related to the characteristics of different immigrant cohorts; a sizable proportion of more recent (post-1965) immigrants from Italy are employed in higher status occupations.

This conforms to the findings on educational attainment where we saw that at the highest levels of education, Italian born fathers compared favorably with their more Americanized counterparts. This suggests that since the earliest periods of mass migration, 1890–1910, a large and significant proportion of the immigrant population had higher socioeconomic status. This might mean several things: (1) higher status Italians have increased their interest in coming to America; (2) there is a higher proportion of higher status persons in the Italian population, reflecting increased opportunity over the decades in Italian society; (3) lower status Italians were less likely to choose America as a destination; (4) some combination of these developments. What is certain is that Italy is not the backward country it is assumed by many to be and that we should expect that some changes in the characteristics of immigrants would have taken place over the past nine or so decades. Unfortunately, most people continue to be under the assumption that Italy offered the United States only low-status migrants.

Noting the differences in the structural changes in the Italian and Italian-American population we should then expect that the generations are not so different from one another as previously posited. We should not

expect such a great advantage to persons of Italian descent who emigrated to America during the earlier periods of mass movement. Descendants of early migrants might be more Americanized but this might not
consistently and directly translate into advantages in educational and occupational achievement. If I might be allowed to speculate at this point, I
would suggest the possibility that for early Italian lower-class immigrants
the American experience was more socially and economically debilitating
than for counterparts who stayed at home and benefited in a more culturally hospitable environment by the eventual modernization of Italy.

We have noted earlier the necessity of seeing Italian Americans from
the perspective of family versus individual attainment. Therefore we
should look at higher education in a family context and compare more
and less Americanized student family settings. The data collected on college education of family members, other than the student him or herself,
shows that if parents were born in Italy then it is more likely that other
family members are either presently attending college or have college degrees. In other words those whose grandparents were born in the United
States are less likely to have other family members presently in college or
with degrees. Of further interest is the fact that it seems as though American born grandmothers are more associated with higher education than
American born grandfathers. In general, American nativity is of greater
advantage to females than to males, although Italian-American females
still do not achieve as well as Italian-American males. In other words, if
you are female it is better to be more American than Italian, but in all
cases it is best to be male.

Let us turn now to a consideration of Table 6; the self-ethnic identification of the sample. Students were given the option of writing their ethnicity or nationality in the following form: Italian, Italian American,
American Italian, and American. As might be expected, there were noticeable differences based on the students' generation. The differences in
ethnic identification are not, however, absolute.

For example, if one's father or mother was born in Italy one was more
likely to respond "Italian" than if one's grandfather or grandmother was
born in America. The proportions were 54% and 59% versus 38% and 30%
respectively. The "American" designation is more interesting. Two percent of students with Italian born fathers and no students with Italian
born grandfathers identified themselves in this way, while none of the
students with Italian born mothers and 10% of those with American born

grandmothers gave "American" for their ethnic group. The intermediary designations Italian American and American Italian conformed closely to expected generation. What is of greatest significance in these responses is the small proportion who answered "American" alone in any case, and the high proportion who answered "Italian." Despite this high rate of Italian identification, it should be noted that in an earlier report by this author (1975) only 19% of the sample reported more than "occasional" use of the Italian language at home. Language use is often given as an indication of cultural identity and commitment. This identification of "Italian" is then much likely to be a response to a question that offers little variation in response than a true indication of cultural similarity. It suggests that Americans are likely to identify themselves by national roots regardless of their awareness and facility with their original national culture. This is not, of course, peculiar to persons of Italian descent.

The students in the survey were also asked to offer what they thought would be the major obstacles to their attaining career or professional goals. Some interesting observations can be made regarding their responses. About 40% of all students reported "no major obstacles," but the most optimistic were those with American grandfathers, and the least optimistic those with Italian born mothers. The more Americanized were more likely to offer "race" as an obstacle, while "ethnicity" was seen as an equal problem by both groups. Interestingly, those with American born grandmothers and Italian born mothers were most likely to see "sex" as a problem. Overall, the less Americanized saw "age" as a major obstacle to goals. To both groups, "religion" was mentioned the least. These data are reported in Table 7.

The students' long-range occupational goals are reported in Table 8. Because of the lack of variety in their responses to this question, it is not possible to make very fine distinctions. Most noteworthy is the fact that those with American born grandfathers and Italian born mothers were most likely to cite professional long-range goals. Those with American grandfathers and grandmothers were also most likely to be "undecided." Since professional careers require graduate education, the data presented in Table 9, on immediate plans after graduation, ought to indicate similar findings. The data show that students with American born grandparents more often plan to attend graduate school immediately after graduation, whereas the least Americanized are more likely to plan to go to work. This might mean, however, that the less Americanized are going into pro-

fessions that do not require as much, or as immediate, graduate education. This may also indicate that the less Americanized are planning to
work full time and go to graduate school on a part-time basis.

Table 10, which reports on the type of graduate program that students
intend to pursue, seems to confirm this expectation as there is little difference in intention to take a graduate program between more and less
Americanized respondents. Students with American born grandmothers
and students with Italian born mothers are the most likely to indicate
medical programs while those with American grandfathers and grandmothers are much more likely to be interested in law programs. Those
with American born mothers and fathers are also most likely to indicate
interest in master's degree programs.

We will now look at how the students responded to questions concerning college education in general and the amount of moral support
they receive from their parents. If we look at profiles of attitudes toward
college education and values associated with higher education, we find
that the more and less Americanized students are very similar. Their responses in all cases are in the same general direction and differ only in
degree of response. In general all students are practical and pragmatic
and do not view the college as a social or cultural opportunity. The students are, in other words, serious minded. It is interesting to note that in
the early 1970s this was only beginning to be typical of American college
youth, as reported by Yankelovich (1974). More recent surveys have been
reported in the media that the practical, non-idealistic trend in college
and youth values has continued. Does this mean that American youth
values have changed, while Italian and Italian-American values have not?
If I could be allowed to be facetious here, I would state that it appears
that American youth have been Italianized over the past generation.

Tables 11–21 summarize student attitudes toward college education.
Although the attitudes of the generations are remarkably similar, some
observations can be made regarding even slight, but regular, differences
between the most and least Americanized groups. In reference to the objectives of all students in their college education, the following are considered "very important" by the majority of all students and could be
ranked, most to least important, in the following order: grades, intellectual pursuits, course work, job training, and earning money. Conversely,
the following were regarded as "least important" in the same order: solving social problems, social activities, cultural activities, and student gov-

ernment. It should be noted here that 40% of the students thought solving social problems was very important while proportions range from 20% to less than 10% for the other activities. With few exceptions, this can be explained by the method of answering the question, the responses of the most and least Americanized are almost identical. The least Americanized seem more practical and those with Italian born mothers the most practical of all. It must be repeated, however, the differences may not be statistically significant. This practical orientation toward college is reflected in Tables 20 and 21, which show that almost three-quarters of the students neither engage in college extracurricular activities nor off campus activities. The more Americanized participating on campus more often and the least Americanized participating more often off-campus.

When asked to agree or disagree with certain statements about the college (see Tables 22–24), many more students totally disagreed than totally agreed with the statements: "I come to Brooklyn College in my spare time," and "If I could get a good job I wouldn't go to college." Students were slightly less emphatic about the latter statement than the former. Interestingly, those with more Americanized fathers and mothers were most likely to agree with the second statement. Again it must be cautioned that the differences are not necessarily statistically significant.

The final tables to be discussed, Tables 25–27, are those reporting on the importance of college education to the students themselves and how important they perceived their education is to their parents. Students were asked to indicate their degree of agreement with statements: "My college education is important to me; my father; my mother." We have focused here only on those responses that indicate "total agreement" with the statements. As we might expect, their education is most important to students themselves. It is virtually identical for mothers and fathers, although the perceptions of mother's support is greater than for fathers. Those with Italian born parents or American born grandparents seem to receive the greatest support, as represented by total agreement to the statements. In almost all cases, American born grandfathers and Italian born mothers seem to give the students the greatest sense of support.

Although the data presented here has severe limitations from a statistical point of view, in combination with other data and studies, I believe many important points concerning Italian Americans and achievement can be made. It is also possible to question some important aspects of general theory about structural and cultural assimilation and Americanization in general. As noted earlier, much of the problem is due to a lack of understanding of what has occurred in Italy since mass migration to America. From the author's point of view, the greatest problem is that our expert notions of Italians and Italian Americans seem to be stuck in a turn of the century scenario.

TABLES

TABLE 1. *Father's Education*

NATIVITY	8 YEARS OR LESS	SOME HIGH SCHOOL	HIGH SCHL GRADUATE	SOME COLLEGE	COLLEGE GRADUATE	GRADUATE SCHOOL	GRADUATE DEGREE
FATHER							
Italy	35.1%	22.1%	26.0%	7.8%	2.6%	0.0%	2.6%
US	9.2%	22.0%	46.8%	8.1%	5.2%	2.3%	2.9%
GRANDFATHER							
Italy	19.6%	22.6%	38.3%	8.3%	3.9%	1.7%	2.6%
US	4.2%	16.7%	62.5%	8.3%	4.2%	-	-
MOTHER							
Italy	43.5%	19.6%	17.4%	8.7%	2.2%	-	2.2%
US	11.7%	21.8%	46.2%	9.1%	4.1%	2.0%	2.5%
GRANDMOTHER							
Italy	23.7%	23.7%	34.9%	8.3%	4.7%	0.6%	1.8%
US	1.9%	19.2%	61.5%	7.7%	1.9%	1.9%	3.8%

TABLE 2. *Mother's Education*

NATIVITY	8 YEARS OR LESS	SOME HIGH SCHOOL	HIGH SCHL GRADUATE	SOME COLLEGE	COLLEGE GRADUATE	GRADUATE SCHOOL	GRADUATE DEGREE
FATHER							
Italy	28.6%	20.8%	40.3%	5.2%	-	-	1.3%
US	5.2%	19.1%	61.3%	7.5%	2.3%	1.2%	0.6%
GRANDFATHER							
Italy	13.5%	20.4%	53.5%	6.1%	0.9%	0.9%	0.9%
US	-	8.3%	70.8%	12.5%	4.2%	-	-
MOTHER							
Italy	43.5%	23.9%	23.9%	2.2%	-	-	-
US	5.1%	18.3%	62.9%	8.1%	1.5%	1.0%	1.0%
GRANDMOTHER							
Italy	16.0%	22.5%	49.7%	5.3%	1.2%	0.6%	1.2%
US	1.9%	15.4%	67.3%	11.5%	1.9%	-	-

TABLE 3. *Father's Occupation*

NATIVITY	PROFSNL	TCHNICL	ADMIN	CLERICAL	SALES	CRAFT	OPERTVE	SERVICE	LABOR
FATHER									
Italy	6.5%	6.5%	2.6%	2.6%	5.2%	5.2%	5.2%	23.4%	5.2%
US	8.1%	8.1%	6.9%	4.6%	5.2%	1.2%	4.0%	34.7%	2.3%
GRANDFATHER									
Italy	7.8%	7.4%	5.2%	3.9%	4.8%	2.2%	4.3%	31.3%	3.5%
US	4.2%	8.3%	-	-	12.5%	4.2%	4.2%	37.5%	4.2%
MOTHER									
Italy	4.3%	6.5%	2.2%	2.2%	6.5%	4.3%	4.3%	21.7%	6.5%
US	6.6%	8.6%	6.1%	4.6%	5.1%	2.0%	4.6%	33.5%	2.5%
GRANDMOTHER									
Italy	7.1%	7.7%	5.3%	5.3%	4.7%	2.4%	4.1%	32.0%	4.1%
US	-	1.9%	3.8%	3.8%	9.6%	1.9%	3.8%	36.5%	3.8%

TABLE 4. *Other Family Members With Degrees*

NATIVITY	YES	NO
FATHER		
Italy	32.5%	64.9%
US	28.9%	67.1%
GRANDFATHER		
Italy	30.4%	66.1%
US	26.7%	79.2%
MOTHER		
Italy	32.6%	65.2%
US	29.4%	66.5%
GRANDMOTHER		
Italy	31.4%	65.7%
US	26.9%	67.3%

TABLE 5. *Other Family Members in College*

NATIVITY	YES	NO
FATHER		
Italy	44.2%	55.8%
US	39.3%	60.7%
GRANDFATHER		
Italy	40.4%	59.6%
US	29.2%	70.8%
MOTHER		
Italy	45.7%	54.3%
US	39.1%	60.9%
GRANDMOTHER		
Italy	39.6%	60.4%
US	38.5%	61.5%

TABLE 6. *Students' Ethnic Identification*

NATIVITY	ITALIAN	ITALIAN-OTHER	ITALIAN AMERICAN	AMERICAN ITALIAN	AMERICAN	OTHER
FATHER						
Italy	54.5%	13.0%	19.5%	7.8%	2.6%	-
US	44.2%	13.3%	21.4%	10.4%	9.2%	1.7%
GRANDFATHER						
Italy	47.4%	13.0%	20.4%	9.6%	7.4%	.4%
US	37.5%	20.8%	16.7%	12.5%	-	8.3%
MOTHER						
Italy	58.7%	13.0%	19.6%	6.5%	-	-
US	44.2%	11.2%	21.3%	10.2%	9.1%	2.5%
GRANDMOTHER						
Italy	55.6%	8.9%	22.5%	7.1%	4.1%	1.2%
US	30.8%	13.5%	21.2%	17.3%	9.6%	5.8%

TABLE 7. *Students' Perceived Major Obstacle to Attaining Career or Professional Goals*

NATIVITY	NONE	AGE	SEX	RACE	ETHNIC	RELIGION	APPEARNC	OTHER
FATHER								
Italy	44.2%	11.7%	14.3%	3.9%	11.7%	2.6%	6.5%	5.2%
US	43.9%	8.7%	13.9%	7.5%	12.7%	1.2%	6.9%	4.6%
GRANDFATHER								
Italy	42.6%	10.4%	14.8%	6.5%	13.0%	1.7%	6.1%	4.3%
US	50.0%	4.2%	12.5%	4.2%	8.3%	-	16.7%	4.2%
MOTHER								
Italy	39.1%	19.6%	17.4%	6.5%	10.9%	-	6.5%	-
US	45.7%	8.6%	12.7%	6.1%	12.7%	2.0%	6.1%	5.6%
GRANDMOTHER								
Italy	44.4%	13.0%	11.8%	4.7%	13.6%	1.8%	7.7%	3.0%
US	42.3%	5.8%	17.3%	11.5%	9.6%	1.9%	3.3%	7.7%

TABLE 8. *Students' Long-range Occupational Goals*

NATIVITY	PROFSNL	MANAGR	ADMIN	PRVT BUS	TECHNCL	CLERICAL	CRAFT	OTHER	UNDECID
FATHER									
Italy	58.4%	3.9%	3.9%	1.3%	-	-	-	7.8%	23.4%
US	58.4%	1.2%	-	3.5%	2.3%	0.6%	0.6%	8.1%	25.4%
GRANDFATHER									
Italy	58.7%	2.2%	1.3%	3.0%	1.7%	0.4%	0.4%	7.8%	23.9%
US	66.7%	-	-	-	-	-	-	-	33.3%
MOTHER									
Italy	63.0%	2.2%	4.3%	2.2%	2.2%	-	-	4.3%	21.7%
US	58.4%	1.5%	-	2.5%	1.5%	0.5%	0.5%	9.6%	25.4%
GRANDMOTHER									
Italy	59.2%	1.8%	1.8%	3.6%	1.8%	0.6%	0.6%	7.1%	23.1%
US	57.7%	1.9%	-	-	1.9%	-	-	9.6%	28.8%

TABLE 9. *Immediate Plans After Graduation*

NATIVITY	GRAD SCHL	WORK	TRAVEL	REST & RELAX	MARRIAGE	OTHER
FATHER						
Italy	22.1%	41.6%	1.3%	6.5%	2.6%	7.8%
US	20.8%	38.7%	6.9%	5.9%	4.0%	6.4%
GRANDFATHER						
Italy	19.6%	40.9%	4.8%	6.1%	3.5%	7.4%
US	33.3%	29.2%	8.3%	4.2%	4.2%	12.5%
MOTHER						
Italy	21.7%	41.3%	2.2%	4.3%	-	6.5%
US	21.3%	38.6%	6.1%	6.6%	4.6%	6.6%
GRANDMOTHER						
Italy	20.1%	42.6%	6.5%	5.3%	2.4%	7.1%
US	25.0%	21.2%	1.9%	7.7%	7.7%	11.5%

TABLE 10. *Type of Graduate Program*

NATIVITY	MASTER'S	MEDICAL	LAW	DENTAL	OTHER
FATHER					
Italy	27.3%	3.9%	-	1.3%	6.5%
US	32.4%	1.7%	1.7%	-	3.5%
GRANDFATHER					
Italy	31.7%	2.6%	-	0.4%	4.3%
US	20.8%	-	12.5%	-	4.2%
MOTHER					
Italy	21.7%	6.5%	-	-	10.9%
US	34.0%	1.5%	1.5%	-	3.0%
GRANDMOTHER					
Italy	31.4%	1.2%	0.6%	-	4.7%
US	26.9%	5.8%	3.8%	-	3.8%

TABLES 11–21
Attitudes Toward College Education

TABLE 11. *Importance of Job Training*

NATIVITY	UNIMPORTANT	NOT VERY	FAIRLY	VERY
FATHER				
Italy	6.5%	14.3%	15.6%	57.1%
US	4.6%	13.9%	27.7%	52.0%
GRANDFATHER				
Italy	5.2%	13.9%	23.0%	54.3%
US	4.2%	8.3%	50.0%	33.3%
MOTHER				
Italy	4.3%	10.9%	19.6%	56.5%
US	5.1%	12.7%	26.4%	53.8%
GRANDMOTHER				
Italy	5.3%	14.2%	21.9%	53.8%
US	3.8%	9.6%	34.6%	50.0%

TABLE 12. *Importance of Earning Money*

NATIVITY	UNIMPORTANT	NOT VERY	FAIRLY	VERY
FATHER				
Italy	1.3%	9.1%	35.1%	46.8%
US	1.2%	8.7%	31.8%	54.9%
GRANDFATHER				
Italy	1.7%	8.3%	33.9%	50.4%
US	-	8.3%	20.8%	70.8%
MOTHER				
Italy	2.2%	4.3%	37.0%	50.0%
US	1.5%	9.6%	31.5%	53.8%
GRANDMOTHER				
Italy	1.8%	9.5%	33.7%	49.7%
US	-	5.8%	34.6%	53.8%

TABLE 13. *Importance of Coursework*

NATIVITY	UNIMPORTANT	NOT VERY	FAIRLY	VERY
FATHER				
Italy	1.3%	9.1%	35.1%	46.8%
US	1.2%	8.7%	31.8%	54.9%
GRANDFATHER				
Italy	1.7%	8.3%	33.9%	50.4%
US	-	8.3%	20.8%	70.8%
MOTHER				
Italy	2.2%	4.3%	37.0%	50.0%
US	1.5%	9.6%	31.5%	53.8%
GRANDMOTHER				
Italy	1.8%	9.5%	33.7%	49.7%
US	-	5.8%	34.6%	53.8%

TABLE 14. *Importance of Grades*

NATIVITY	UNIMPORTANT	NOT VERY	FAIRLY	VERY
FATHER				
Italy	1.3%	6.5%	24.7%	61.0%
US	4.6%	4.0%	28.9%	60.1%
GRANDFATHER				
Italy	3.0%	4.3%	27.0%	61.7%
US	12.5%	8.3%	33.3%	45.8%
MOTHER				
Italy	2.2%	2.2%	21.7%	65.2%
US	4.6%	4.1%	29.9%	58.9%
GRANDMOTHER				
Italy	3.6%	5.3%	29.0%	57.4%
US	3.8%	-	26.9%	65.4%

TABLE 15. *Importance of Intellectual Pursuits*

NATIVITY	UNIMPORTANT	NOT VERY	FAIRLY	VERY
FATHER				
Italy	2.6%	2.6%	26.0%	64.9%
US	4.6%	6.4%	30.6%	56.6%
GRANDFATHER				
Italy	3.5%	4.3%	30.0%	59.1%
US	8.3%	16.7%	16.7%	58.3%
MOTHER				
Italy	4.3%	2.2%	34.8%	54.3%
US	4.1%	6.1%	28.9%	58.9%
GRANDMOTHER				
Italy	3.6%	5.3%	33.1%	55.1%
US	5.8%	7.7%	26.9%	53.8%

TABLE 16. *Importance of Cultural Activities*

NATIVITY	UNIMPORTANT	NOT VERY	FAIRLY	VERY
FATHER				
Italy	16.9%	27.3%	33.8%	18.2%
US	14.5%	30.1%	37.0%	16.8%
GRANDFATHER				
Italy	14.8%	28.7%	35.7%	17.4%
US	20.8%	29.2%	33.3%	12.5%
MOTHER				
Italy	19.6%	26.1%	37.0%	10.9%
US	14.2%	29.9%	36.5%	17.3%
GRANDMOTHER				
Italy	16.6%	26.6%	37.3%	15.4%
US	17.3%	28.8%	30.8%	19.2%

TABLE 17. *Importance of Student Government*

NATIVITY	UNIMPORTANT	NOT VERY	FAIRLY	VERY
FATHER				
Italy	32.5%	40.3%	18.2%	5.2%
US	31.8%	41.0%	18.5%	6.9%
GRANDFATHER				
Italy	31.3%	39.1%	19.6%	7.0%
US	41.7%	41.7%	12.5%	4.2%
MOTHER				
Italy	30.4%	37.0%	23.9%	4.3%
US	31.5%	41.6%	17.3%	7.6%
GRANDMOTHER				
Italy	33.7%	40.2%	17.2%	5.9%
US	25.0%	46.2%	17.3%	7.7%

TABLE 18. *Importance of Solving Social Problems*

NATIVITY	UNIMPORTANT	NOT VERY	FAIRLY	VERY
FATHER				
Italy	7.8%	10.4%	31.2%	42.9%
US	11.0%	15.0%	28.3%	40.5%
GRANDFATHER				
Italy	10.0%	14.3%	29.6%	39.6%
US	8.3%	8.3%	37.5%	41.7%
MOTHER				
Italy	8.7%	17.4%	21.7%	45.7%
US	10.2%	13.2%	30.5%	40.6%
GRANDMOTHER				
Italy	10.1%	13.0%	28.4%	40.8%
US	3.8%	17.3%	32.7%	38.5%

TABLE 19. *Importance of Social Activity*

NATIVITY	UNIMPORTANT	NOT VERY	FAIRLY	VERY
FATHER				
Italy	20.8%	31.2%	23.4%	19.5%
US	17.3%	31.8%	25.4%	24.9%
GRANDFATHER				
Italy	17.8%	33.0%	23.9%	22.2%
US	25.0%	20.8%	33.3%	20.8%
MOTHER				
Italy	21.7%	30.4%	21.7%	19.6%
US	15.7%	33.0%	25.9%	23.9%
GRANDMOTHER				
Italy	16.6%	31.4%	26.6%	22.5%
US	15.4%	30.8%	28.8%	23.1%

TABLE 20. *Student Engages in Extracurricular Activities*

NATIVITY	YES	NO
FATHER		
Italy	26.0%	71.4%
US	25.7%	73.4%
GRANDFATHER		
Italy	25.7%	72.6%
US	29.2%	66.7%
MOTHER		
Italy	23.9%	71.7%
US	25.9%	73.1%
GRANDMOTHER		
Italy	27.8%	70.4%
US	26.9%	73.1%

TABLE 21. *Student Engages in Off-campus Activities*

NATIVITY	YES	NO
FATHER		
Italy	22.1%	70.1%
US	17.9%	78.0%
GRANDFATHER		
Italy	19.6%	74.3%
US	12.5%	83.3%
MOTHER		
Italy	19.6%	76.1%
US	17.8%	77.2%
GRANDMOTHER		
Italy	18.9%	75.7%
US	17.3%	80.8%

TABLES 22–27
Students' Agreement with Statements Concerning College Education and Brooklyn College

TABLE 22. *"I Come to Brooklyn in My Free Time."*

NATIVITY	TOTALLY DISAGREE	GREATLY DISAGREE	MILDLY DISAGREE	MILDLY AGREE	GREATLY AGREE	TOTALLY AGREE
FATHER						
Italy	9.1%	11.7%	7.8%	13.0%	1.3%	6.5%
US	9.8%	6.9%	10.7%	8.7%	5.8%	3.5%
GRANDFATHER						
Italy	8.7%	7.8%	11.3%	7.4%	5.2%	5.2%
US	8.3%	12.5%	4.2%	25.0%	-	-
MOTHER						
Italy	6.5%	6.5%	10.9%	10.9%	6.5%	8.7%
US	10.2%	8.6%	9.6%	9.6%	4.1%	3.0%
GRANDMOTHER						
Italy	10.7%	9.5%	11.8%	8.9%	4.1%	6.5%
US	7.7%	3.8%	9.6%	9.6%	3.8%	1.9%

TABLE 23. *"If I Could Get a Good Job, I Wouldn't Go to College."*

NATIVITY	TOTALLY DISAGREE	GREATLY DISAGREE	MILDLY DISAGREE	MILDLY AGREE	GREATLY AGREE	TOTALLY AGREE
FATHER						
Italy	11.7%	9.1%	7.8%	7.8%	3.9%	6.5%
US	11.6%	10.4%	5.2%	12.7%	4.6%	10.4%
GRANDFATHER						
Italy	11.3%	9.6%	6.1%	12.2%	4.3%	8.7%
US	16.7%	12.5%	-	4.2%	4.2%	12.5%
MOTHER						
Italy	10.9%	13.0%	6.5%	4.3%	2.2%	10.9%
US	10.7%	9.1%	5.1%	13.2%	5.1%	9.1%
GRANDMOTHER						
Italy	11.8%	11.2%	6.5%	13.0%	3.0%	10.1%
US	5.8%	3.8%	3.8%	9.6%	7.7%	7.7%

TABLE 24. *"The College Should Prepare Students for Jobs."*

NATIVITY	TOTALLY DISAGREE	GREATLY DISAGREE	MILDLY DISAGREE	MILDLY AGREE	GREATLY AGREE	TOTALLY AGREE
FATHER						
Italy	3.9%	11.7%	3.9%	14.3%	19.5%	37.7%
US	2.9%	4.6%	5.8%	24.3%	20.2%	37.0%
GRANDFATHER						
Italy	3.5%	6.1%	5.7%	20.9%	19.6%	37.8%
US	-	4.2%	-	20.8%	29.2%	33.3%
MOTHER						
Italy	2.2%	6.5%	2.2%	13.0%	23.9%	45.7%
US	2.5%	4.6%	6.1%	23.4%	20.3%	37.1%
GRANDMOTHER						
Italy	3.0%	4.7%	4.1%	19.5%	23.1%	37.1%
US	1.9%	7.7%	5.8%	28.8%	17.3%	36.5%

TABLE 25. *"My College Education is Important to Me"*

NATIVITY	TOTALLY DISAGREE	GREATLY DISAGREE	MILDLY DISAGREE	MILDLY AGREE	GREATLY AGREE	TOTALLY AGREE
FATHER						
Italy	-	2.6%	2.6%	6.5%	23.4%	62.3%
US	0.6%	1.2%	2.9%	11.0%	22.5%	57.8%
GRANDFATHER						
Italy	0.4%	1.7%	3.0%	8.7%	24.3%	57.8%
US	-	-	-	16.7%	4.2%	75.0%
MOTHER						
Italy	-	2.2%	4.3%	-	28.3%	63.0%
US	0.5%	1.5%	2.5%	11.7%	21.3%	58.9%
GRANDMOTHER						
Italy	-	1.2%	3.0%	10.1%	26.6%	54.4%
US	-	3.8%	-	11.5%	15.4%	67.3%

TABLE 26. *"My College Education is Important to My Father"*

NATIVITY	TOTALLY DISAGREE	GREATLY DISAGREE	MILDLY DISAGREE	MILDLY AGREE	GREATLY AGREE	TOTALLY AGREE
FATHER						
Italy	1.3%	2.6%	6.5%	14.3%	18.2%	44.2%
US	0.6%	4.0%	14.5%	15.6%	16.2%	45.1%
GRANDFATHER						
Italy	0.9%	3.5%	11.3%	16.5%	17.4%	43.0%
US	-	4.2%	12.5%	8.3%	20.8%	50.0%
MOTHER						
Italy	-	2.2%	13.0%	6.5%	15.2%	50.0%
US	0.5%	3.6%	11.7%	18.3%	17.3%	45.2%
GRANDMOTHER						
Italy	0.6%	1.8%	10.1%	18.3%	17.2%	45.0%
US	-	9.6%	15.4%	13.5%	17.3%	42.3%

TABLE 27. *"My College Education is Important to My Mother"*

NATIVITY	TOTALLY DISAGREE	GREATLY DISAGREE	MILDLY DISAGREE	MILDLY AGREE	GREATLY AGREE	TOTALLY AGREE
FATHER						
Italy	1.3%	1.3%	7.8%	11.7%	27.3%	40.3%
US	1.2%	6.4%	9.8%	16.2%	19.7%	43.9%
GRANDFATHER						
Italy	1.3%	4.3%	9.1%	15.7%	21.7%	41.7%
US	-	8.3%	12.5%	12.5%	20.8%	45.8%
MOTHER						
Italy	-	-	10.9%	6.5%	28.3%	43.5%
US	1.5%	5.6%	8.6%	17.8%	20.8%	43.7%
GRANDMOTHER						
Italy	1.2%	3.6%	7.7%	15.4%	23.1%	43.2%
US	-	7.7%	9.6%	15.4%	21.2%	44.2%

Selected Bibliography

Abrahmson, H. J. (1973). *Ethnic Diversity in Catholic America*. New York: John Wiley and Sons.

Alba, R. D. (1981). "The Twilight of Ethnicity Among American Catholics of European Ancestry." *Annals*, 454 (March): 86–97.

Banfield, E. C. (1958). *The Moral Basis of a Backward Society*. Glencoe: Free Press.

Child, I. L. (1943). *Italian or American? The Second Generation in Conflict*. New York: Russell and Russell.

Cohen, M. J. (1978). *From Workshop to Office: Italian Women and Family Strategies in New York City, 1900–1950*. Doctoral dissertation, University of Michigan, Ann Arbor.

Covello, L. (1977). *The Social Background of the Italo-American School Child*. Totowa, New Jersey: Rowan and Littlefield.

Dyer, E. D. (1979). *The American Family: Variety and Change*. New York: McGraw-Hill.

Egelman, W. (1982a). "Family Values and Educational Attainment: Intergenerational Change Among Italian Americans." Paper presented at a meeting of the Eastern Sociological Society, Philadelphia, Pennsylvania.

Egelman, W. (1982b). "Italian-American Educational Attainment: An Introductory Analysis Utilizing Recent Current Population Survey Data." Paper presented at a meeting of the American Italian Historical Association, Jamaica, New York: St. John's University.

Egelman, W. and DeVito-Egelman, C. (1981). "Ethnicity and Education: A Review of the Italian-American Experience." Paper presented at "Preventing Psychosocial Malfunctioning in Ethnic Families: An Interdisciplinary Symposium." Brooklyn, New York: Brooklyn College.

Gans, H. J. (1962). *The Urban Villagers*. New York: Free Press.

Gordon, M. (1964). *Assimilation in American Life*. New York: Oxford University Press.

Greeley, A. M. (1969). *The Catholic Experience*. Garden City, New Jersey: Doubleday.

Greeley, A. M. (1974). *Ethnicity in America. A Preliminary Reconnaissance*. New York: Wiley.

Greeley, A. M. (1977). *The American Catholic: A School Portrait*. New York: Basic Books.

Kessner, T. (1977). *The Golden Door: Italian and Jewish Immigrant Mobility in New York City, 1890–1915*. New York: Oxford University Press.

Krase, J. (1978). "Italian-American Female College Students: A New Generation Connected to the Old." In B. B. Caroli, R. F. Harvey, and L. F. Tomasi (Eds.) *Annual Conference of the American Italian Historical Association, Vol. 10, The Italian-American Immigrant Woman in North America* (pp 246–251). Toronto, Canada: Multicultural History Society of Ontario.

Krase, J. (1982). "The Mediterranean-American Neighborhood." *Proceedings of the Mediterranean Sociopsychiatric Association, Second Mediterranean Congress of Social Psychiatry*, Udine, Italy.

Krase, J. and Fuccillo, V. J. (1975). "Italian-Americans and College Life: A Survey of Student Experiences at Brooklyn College." Unpublished manuscript, Brooklyn College, City University of New York, Department of Sociology and Center for Italian American Sudies.

Levi, C. (1947). *Christ Stopped at Eboli*. New York: Farrar, Strauss.

Lopreato, J. (1970). *Italian Americans*. New York: Random House.

Parillo, V. N. (1980). *Strangers to These Shores: Race and Ethnicity in the United States*. Boston: Houghton Mifflin.

Pisani, L. (1957). *The Italians in America*. New York: Exposition Press.

Rolle, A. (1980). *The Italian Americans: Troubled Roots*. New York: Free Press.

Rosen, B. (1959). "Race, Ethnicity and the Achievement Syndrome." *American Sociological Review* 24 (February): 47–60.

Sennett, R. and Cobb, J. (1972). *The Hidden Injuries of Class*. New York: Alfred A. Knopf.

Stryker, R. (1981). "Religio-Ethnic Effects on Attainments in the Early Career." *American Sociological Review*, 46, 212–231.

Tomasi, L. F. (1972). *The Italian-American Family*. Staten Island, New York: Center for Migration Studies.

Williams, R. M. (1963). *American Society: A Sociological Interpretation*. New York: Knopf.

Whyte, W. F. (1943). *Street Corner Society*. Chicago: University of Chicago Press.

Yankelovich, D. (1974). *Changing Youth Values in the 70s*. New York: McGraw-Hill.

Acknowledgements

As it is only with extreme difficulty that one is able to gather support for conducting research on Italian Americans, it is most necessary to cite the contributions of all those who assisted the author in this study. As the data for this paper was collected several years ago, the list of people who made it possible is long. Professor Vincent Fuccillo, the first Director of the Center for Italian American Studies gave initial, invaluable support, along with Ms. Lillian Viola, the center coordinator. Mary Sansone, Director of the Congress of Italian-American Organizations, provided the stimulus for the project and staff assistance. The student organizations, Italian-American Student Union and Circolo Italiana, helped in the collection of the data. Ms. Maria Vuono, a student, and Mrs. Suzanne Nicolleti Krase, my wife, helped with the original coding. The second phase of the project took place in 1982 with the aid of a small grant from the Italian American Institute to Foster Higher Education, and for this support I am in debt to Mrs. Rosemarie Pietanza, a member of the board and advocate of Italian-American excellence in education. Finally, to Ms. Pat Milner, my research assistant who was responsible for the recoding, re-entry of the data, and programming, I owe a great debt.

Italian-American Students at the City University of New York: A Socioeconomic and Educational Profile

AUDREY BLUMBERG
DAVID E. LAVIN

In the history of the City University of New York (CUNY), the theme of ethnicity looms large. The origins of the university coincided in a rough way with the emergence of New York City as the major funnel of immigration in the United States. Beginning in the 1840s over a million Irish from agricultural origins made their way to New York. Later in the century, they were joined by waves of Jewish immigrants from Russia and Eastern Europe, and by vast numbers of Italians who came overwhelmingly from peasant origins in the southern region of that country.

Partly as a result of cultural differences, these groups varied markedly in their utilization of City University. From the early 1900s up to the 1960s, Jewish students were by far the dominant presence on the various campuses of the municipal college system. In part, Jewish enrollments were a result of heavy emphasis in their culture upon the importance of education. During this period, the university established its reputation as a major avenue of social and economic mobility. This image of the university resulted largely from the achievements of many Jewish graduates in the professions, business, academe, the arts, and in public life. Relative to their proportions in the population of the city, the representation at CUNY of the major Catholic groups, the Irish and the Italians, was very low. In part this was due to the presence of several Catholic colleges in the area. Intrinsic to Catholic religious doctrine was a perception that secular education was a threat to religiosity, and so, if Catholics went to college, they were likely to attend church-sponsored institutions. In addition, the ethnic cultures of these groups did not place the heavy emphasis on education that was displayed among Jews. Indeed among those of southern Italian origin, ". . . educational aspirations were thwarted by cultural values, such as an emphasis on loyalty to the family above all else, that were finely tuned to the needs of a rural folk society but were very dysfunctional in a highly industrialized urban setting."[1] These factors so reduced the attendance of Italians at CUNY that in 1930 they comprised only 3% of the graduating class at City College.[2]

But as the forces of assimilation made themselves felt, Catholics, including those of Italian ancestry, began to attend college in sizeable numbers. Indeed, by the mid to late 1960s Catholics comprised between one-third and 40% of entering classes at some CUNY colleges.[3] This trend accelerated in the early 1970s as a result of CUNY's open admissions policy. Though the policy was designed to increase the representation in CUNY of newer migrants (blacks and Hispanics) to the City (and it did so dramatically), the major beneficiaries of the policy were white ethnics, in particular Irish and Italian Catholics. While the enrollment of whites in CUNY fell off substantially after the fiscal crisis of 1975–76, the proportions of Italian Americans among whites continued to increase, so that by 1980 they were the largest single white group enrolling in that fall's freshman class, surpassing Jews as the numerically most important white group among entering classes.

In the years after World War II and especially since the 1960s, much research has been conducted and a great deal written about CUNY's efforts to expand educational opportunity for impoverished minority groups, primarily blacks and Hispanics. And the utilization of the university as an instrument for assimilation and social mobility has been well documented for Jewish students. By contrast, relatively little attention has focused on students from other ancestries whose representation in CUNY has increased. An important example is that of Italian Americans who are the largest white group within CUNY, just as they are the largest ethnic bloc within the American Catholic population.[4]

The educational achievements of Italians have been viewed as attenuated because of the constraints of southern Italian folk culture which placed little emphasis on formal schooling, since education was seen as conflicting with urgent practical demands of rural life.[5] Notwithstanding these initial dissonances of Italian and American culture, there is considerable evidence suggesting the assimilation of Italians in the United States. For example, one important index, intermarriage, indicates considerable assimilations.[6] There is less known about the more recent achievements and aspirations in the educational arena, particularly in higher education, which has become almost a prerequisite for entry into the more rewarding positions in the American occupational system.

What are the achievements of Italian Americans in high school? Do they typically enter college via institutions that lead to bachelor's degrees or are they more likely to begin in two-year community colleges? What are their educational aspirations and what do they want from college? How do their family backgrounds affect their educational life chances? Are traces of earlier cultural constraints still visible among college entrants? These are some of the questions considered in this study. In addressing them we shall contrast the Italian-American group with others, in particular other white groups and minority students. Drawing such a profile will ultimately provide a baseline for understanding the educational attainments of Italian Americans in CUNY.

DESIGN OF THE STUDY AND NATURE OF THE DATA

The data presented in this report are taken from a longitudinal study that is following the academic careers of freshmen who entered the university in fall 1980.* The point of departure for the broader study is a detailed social background survey mailed in summer 1980 to 52,366 students who had applied to CUNY as first-time freshmen. The survey requested a wide range of information about students' social origins, financial resources, employment situations and educational attitudes and aspirations. The number of respondents to the survey questionnaire was 15,727. Of these, 11,625 subsequently enrolled in CUNY. This report draws on the data collected for these enrollees. The sample represents about 36% of the total freshman class of 31,890.

A second type of data used in this report are high school background records. This information, collected by CUNY's centralized admissions office for the 52,366 freshman applicants, contains data on numerous variables including: (1) college admissions average, a measure of the students' grades in all academic courses deemed by the university to be college preparatory in nature (e.g., English, mathematics, science, etc.); (2) the number of college preparatory courses taken (this variable reflects the breadth of students' exposure to college preparatory work); (3) the number of college preparatory courses taken in two subject matter areas: math and science.

---

* This study was conducted in conjunction with the City University Office of Institutional Research and Analysis; it was supported, in part, by the Italian American Institue of CUNY.

To obtain an overview of students' academic preparedness and for purposes of placement into remedial courses, CUNY administers to entering freshmen university-wide tests in mathematics, reading and writing. Our files contain the raw scores for each test and indicate whether the student passed or failed each.

A fourth data source is the registration file assembled for the freshman population by the university's Office of Institutional Research and Analysis from information transmitted to it by each of the CUNY colleges. This file indicates the level of enrollment in the university (senior or community college).

The registration data, high school transcript information, skills assessment test scores and social background survey have been combined so that the record of each enrollee who responded to the survey also contains all of the other information. This merged file is used to describe and compare the characteristics of Italian-American students, other white students, and minority students in the senior and community colleges.

Though the sample of 11,625 students is a large one, it is being used to generalize to the 1980 cohort population of 31,890 cases, and it is necessary to determine whether the sample is representative by comparing it with the population, using measures common to both. The details of the comparison have been presented elsewhere.[7] Overall, the pattern is clear. The sample contains a greater proportion of females, and among students in the senior colleges, the sample contains a greater proportion of more able students than the population. In all cases, however, the sample/population differences are small. In short, the comparisons indicate that the sample provides a good representation of the population.

SOCIAL ORIGINS
INTRODUCTION

Social origins are known to have important effects upon students' academic careers. In so far as ethnic groups differ in aspects of their social backgrounds, it would be expected that their grades, rates of progress toward a degree, and likelihood of graduation would also differ. Thus, the social advantages and disadvantages with which Italian-American students enter college will help to predict how they will fare in higher education. For this reason it is important to consider social background profiles. We shall examine several social origins factors including gender, age, marital status, and economic situation.

In each of the following analyses, we compare Italian-American entrants with two other categories: "other whites" and minorities. Each of the latter are an aggregation of specific groups. The minority category includes blacks and Hispanics (Asians are not included in this report). The other white classification includes Jewish students, Irish Catholics, white Catholics of other ancestry, and whites of diverse religious/ethnic backgrounds. Students entering via special admissions programs (i.e., SEEK and College Discovery) are not included in this report.

The distribution of these three groupings across the two levels of CUNY (senior and community colleges) is shown in Table 1. Among entering classes, minorities have become the numerically predominant category, particularly in CUNY's two-year schools. Italian Americans now comprise 10% of all entrants, and about 25% of all whites.

DEMOGRAPHIC PROFILE

Nationally, about half of all college entrants are female.[8] At CUNY, females predominate for all groups, comprising 60% of entering students (Table 2). The proportion of females among minority entrants is higher than for Italian Americans or other whites. The racial disparity is partly a consequence of gender differences in high school dropout rates. Minority females predominate over minority males because the latter are more likely to drop out of high school. Among the white groups, including Italian Americans, we speculate that a different process is involved: limited financial resources are expended in sending males to more prestigious and expensive colleges than CUNY, since their educations are assumed to be the basic determinants of the financial status of their future families.

Although the representation of females among Italian-American students is not much different from other whites, they do stand apart in one respect: the proportion of females is constant for the other white students in both senior and community colleges, but the sex distribution of Italian Americans differs by institution type. Sixty-one percent of the Italian Americans at the senior colleges are female, compared with 53% at community colleges. The reason for this difference in sex ratios among Italian Americans is not immediately apparent from our data, but we speculate that compared with other whites, a higher proportion of males see community college as the route to clearly defined vocational goals.

In the conventional view, college going is a life cycle event, which occurs immediately after high school graduation. Thus, the typical college student is thought to be 18 years old, unmarried and childless. National data confirm that these are, overwhelmingly, the typical characteristics of college freshmen. This national picture does not fit the realities at CUNY, as is shown in Tables 3, 4 and 5. For example, nationally, 8 of 10 entering senior college freshmen are 18 or younger, and less than 1% are married. At CUNY, only 7 of 10 entrants are 18 or less (16% are 20 or older), 4% are married, and 5% have children. The corresponding percentages are substantially higher in the community colleges. These differences between freshmen nationally and those at CUNY are accounted for largely by the variance of minority students from the national norm and to a lesser extent by other whites. Italian Americans, on the other hand, stand out as the group approximating most closely the traditional picture of college going in America. They are younger, the least likely to be married and the least likely to be supporting children.

These characteristics of Italian Americans may place them at an advantage relative to other groups, at least in terms of ultimate educational attainment. Students who complete college at age 21 or 22 are more likely to consider going on for further education than those who do not finish until 25 or older.

ECONOMIC BACKGROUND

The single most direct indicator of economic class is family income. It is an indication of ability to enter and continue in higher education, as well as to meet the routine exigencies of daily life.

As Table 6 shows, minority students are markedly more disadvantaged by low income than are white students. Overall, 91% of all minority students have family incomes of less than $20,000. Among Italian Americans and other white students, only about 60% have incomes of less than $20,000.

The proportion of lower income students is significantly greater at community colleges than at the senior colleges. If we consider the lowest income group, (less than $10,000), we find that while over two-thirds of the minority students at community colleges fall in this income bracket, one-third of the white students and only one-quarter of the Italian Americans report such low income. However, the apparent income advantage of Italian-American students over other whites is offset to some extent by the fact that the former are slightly more likely than other white students to have five or more people supported by the reported family income (see Table 7).

As one might expect, given group differences in income, there are substantial disparities in the proportions receiving public assistance. Table 8 shows that at the four-year colleges only 2% of Italian Americans and other whites receive welfare and, at the two-year colleges 5% of the former and 7% of the latter are welfare recipients. The proportions of black and Hispanic students who receive public assistance are significantly higher: 15% at the four-year schools and 24% at two-year colleges.

These differences in economic status are reflected in the likelihood of receiving financial aid (in the form of New York State Tuition Assistance Program (TAP) awards, Pell grants, and other aid). Minority students, at both senior and community colleges, are far more likely to receive aid, and they receive it from more numerous sources than do white students (see Table 9).

Slightly more than half of Italian-American students receive financial aid at senior colleges. In this respect, they are very similar to other white students. In the community colleges, 60% of Italian Americans receive aid, somewhat less than the proportion of other white recipients. This difference between the two white groups may be a reflection of the fact that Italian-American students in the two-year schools are less likely than other whites to come from very low income families.

As expected in a university where so many students come from families of modest and low income, a high proportion of students reported that they were working (full or part-time) or looking for work at entry to college (Table 10). Overall, three-fourths of students were working or looking for work. Minority students were more likely than whites to be working full-time. In senior colleges, the work situations of Italian-American students were little different from their other white counterparts. In the two-year schools, however, the Italian Americans were more likely to be working part-time than either minorities or other whites. Employment has negative effects on success in college and, in this regard, CUNY students carry a heavier burden than is true for college students in general.[9]

Despite the fact that CUNY students are likely to be labor force participants, they appear, in general, to be living in traditional family settings. The majority of these students live with parents or other relatives.

Not unexpectedly, given their age and marital status, Italian Americans, even more than the other two groups, live with their families: 97% at senior colleges and over 80% of those at community colleges do so (see Table 11).

In summary, this is the picture of Italian-American students that emerges from our data: They are younger, less likely to be married, less likely to be in the lowest income category, or have multiple sources of financial aid, and in the community colleges they are less likely to have any financial assistance than are minorities and the composite group of other white students. They are more likely to be living at home and to be working part-time than are the other student groups. They present themselves as solidly from working class or lower middle class backgrounds. By most criteria, they are advantaged by comparison with minority students and they tend to be similar to the other white students.

EDUCATIONAL BACKGROUND
FAMILY EDUCATIONAL HISTORY

Demographic status and economic context are only part of the life histories, which affect students' educational chances in college. There are also family cultural resources (such as parental educational background) that can enhance childrens' school achievements. Then, there are actual school environments, which can affect students' academic self-concepts, aspirations, and basic skills. We now consider several aspects of family and school background, which may differ between groups, thus affecting chances for success in college.

The educational background of parents can have important effects on school achievement, aspirations, expectations and knowledge about college. Better educated parents presumably bring to their children a wider range of information, interests and cognitive competencies that add to skills children carry with them when they start school. They also may be better able to provide their offspring with important daily advantages; for example, helping with homework.

As shown in Table 12, the educational attainments of parents of Italian-American students are noticeably lower than those of parents of other white students. Indeed, with regard to college attendance, mothers and fathers of Italian-American students are more similar to minority parents than to other whites. At the senior colleges almost half of the fathers of the other white students have had some college, compared to about a quarter of Italian American and minority student fathers. A similar pattern is evident in the community colleges, although group differences are smaller. In all groups, mothers are less likely to have attended college than fathers, but those of Italian-American students are considerably less likely to have attended than the mothers of other whites.

Italian-American students are more likely than minorities and other whites to represent the first generation of their families to be attending college (Table 13). More than 90% of Italian-American students are first generation college-goers.

Whether students have siblings, who are or were in college partly conditions expectations that college is a natural stage in the life cycle. To possess such an expectation may well enhance the student's chances of adapting to the collegiate setting. In CUNY's senior colleges there are no important differences among groups in the likelihood of having college-attending siblings (Table 14). Overall, about half of the students had brothers or sisters with college experience. In community colleges, about 40% of Italian-American students had college-going siblings. In this respect, they more closely resembled minority students than other whites.

HIGH SCHOOL BACKGROUND

It is well documented that students from different socioeconomic and ethnic backgrounds are differentially prepared for college careers. Because they typically come from poverty backgrounds and because of educational disadvantage stemming from attendance in ghetto high schools, minority students generally graduate high school less well prepared than others. In contrast, white students, and especially Italian Americans, are markedly more likely to have graduated from private high schools (most commonly Catholic, parochial ones). Almost half of the Italian Americans at senior colleges and one-third of those at the two-year colleges are graduates of private high schools (see Table 15). The effect of having attended private schools is unclear. Whether Italian-American students enter CUNY prepared by a strong high school background relative to that of other white and minority students is a question we now address.

An overview of CUNY students' high school backgrounds is given in Table 16, showing the average number of college preparatory courses taken. Large disparities exist in the extent of college preparation. At both senior and community colleges, minority students take fewer college preparatory courses than Italian Americans or other whites. Both white groups closely resemble each other. On average, they finish high school having taken a semester more of college preparatory work than their minority counterparts. Community-senior college differences are also evident. Generally, community college entrants have had almost a year less academic coursework than their senior college peers. For example, other whites in two-year schools average less than 11 college preparatory credits, while in the senior colleges they earned about 14 credits.

How these summary differences in preparation translate into substantive course exposure is revealed clearly in Tables 17 and 18 that show differences among groups in math and science preparation. In the senior colleges, the differential between minority students and the other white and Italian-American groups is marked: over two-thirds in these groups have completed algebra and/or trigonometry (eleventh year high school mathematics) and well over half have completed chemistry and/or physics. Only about one-third of minority students had this much math and science preparation.

Among community college entrants, all groups have had less exposure to math and science than their counterparts in senior colleges. Nonetheless, the pattern of differences observed in the former is again observed. Relative to Italian Americans and other whites (who, for the most part are similar in preparation), minority students are considerably less likely to have taken math or science courses beyond the ninth grade level. For example, 63% of minority students did not go beyond ninth grade math, compared with 49% of Italian Americans and other whites.

Overall, then, our analyses of high school academic preparation suggest two major themes. First, Italian-American students appear very similar to other whites, and both groups seem considerably better prepared than minority students. Second, senior college entrants exhibit stronger preparation than their community college peers.

These differences in high school background may have important effects on students' chances of clearing their first major hurdle after acceptance at CUNY: the Freshman Skills Assessment Tests. These tests in math, reading, and writing are administered to all CUNY entrants and must be passed in order to move directly into the mainstream of college work. Failing two or three of the basic skills tests leads to placement in remediation courses. A program saturated with such courses (typically for no credit) for the first year or two of college, may, in a student population already burdened by financial difficulties and social pressures, act as a deterrent to remaining in college.

As one might expect from the preceding discussion there are marked group differences in performances on the skills tests. Table 20 shows that in the senior colleges about two-thirds of Italian-American students and other whites *passed all* three tests. In sharp contrast, only a quarter of minority students did this well. In community colleges, there were also no differences between the white groups: about one-fourth passed all of the tests. This was true for only 5% of minority students.

The data in Table 20 can also be viewed in terms of this question: what proportions of each group *failed all* of their skills tests? In the senior colleges, very few Italian-American students or other whites fared this poorly (only 2–3%). On the other hand, 20% of minorities passed none of the tests. In community colleges, almost half of the minority students failed all three tests. This was true for less than 20% of the white groups.

A fuller picture of students' academic skills upon entry to CUNY is given in Table 22, showing the performance of each group for each skill area. Generally, there is little difference between Italian-American students and other whites in the proportions passing each type of test. Both groups have higher pass rates on every type of test than do minority students. Overall, students were most likely to pass the writing test and least likely to pass the math assessment, though it is true that in the senior colleges white groups did about equally well on math and reading.

SELF-ASSESSMENT

These test score results are reflected in students' self-assessments as shown in Table 23. Students were asked if they felt that they needed any special tutoring or extra help in the three areas of the basic skills tests. In the senior colleges, students reported needing extra help in mathematics in proportions approximating those in each group that failed the test. However, this pattern did not hold throughout. Students reported needing help in writing in proportions that generally matched or exceeded those whose test scores showed a need for help. The opposite was true for reading: students were less likely to think they should have help when their scores indicated a need for it. Generally, other whites and Italian Americans, who did better on the tests than minorities, were less likely to report needing help.

In the community colleges, where pass rates on the skills tests were substantially lower, all groups were more likely to think they needed extra help. As in senior colleges, other whites and Italian Americans were less likely to report needing help than were minorities. (This, of course, is a function of the different pass rates between the two groups.) The pattern of relationship between scores and reported need differed somewhat from senior college students. Students were somewhat less likely to think they needed help in math even if they needed it. The slippage was even greater in the reading area. In writing, the reported need for help dovetailed quite well with the percentages in each group that failed the test.

As a way of summarizing students' academic self-concept, they were asked to rate their ability relative to other students who had entered college with them. The results are shown in Table 24. There were no large differences observed between Italian Americans and the other whites at the four-year schools. Sixty percent of these white students felt that they were above average, while less than half of the minority students rated themselves above average. At the two-year colleges, there were essentially no differences among groups. A little more than one-third of the students rated themselves above average. Practically no students felt that they were below average in comparison to other students at their school. In short, student academic self-concepts seem to reflect, at least in senior colleges, the realities of their actual preparation. Italian Americans and other whites entered four-year schools better prepared than minorities and their self-estimates reflect this reality.

Upon entry all groups showed considerable optimism that they would persist in their collegiate studies. Ninety percent or more felt that there was little chance they would drop out, either permanently or temporarily (see Table 25). Much higher proportions expected that they would transfer to another college before graduating from the one in which they started. In both senior and community colleges, other white students were more likely than Italian Americans to think they would transfer. The latter were more similar to minorities in their transfer expectations. We speculate that because Italian Americans are more vocationally focused in their orientation to college, they are less apt to see transfer as an appropriate option.

THE MEANING OF COLLEGE FOR STUDENTS

Higher Education in the United States has traditionally been per-ceived as an avenue of upward social mobility. The extent to which going to college continues to provide opportunities for working class and lower class people is the subject of much ongoing investigation. Whatever the actual advantages of a college education, students come to college with certain expectations and goals. How such orientations are altered or sup-ported during the course of their student careers is a result of a variety of circumstances: the real or imagined success students feel in their studies, the requirements placed on them by family and friends, the subtle or overt support of school personnel (or lack of such support), and so forth. At this point, we are not addressing what transpires during the college years to reinforce or reshape the original meaning going to college has for students. We can, however, locate CUNY students in their initial defini-tion of what college holds for them.

Most striking in the data are the high aspirations held by all students. At the senior colleges, 60% or more of the students aspire to master's de-grees or higher. Minority students and other whites are most likely to as-pire to these higher degrees (66%) and Italian Americans are least likely to aim for such additional credentials (60%). The most notable difference between Italian Americans and the other two groups involves aspirations for the doctoral or professional degree: Almost 30% of minorities and other whites hold such aspirations compared with only 18% of Italian-American students (see Table 26).

High aspirations are also the rule in community colleges, but, again, Italian Americans hold more modest goals than others. Sixty-seven per-cent of the Italian-American students indicated wanting to continue to-ward a bachelor's degree or higher compared with 79% of other white students and 80% of the minority students. Italian Americans were also more likely than others to hold aspirations no higher than an associate's degree (33%, compared with about 20% for other whites and minorities). One can only speculate about the reasons for Italian-American students' more modest aspirations. But we believe that their closer ties to family (Table 11), the lower educational attainments of their parents (Table 12), and a clearer vocational orientation to college may, in part, be an explana-tion. Perhaps it is stretching the point, but it is possible that these findings indicate the traces of earlier cultural orientations.

In conducting our survey of entrants, we assessed the reasons why students wanted to go to college. Did they see it as having mainly vocational utility? Was it a stepping-stone to graduate school? Did they simply want to know more? We asked students to pick from such a list the two most important reasons for going to college. Table 27 gives their most important reason for attending.

In senior colleges, three-quarters of Italian Americans reported that their first reason was to "get a better job," compared with less than two-thirds of other white and minority students. At the community colleges, Italian Americans were also more likely than other students to consider getting a better job the primary reason for going to college, but differences were narrower than in four-year schools.

Few students in any group stated that preparing for graduate school was an important reason for going to college (less than 10% of the senior college students, and less than 5% of the junior college students). Given the fact that such large proportions of students reported earlier that they aspired to graduate degrees, it is surprising that so few found it a primary motivation.

Generally, then, CUNY students are motivated to go to college to get a better job. Our data (Table 28) also show that they have considerable faith that college will further this aim. In all groups, close to 90% believed that their education would advance their job prospects.

INITIAL COLLEGE PLACEMENT

Considerable controversy exists among social scientists about the relative merits of attendance at senior or community colleges. Some have argued that two-year schools are a good place to start college, especially in the case of students with weak high school preparation and poor economic circumstances. Others ague that in the long run, community colleges have negative impacts: they tend to depress aspirations and lead to lower educational attainment, and they tend to sort people into dead-end jobs. While the controversy is far from resolved, most social scientists side with the latter view. Evidence at CUNY is sparse at this point, but one systematic study indicates that those who begin in two-year schools do not go as far in higher education as comparable students who begin in senior colleges.[10]

In the context of this debate, where groups are placed is of some importance. It is clear from an examination of Table 1 that different groups have different probabilities of attending senior and community colleges. Most unequally distributed are minority students: three-fourths of them are found in the two-year tier. Other whites are the group most likely to attend senior colleges: 44% are found there. Italian Americans are less likely than other whites to go to a four-year institution: slightly less than 4 out of every 10 enroll in one, while 6 in 10 go to a community college.

One should not assume that placement in the two-year college is something necessarily done against the wishes of unwilling students. To some degree, where students begin their college careers is also a reflection of their preferences. For example, our data show that of all groups in community colleges, Italian Americans are the ones most likely to have picked that college level as their first choice (Table 30). Indeed, regardless of level, Italian Americans are more likely to prefer being where they are placed. On the other hand, even though their educational aspirations are not as high as other groups, the majority of those in community colleges aspire to credentials beyond the associate's degree. If the critics of community colleges are right, these students' chances of realizing their ambitions are, in part, constrained by community college placement.

CONCLUSION

Over the past twenty years the composition of the CUNY student body has changed dramatically. The university's student mix has become much more diverse in terms of economic status, educational background, race and ethnicity. The conventional wisdom holds that a very large increase in the enrollment of minority students has been the main racial/ethnic change. While this has occurred, other changes have also taken place. White groups such as Italian Americans have come to the university in large numbers, but very little is known about them. This report has aimed to fill this vacuum by presenting a profile of their socioeconomic backgrounds, their educational histories, and their attitudes and aspirations.

The sharpest differences revealed in this report are those distinguishing minority students from both Italian Americans and other white groups. In terms of economic status and educational preparation, whites are far more advantaged than minorities.

Although in most respects Italian-American students are very much like other whites, there are some important ways in which they differ. One is that they more closely approximate the traditional demographic profile of the beginning college student: they are younger, single, and more likely to be living with their parents. They are also more likely to have graduated from a private (presumably parochial) high school. The educational attainments of their parents are somewhat below the parents of other white students, especially in terms of college attendance. Possibly, as a consequence, Italian-American students hold more modest educational aspirations for themselves. They also have a somewhat more vocational orientation to college and perhaps this orientation has led them more often to prefer a community rather than a senior college.

Whether the differences we have noted have consequences for success in college is not a question addressed in this report. It remains a topic requiring additional analysis.

TABLES

TABLE 1. *College Type by Ethnic Group*

	SENIOR COLLEGES			COMMUNITY COLLEGES		
	MINORITIES	OTHER WHITES	ITALIAN AMERICANS	MINORITIES	OTHER WHITES	ITALIAN AMERICANS
Percentage	46%	43%	12%	67%	25%	9%
% of group at each CUNY level	24	44	38	76	56	62
(N)*	(1237)	(1154)	(323)	(3941)	(1459)	(521)

These numbers are the maximum possible bases for all subsequent tables. The actual basis for specific tables may be slightly reduced by missing values of the variable in question.

TABLE 2. *Percentage of Female Students by College Type and Ethnic Group*

SENIOR COLLEGES			COMMUNITY COLLEGES		
MINORITIES	OTHER WHITES	ITALIAN AMERICANS	MINORITIES	OTHER WHITES	ITALIAN AMERICANS
65	57	61	63	57	53

TABLE 3. *Age of Enrollment by College Type and Ethnic Group*

	SENIOR COLLEGES			COMMUNITY COLLEGES		
AGE	MINORITIES	OTHER WHITES	ITALIAN AMERICANS	MINORITIES	OTHER WHITES	ITALIAN AMERICANS
18 or younger	69%	84%	93%	33%	55%	62%
19	11	6	3	13	11	10
20–29	14	9	4	36	23	20
30 or older	6	2	-	18	12	9

TABLE 4. *Percentage of Married Students*

SENIOR COLLEGES			COMMUNITY COLLEGES		
MINORITIES	OTHER WHITES	ITALIAN AMERICANS	MINORITIES	OTHER WHITES	ITALIAN AMERICANS
7	3	1	19	12	8

TABLE 5. *Percentage of Students Supporting Children*

SENIOR COLLEGES			COMMUNITY COLLEGES		
MINORITIES	OTHER WHITES	ITALIAN AMERICANS	MINORITIES	OTHER WHITES	ITALIAN AMERICANS
11	2	1	31	12	11

TABLE 6. *Family Income*

	SENIOR COLLEGES			COMMUNITY COLLEGES		
INCOME	MINORITIES	OTHER WHITES	ITALIAN AMERICANS	MINORITIES	OTHER WHITES	ITALIAN AMERICANS
Less than $10,000	44%	19%	16%	65%	32%	24%
$10,000–$19,000	41	30	39	28	38	44
$20,000 or more	15	51	45	7	31	33

TABLE 7. *Number of Persons Income Supports*

	SENIOR COLLEGES			COMMUNITY COLLEGES		
NUMBER OF PERSONS	MINORITIES	OTHER WHITES	ITALIAN AMERICANS	MINORITIES	OTHER WHITES	ITALIAN AMERICANS
1	6%	5%	3%	15%	11%	8%
2–4	52	60	57	58	60	56
5–6	30	28	37	21	23	31
7 or more	12	6	4	6	5	4

TABLE 8. *Percentage of Students Whose Family Receives Public Assistance*

SENIOR COLLEGES			COMMUNITY COLLEGES		
MINORITIES	OTHER WHITES	ITALIAN AMERICANS	MINORITIES	OTHER WHITES	ITALIAN AMERICANS
15	2	2	24	7	5

TABLE 9. *Number of Sources of Financial Aid*

NUMBER OF SOURCES	SENIOR COLLEGES			COMMUNITY COLLEGES		
	MINORITIES	OTHER WHITES	ITALIAN AMERICANS	MINORITIES	OTHER WHITES	ITALIAN AMERICANS
None	16%	47%	45%	13%	36%	41%
One	12	19	25	13	17	19
Two	50	25	23	45	29	27
Three or more	21	9	7	30	18	13

TABLE 10. *Students' Work Situation*

WORK STATUS	SENIOR COLLEGES			COMMUNITY COLLEGES		
	MINORITIES	OTHER WHITES	ITALIAN AMERICANS	MINORITIES	OTHER WHITES	ITALIAN AMERICANS
Working/looking full-time	11%	6%	3%	25%	17%	16%
Working/looking part-time	64	72	75	52	61	70
Not working	26	23	22	23	22	14

TABLE 11. *Where Students Expect to Live Upon College Entrance*

LIVE WITH	SENIOR COLLEGES			COMMUNITY COLLEGES		
	MINORITIES	OTHER WHITES	ITALIAN AMERICANS	MINORITIES	OTHER WHITES	ITALIAN AMERICANS
Parents or other relative	84%	88%	97%	58%	73%	81%
Spouse	5	2	-	12	11	7
Friends	2	4	1	3	3	2
Alone	9	5	2	27	12	10

TABLE 12. *Father's and mother's education*

	SENIOR COLLEGES			COMMUNITY COLLEGES		
	MINORITIES	OTHER WHITES	ITALIAN AMERICANS	MINORITIES	OTHER WHITES	ITALIAN AMERICANS
FATHER'S EDUCATION						
Less than high school	51%	24%	39%	59%	36%	50%
High school graduate	25	29	38	25	38	32
Some college or more	24	48	23	16	26	18
MOTHER'S EDUCATION						
Less than high school	53	19	32	58	29	41
High school graduate	29	45	51	27	50	49
Some college or more	18	36	18	15	21	10

TABLE 13. *Percentage of First Generation College Entrants*

	SENIOR COLLEGES			COMMUNITY COLLEGES		
MINORITIES	OTHER WHITES	ITALIAN AMERICANS	MINORITIES	OTHER WHITES	ITALIAN AMERICANS
85	70	89	85	85	93

TABLE 14. *Percentage of Students With Siblings Who Attended or Are Attending College*

	SENIOR COLLEGES			COMMUNITY COLLEGES		
MINORITIES	OTHER WHITES	ITALIAN AMERICANS	MINORITIES	OTHER WHITES	ITALIAN AMERICANS
47	52	52	40	49	42

TABLE 15. *Percentage of Students Who Attended Private High School*

	SENIOR COLLEGES			COMMUNITY COLLEGES		
MINORITIES	OTHER WHITES	ITALIAN AMERICANS	MINORITIES	OTHER WHITES	ITALIAN AMERICANS
14	37	45	17	25	31

TABLE 16. *Average Number of College Preparatory Courses**

	SENIOR COLLEGES			COMMUNITY COLLEGES		
MINORITIES	OTHER WHITES	ITALIAN AMERICANS	MINORITIES	OTHER WHITES	ITALIAN AMERICANS
11.6	13.8	13.5	8.8	10.8	10.9

*The number of courses shown is based upon those completed at the time of application to CUNY and, thus, do not necessarily reflect all work done in the senior year of high school.

TABLE 17. *High School Mathematics Preparation*

	SENIOR COLLEGES			COMMUNITY COLLEGES		
	MINORITIES	OTHER WHITES	ITALIAN AMERICANS	MINORITIES	OTHER WHITES	ITALIAN AMERICANS
9th year math not completed	13%	2%	5%	26%	17%	14%
Completed 9th year math	26	8	12	37	32	35
Completed 10th year math	24	21	15	18	20	30
Completed 11th year math	37	69	68	19	31	21

TABLE 18. *High School Science Preparation*

	SENIOR COLLEGES			COMMUNITY COLLEGES		
	MINORITIES	OTHER WHITES	ITALIAN AMERICANS	MINORITIES	OTHER WHITES	ITALIAN AMERICANS
Intro science not completed	4%	-	-	3%	2%	3%
Intro science completed	31	10	10	65	44	37
Biology completed	31	32	34	22	37	38
Chem/Physics completed	34	57	55	10	17	22

TABLE 19. *College Admissions Average (CAA)**

	SENIOR COLLEGES			COMMUNITY COLLEGES		
CAA	MINORITIES	OTHER WHITES	ITALIAN AMERICANS	MINORITIES	OTHER WHITES	ITALIAN AMERICANS
Less than 70	6%	3%	4%	28%	28%	25%
70–74.9	12	4	5	46	34	33
75–79.9	20	16	10	17	22	24
80 and over	62	77	82	9	17	18
$\overline{X}$ CAA	80	82	82	65	69	70

*Students with GEDs are excluded from this analysis.

TABLE 20. *Number of Basic Skills Tests Passed*

	SENIOR COLLEGES			COMMUNITY COLLEGES		
TESTS PASSED	MINORITIES	OTHER WHITES	ITALIAN AMERICANS	MINORITIES	OTHER WHITES	ITALIAN AMERICANS
None	20%	2%	3%	49%	12%	18%
One	23	8	7	30	27	24
Two	31	24	27	17	39	33
Three	26	66	63	5	22	24

TABLE 21. *Average Scores on First Basic Skills Test*

	SENIOR COLLEGES			COMMUNITY COLLEGES		
AVERAGE SCORES	MINORITIES	OTHER WHITES	ITALIAN AMERICANS	MINORITIES	OTHER WHITES	ITALIAN AMERICANS
Math test*	24.4	31.1	30.4	16.5	21.8	21.7
Reading test**	29.7	36.3	36.0	24.3	32.1	31.6
Writing test***	6.4	8.1	8.3	5.4	7.1	7.0

*Highest possible score = 40.   **Highest possible score = 45.   ***Highest possible score = 12.

TABLE 22. *Percentage of Students Who Passed Basic Skills Test*

	SENIOR COLLEGES			COMMUNITY COLLEGES		
SKILL AREA	MINORITIES	OTHER WHITES	ITALIAN AMERICANS	MINORITIES	OTHER WHITES	ITALIAN AMERICANS
Math	51	85	78	14	35	37
Reading	41	75	77	25	57	54
Writing	68	92	95	40	81	77

TABLE 23. *Percentage of Students Who Feel They Need Tutoring or Extra Help*

	SENIOR COLLEGES			COMMUNITY COLLEGES		
SKILL AREA	MINORITIES	OTHER WHITES	ITALIAN AMERICANS	MINORITIES	OTHER WHITES	ITALIAN AMERICANS
Math	48	22	20	66	41	39
Reading	25	7	4	39	12	12
Writing	40	16	11	53	21	17

TABLE 24. *Self-rating of Academic Ability*

	SENIOR COLLEGES			COMMUNITY COLLEGES		
SELF-RATING	MINORITIES	OTHER WHITES	ITALIAN AMERICANS	MINORITIES	OTHER WHITES	ITALIAN AMERICANS
Above average	46%	61%	60%	35%	39%	34%
Average	53	38	40	62	60	64
Below average	2	1	0	4	2	2

TABLE 25. *Percentage of Students Who Estimate a Strong Chance or Some Chance They Will Drop Out or Transfer to Another College*

	SENIOR COLLEGES			COMMUNITY COLLEGES		
	MINORITIES	OTHER WHITES	ITALIAN AMERICANS	MINORITIES	OTHER WHITES	ITALIAN AMERICANS
Drop out temporarily	8	10	7	8	11	10
Drop out permanently	5	8	7	5	8	7
Transfer to another college	42	54	38	38	42	37

TABLE 26. *Degree Aspirations**

	SENIOR COLLEGES			COMMUNITY COLLEGES		
DEGREE WANTED	MINORITIES	OTHER WHITES	ITALIAN AMERICANS	MINORITIES	OTHER WHITES	ITALIAN AMERICANS
Associate	1	-	2	20	21	33
Bachelor	33	34	38	36	47	39
Master	37	39	42	32	23	19
Doctoral or equivalent**	29	27	18	12	9	9

*Data have been recalculated with responses of "don't know" and "other" removed.   **e.g., law, medical degree.

TABLE 27. *Most Important Reasons for Going to College*

	SENIOR COLLEGES			COMMUNITY COLLEGES		
REASON	MINORITIES	OTHER WHITES	ITALIAN AMERICANS	MINORITIES	OTHER WHITES	ITALIAN AMERICANS
Get better job	60%	63%	72%	65%	70%	73%
Prepare for graduate school	8	8	7	4	3	3
General education	16	16	10	15	12	11
Contribute to community	7	3	3	6	3	3
Other	9	10	8	10	12	10

TABLE 28. *Percentage of Students Who Feel That Graduating From This College Will Help Them Get a Better Job*

SENIOR COLLEGES			COMMUNITY COLLEGES		
MINORITIES	OTHER WHITES	ITALIAN AMERICANS	MINORITIES	OTHER WHITES	ITALIAN AMERICANS
93	89	94	91	86	88

TABLE 29. *Most Important Reason for Choosing This College*

	SENIOR COLLEGES			COMMUNITY COLLEGES		
REASON	MINORITIES	OTHER WHITES	ITALIAN AMERICANS	MINORITIES	OTHER WHITES	ITALIAN AMERICANS
Academic or program reputation	64%	48%	53%	46%	31%	35%
Financial reasons	12	27	28	10	21	23
Near home	16	18	14	26	33	30
Other	8	7	5	18	15	12

TABLE 30. *Percentage of Students Enrolled in First Choice College Type*

	SENIOR COLLEGES			COMMUNITY COLLEGES		
FIRST CHOICE	MINORITIES	OTHER WHITES	ITALIAN AMERICANS	MINORITIES	OTHER WHITES	ITALIAN AMERICANS
Four-year CUNY college	64	64	71	-	-	-
Two-year CUNY college	-	-	-	43	46	52

TABLE 31. *Percentage With Friends at College of Attendance*

SENIOR COLLEGES			COMMUNITY COLLEGES		
MINORITIES	OTHER WHITES	ITALIAN AMERICANS	MINORITIES	OTHER WHITES	ITALIAN AMERICANS
66	77	83	45	62	67

TABLE 32. *Percentage With Friends at Other Colleges*

	SENIOR COLLEGES			COMMUNITY COLLEGES	
MINORITIES	OTHER WHITES	ITALIAN AMERICANS	MINORITIES	OTHER WHITES	ITALIAN AMERICANS
92	96	97	80	84	88

TABLE 33. *Participation in High School Extracurricular Activities*

	SENIOR COLLEGES			COMMUNITY COLLEGES		
PARTICIPATED	MINORITIES	OTHER WHITES	ITALIAN AMERICANS	MINORITIES	OTHER WHITES	ITALIAN AMERICANS
A lot	23%	23%	21%	18%	14%	15%
To some extent or a little	57	60	61	55	53	56
Rarely	20	17	18	27	34	29

Notes

1. D. E. Lavin, R. D. Alba, and Richard A. Silberstein, *Right Versus Privilege: The Open Admissions Experiment at the City University of New York.* (New York: The Free Press, 1981), p. 4.

2. Lavin, Alba, and Silberstein, pp. 22–23, note 23.

3. J. E. Rossman, H. S. Astin, A. W. Astin, and E. H. El-Khawas, *Open Admissions at City University of New York: An Analysis of the First Year.* (Englewood Cliffs: Prentice Hall, 1975), see Tables 3.4–3.6, pp. 35–37.

4. As reported in S. Steinberg, *The Academic Melting Pot.* (New York: McGraw-Hill, 1974), p. 63.

5. See, for example, N. Glazer and D. P. Moynihan, *Beyond the Melting Pot, Second Edition* (Cambridge: M.I.T. Press, 1970). See also L. Covello, *The Social Background of the Italo-American School Child* (Leiden: Brill, 1967); R. Gambino, *Blood of My Blood: The Dilemma of the Italian Americans* (New York: Doubleday, 1974).

6. R. D. Alba, *Italian Americans: Into the Twilight of Ethnicity* (Englewood Cliffs: Prentice Hall, 1985).

7. See D. E. Lavin and others, "Socioeconomic Origins and Educational Background of an Entering Class at CUNY: A Comparison of Regular and Special Program Enrollees" (New York: City University of New York, 1983), pp. 46–49.

8. See A. W. Astin, M. R. King, and G. T. Richardson, "The American Freshman: National Norms for Fall 1980" (Los Angeles: Cooperative Institutional Research Program, U.C.L.A. and American Council on Education).

9. Lavin, Alba, and Silberstein, Chapter 7.

10. R. D. Alba and D. E. Lavin, "Community College and Tracking in Higher Education," *Sociology of Education,* 54 (1981: 223–237).

Italian-American Students at CUNY:
A Psychoeducational Profile

JAMES PERRONE

PREFACE

From the outset of this endeavor, it was my intention that this research would be primarily descriptive, exploratory, and applied, with outcomes that would lead to improved services for Italian-American students. Thus, this report was not written in APA journal style but rather was designed for counselors and teachers to read. For this reason, I made every attempt to reduce or explain some of the technical jargon ever present in psychological research reports and have relegated the specifics of the statistical methodology to a section in the appendix. I have also kept most of the tables and figures brief and filled with only information relevant to the results narrative. I have, however, gone to some lengths to present a comprehensive, heavily documented review of the research in the psychoeducational areas examined. I did this with the hope that others might follow-up or replicate some of these exploratory findings not only with Italian Americans but with other ethnic and racial groups as well.

I gratefully acknowledge the help and support of the following persons in the implementation of this project: the administrators at Baruch College for granting me the release time from my professional duties and the incentive to spend the past academic year on this research project; the counselors and teachers throughout the CUNY system who generously took time out from their busy professional schedules to help me obtain the sample I had projected; Frank Di Bennardo, Rosemary McNamara, Rose Ann Rizzo Keane, Gloria Salerno, Joseph Grosso, Nancy Lippa-Ziehler, Pat Imbimbo and Emelise Aleandri from the Italian American Institute whose professionalism and competence in obtaining the sample and conducting the interviews made my work easier and enjoyable; Larry Castiglione, Bill Avrimedes and Jim Crispino who consulted with me at various times in the design of the study and interpretation of the results; Wendy Heyman, Eli Maier, Gloria Salerno and Jenny Roman who were responsible for helping me obtain the non-Italian data; Maria Victoria, my research assistant, who worked tirelessly and efficiently to score the inventories, prepare the data for analysis, enter it into the computer and search for non-existent research articles; Gerry Lanzilli, Maria Fosco, Diane Galemmo and Natalie Marden, who provided me with the administrative and clerical support I needed to implement this comprehensive study; Dr. Joseph Scelsa, the director of the Italian American Institute, whose enthusiasm and commitment to this project and to Italian-American students, in general, rekindled my own sense of ethnicity and gave me the energy to accomplish my objectives; and, finally, the 217 students who completed the lengthy research packets and sat for the interviews without complaint and with the seriousness of purpose that typifies their approach to education. They are the institution; we just manage and teach here. —JVP, July 1986

The City University of New York
Italian American Institute • Graduate Center • 33 West 42nd Street • New York, NY 10036

October 1986

Dear Colleague,

It is a pleasure to be able to provide you and the university community with a report on "The Psychoeducational Profile of the Italian-American Student."

This report was conducted by the Institute's first Faculty Fellow, Dr. James Perrone, Associate Professor of Student Personnel services at Baruch College and is the result of his year long research project in which he examined the current state of motivation, values and concerns among Italian-American students at the City University of New York. Through four educational profiles, Dr. Perrone has determined a pattern among Italian-American students that reveals a strong emphasis on personal growth, financial independence through part-time employment and a desire to achieve success. The report reveals not only that Italian-American students in some areas have culturally distinct profiles as compared to the rest of CUNY students, but also that Italian-American women are statistically different in their motivation, values and concerns from Italian-American men.

We are particularly grateful to Dr. Perrone for his willingness to undertake this important work. We also wish to thank all those who assisted him: the faculty, counselors, and staff at various CUNY campuses, the Italian-American Institute staff and, especially, the students without whose participation this report would not have been possible.

We hope you find this report of interest.

Sincerely,
JOSEPH V. SCELSA
Director   JVS: mf

PART 1: RATIONALE

> There are few serious studies of Italian Americans, particularly current
> ones. It is easy to see why this has left accounts of their past, their pre-
> sent, and their future expressed almost always in the dubious logic of
> stereotypes (Gambino, 1975, p. 38).

Italian Americans are the largest White ethnic group attending City
University and yet we know very little about their needs and concerns as
students. The general purpose of this research project is to identify some of
these areas of need so that programs and services can be developed to
make their educational experience at CUNY a rewarding and fulfilling one.

Research on the developmental and educational needs of racial or
ethnic groups is hardly a new phenomenon. Reports and studies on the
effects of acculturation on European immigrant groups, including Italian
Americans (cf. Cordasco and LaGumina, 1972), date back to the last century. Since the Brown Supreme Court decision on the racial integration of
schools, scores of studies have been conducted on the social and psychological effects of the American experience on Blacks and other minority
groups in this country. From the early work of psychologists like Kenneth
Clark (1947) and Martin Deutsch (1960) on self-concept and achievement
motivation in Blacks to the more recent profiles developed by Sue, et al.
(1975) on Asian-Americans, Ruiz, et al. (1977) on Chicanos, Canino and
Canino (1980) on Puerto Ricans, Epstein (1979) on Jews and McGoldrick
and Pearce (1981) on Irish-Americans, ethnic groups have been the focus
of study for the expressed purpose of utilizing the results to develop educational and counseling programs to enhance their status in society. Unfortunately, very little extensive research of this nature has been conducted on Italian Americans.

A computer search of the social sciences research on Italian Americans in the past ten years yielded less then 100 separate studies and articles on this ethnic group. A review of the abstracts reveals that only a
small percentage of these studies could even loosely be considered psychological in nature. Many were written by psychiatric professionals interested in abnormal behavior patterns and hospitalization trends among
the different ethnic groups (Mintz and Schwartz, 1976; Murphy, 1978).
Others focused on providing ethnocultural, information on Italian Americans and other groups relevant to the interests of family therapists (cf.

McGoldrick, Pearce and Giordano [1982] and Giordano and Giordano [1976] for a review of the research).

There has, however, been no dearth of interest in Italian Americans, recent or past, among sociologists, historians and educators. The focus of most of these studies and articles was centered around Italian family dynamics and the impact of acculturation on ethnic values and practices. Over three decades ago, Irwin Child (1943) and Paul Campisi (1948) discussed the significant influence of the American experience on first and second generation Italian families. This was followed by a host of books, articles and research studies on this subject. Among the more well known, were the books and articles of Richard Gambino (1973, 1974) at Queens College who focused his attention on the Sicilian-American experience and generational differences among Italian Americans. The ethnicity movement in the 1970s also spawned some excellent analyses of the Italian-American experience in contemporary America (Ianni and Ianni, 1972; Tomasi, 1972; Lopreato, 1970). Two most recent studies of Italian Americans (Crispino, 1980; Alba, 1985) present some convincing evidence for what appears to be the twilight of the old ethnicity and the beginning of a new ethnicity. Italian Americans, among other ethnic groups, also drew the attention of several prominent sociologists including Andrew Greeley (1974), Herbert Gans (1962) and Papajohn and Speigel (1975) all of whom have contributed significantly to our understanding of their accomplishments, acculturation and structural assimilation.

Early interest in the academic achievement and aspirations of the Italian American is best represented in the sensitive, insightful works of the Italian-American educator, Leonard Covello. In his book on the Italo-American school child he wrote:

> The retention of alien concepts of education is a stumbling block for the Italo-American. In Southern Italy the *contadino* concept of education was based on character education (*l'uomo buen educate*), or the moral content of education. There was little or no concern or appreciation for intellectual interests. The early social maturity of southern Italian children, as a result of their economic worth or value, is a concept which was brought to America, and remains, in spite of modification, basic to their attitude toward the education of their children (Covello, 1967, p. 421).

In similar manner, Italian Americans have been described in the past literature as being slow to assimilate and limited in social mobility by the traditional bounds of family and neighborhood (Glazer and Moynihan, 1963). Work and family are valued over education and career. Children are not encouraged to pursue education and advancement if it results in taking them away from their family (Papajohn and Speigel, 1975). As a result, some writers purport that many Italians have not tended to do well academically (Ragucci, 1981; Vecoli, 1978) and do not adopt the future-oriented schema so much a part of the typical American Dream.

In a paper presented at the 1982 annual conference of the American-Italian Historical Association, sociologist Jerome Krase (1983) challenged this stereotypical, outdated profile of the Italian-American student as well as the purportedly negative impact of Italian-American cultural and family values on educational aspiration and achievement. He cites the statistical reviews by Egelman (1982a & b), Greeley (1977) and Alba (1981) to show that Italians as a group have scored at or above the national average for achievement. Krase maintains that when real opportunities for higher education exist for Italian Americans of all socioeconomic and cultural backgrounds, they will be taken advantage of with great "gusto and success" (pp. 7–8). His own survey of Italian-American students at CUNY in 1975 reinforces his contention. The young people who responded to this survey present themselves as very pragmatic and serious about their education. They feel greatly supported by their families in this endeavor but are basically "doing this for themselves." This profile of the achievement oriented Italian-American college student is further corroborated in studies conducted at CUNY by Castiglione (1982) Blumberg and Lavin (1985).

What Krase and others are saying is that a great deal has happened and changed since the early immigration of Italian Americans to this country and that many of our assumptions about Italian-American life, in general, and the Italian-American student, in particular, may be "stuck in a turn of the century scenario" (Krase, 1983, p. 24). Even the hypotheses and speculations of contemporary analysts about the impact of family values and culture on the educational pursuits of Italian Americans tend to be based on personal observation and intuition rather than on empirical research. This is especially true in the area of educational psychology where there is a notable paucity of research on Italians. This poses problems for those professionals who must work with these students in the areas of personal, academic and vocational counseling. Assumptions are made and generalizations acted upon that could render services and programs for Italian-American students, at the very least, ineffective and at the most, destructive.

As a result, many questions arise about the Italian-American college student of the '80s, especially those young people from the urban environs of New York City who more than any other ethnic group have taken advantage of the low cost higher education opportunity offered to them by the City University of New York. What are the educational and career aspirations of this new breed of Italian-American student? How motivated are they to achieve in American society and how do they go about making their choices for life and career? Is work and family still valued over education and career? What are the basic values and needs that influence their decisions? Do family and culture continue to exert a major influence as has been reported in the past, or are they able to make decisions independent of outside influences?

Even further questions arise. If this group is structurally and educationally assimilating as quickly as recent investigators claim, how culturally different are these students from other ethnic groups, especially those who attend the various CUNY colleges? Are there any special stressors attached to this recent thrust of social and educational mobility? Are there any conflicts or anxieties centered around family needs and demands? Do the values orientation and motivational profiles of this group differ internally with respect to gender and acculturation? More specifically, is the impact of family and culture different for males than for females or do the differences between the sexes mirror the general American population? With respect to assimilation, is a first generation Italian-American college student in 1985 driven by the same motivational forces and stressors as a student whose family has been in America for several generations, or are the generational differences that were so prominent thirty years ago confounded by contemporary factors like the effects of social class and changing immigration patterns? Finally and most importantly, if we are to counsel in the "cultural context" as recommended by Sue (1981) and others, what is that context for the Italian-American college student attending CUNY in 1985?

All of these questions require analysis and study so that we can proceed with our efforts to educate, counsel and develop effective programs and services to help these young people grow and develop as students and as achieving citizens of this country. This study explores and examines some of these questions and, in this report, communicates its findings to the professional community at the university. It has been designed as action-oriented research and exploratory in nature with each of the factors studied related to the professional interests and needs of counselors and student development professionals so that they can, in turn, improve and target their services for Italian-American students.

The design focuses its attention on the three major psychoeducational constructs: locus of control, values and stress. Each of these constructs are introduced and discussed in greater detail in parts 2, 3, 4 and 5 of this report. In general, all are associated in some way with the personal, educational and vocational growth of students and are heavily researched concepts in the educational and psychological literature. Most importantly, they are most useful in helping us to develop a profile of this student group for the purposes of needs analysis in a higher educational setting. In addition to the quantitative profile of this group, interviews and focus groups were conducted with a small sub sample of this sample to provide some qualitative understanding of the results. Part 6 summarizes the results and presents their implications for further analysis and research. In addition, this section makes recommendations for improving or initiating programs and counseling services based on the findings of the study.

PART 2: THE DESIGN
DATA COLLECTION

Beginning in September 1985, 435 packets containing the research inventories were distributed to counselors and teachers at 14 City University senior and community colleges for dissemination to Italian-American students willing to participate in the research project. Each packet contained a biographical information sheet, the IPC Scale (Levenson, 1972), the Scale of Values (Rokeach, 1973), and a Personal Problems Checklist (Schinka, 1986). Students were informed about the project through classroom announcements or personal contact. They were made aware of the purposes and objectives of the research both in writing and verbally and were advised that the data would be reported as group results protecting the anonymity of their individual responses. Of the 435 original packets, 330 were actually given to students to be completed. Completion time for each of the packets was approximately 45 minutes. Most were completed individually or in groups at the time of distribution; a small percentage returned them at a later date. A total of 269 were returned resulting in a return rate of 81%. After an examination of the packets, 217 met the criteria for inclusion in the study.

A review of the feedback from the counselors and teachers indicated that over 65% of the sample were not affiliated with an Italian student organization in any way and only a very small number of the total were well known to the counselors or teachers. This left the large majority of the sample representing the typical commuter student who attends classes and returns home or, more likely, to work. Even many of the club-affiliated subjects could not be described as active in the leadership or administration of the activities.

This data collection process did not exclude the operation of a self-selection factor among participants; only random selection could achieve that end. Because random selection was not possible, the best available solution was to collect data so as to eliminate any obvious source of systematic bias. The return rate on a mail distribution of such a large packet would have been considerably lower and self-selected even if the targeted sample were larger and systematically selected. Moreover, the absence of a reliable database on Italian-American students at CUNY makes any attempt to use randomization with mailed surveys an extremely questionable procedure.

THE SAMPLE

There are no population statistics available for Italian-American students at CUNY. The only recent breakdown of Italian-American students that could be used for comparison purposes is itself a sample. Audrey Blumberg and David Lavin (1985) conducted a longitudinal study on the class of 1980–1984 and obtained a final sample of over 11,000 students that included 846 Italian-American respondents. They estimate that that their total sample (which included non-Italians) approximates 36% of the entering class. In comparing this to the population, they conclude that "in all cases, however, the sample/population differences are small . . . the sample provides a good representation of the population" (p. 6). For these reasons, the Blumberg and Lavin data will be used as a standard against which the accuracy of the results in this investigation may be judged.

TABLE 1. *Demographics of Sample*

	NUMBER OF STUDENTS			PERCENTAGE OF TOTAL SAMPLE		
	MALES	FEMALES	TOTAL	MALES	FEMALES	TOTAL
GENERATION						
First	11	15	26	5.1%	6.9%	12.0%
Second	31	41	72	14.3%	18.9%	33.2%
Third	60	59	119	27.6%	27.2%	54.8%
GRADE POINT AVERAGE						
< 2.00	1	1	2	0.5%	0.5%	1.0%
2.00–2.49	16	10	26	8.7%	5.4%	14.1%
2.50–2.99	22	27	49	12.0%	14.72%	26.7%
3.00–3.49	38	41	79	20.7%	22.3%	43.0%
> 3.50	12	16	28	6.5%	8.7%	15.2%
No response	13	20	33			
YEAR IN COLLEGE						
Freshman	22	32	54	10.1%	14.7%	24.8%
Sophomore	25	28	53	11.5%	12.9%	24.4%
Junior	26	25	51	12.0%	11.5%	23.5%
Senior	29	30	59	13.4%	13.8%	27.2%
COLLEGE MAJOR						
Computer science	6	3	9	0.9%	3.3%	4.2%
Engineering, et al.	15	1	16	7.0%	0.5%	7.5%
Community services	6	7	13	2.8%	3.3%	6.1%
Business programs	32	32	64	15.0%	15.0%	30.0%
Health sciences	2	14	16	0.9%	6.6%	7.5%
Liberal arts	27	38	65	12.7%	17.8%	30.5%
Undecided	12	9	21	5.6%	4.2%	9.9%
No response	0	4	0			
INCOME						
Under $10,000	4	6	10	2.0%	3.0%	5.0%
$10,000–$19,000	9	21	30	4.5%	10.4%	14.9%
$20,000–$29,000	34	36	70	16.8%	17.8%	34.6%
$30,000–$39,000	24	24	48	11.9%	11.9%	23.8%
$40,000–$75,000	22	13	36	10.9%	6.4%	17.3%
Over $75,000	6	3	9	3.0%	1.5%	4.5%
No response	2	12	14			
COLLEGE TYPE						
Senior college	75	85	160	35.0%	39.7%	74.7%
Community college	27	27	54	12.6%	12.6%	25.2%

The final sample in this study consists of 217 subjects who identified themselves as Italian or Italian American. It includes students from every college in the CUNY system except Bronx Community College, Medgar Evers Community College and Hostos Community College. These colleges were not included in the distribution process because of the small numbers of Italian Americans in attendance. Table 1 summarizes the demographics of this sample.

Gender Breakdown

Figure 1 illustrates the gender breakdown of this sample and compares it to the Blumberg and Lavin Sample (1985). The female majority is almost identical in both samples reflecting the same ratio of men to women in the general population of students.

FIGURE 1. *Comparison With Blumberg and Lavin Sample by Gender*

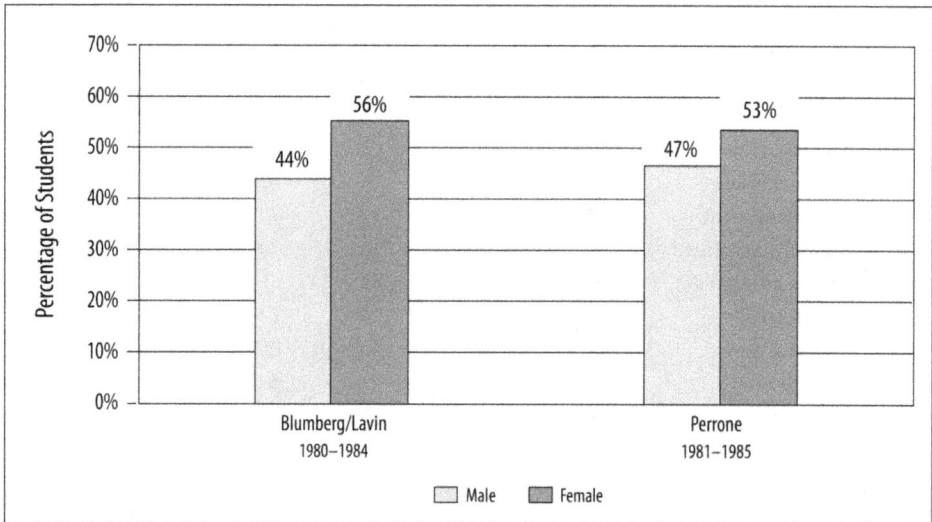

Generational Breakdown

In this study, students were categorized into three generational levels. The first generation includes students who were born in Italy and migrated to this country. The second generation includes students who were born in the United States and had one or more parents who were born in Italy. The third generation includes students who had both parents born in the United States. The second and third generation subsamples include students who came from exogamous marriages — i.e., marriages in which one partner is non-Italian. This group comprises over 23% of the total sample in this study. The degree of marital assimilation among Italian Americans has increased steadily over the years. In the 1980 census, 18% of the Italian Americans in New York State were from mixed ancestry (Egelman and Salvo, 1984). Not to include a sizeable group of students of this nature in this study would provide an incomplete profile of the Italian-American student at CUNY, moreover, an analysis of the data reveals that there are no significant differences in any of the variables measured between students from mixed ancestry and their generational counterparts who are from full Italian ancestral backgrounds.

FIGURE 2. *Sample Data, Gender by Generation*

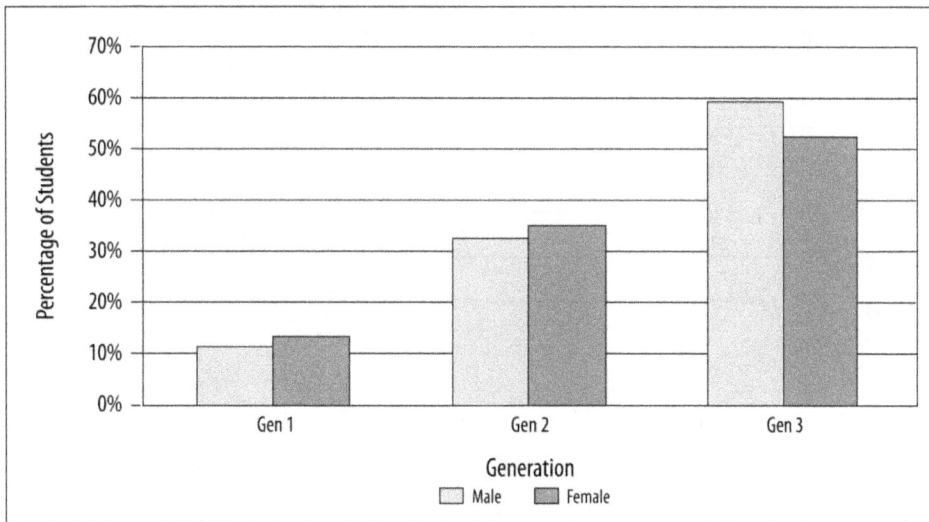

Figure 2 presents a picture of this distribution in the sample. For reasons of statistical analysis, the size of the total sample precluded any further breakdown of total generational categories or the ethnic origin of non-Italian parents. A sample of closer to 1,000 students would have permitted this detailed an analysis.

Although there is no previous database with which to compare this distribution, the preponderance of later generation students and students of mixed ethnic heritage in the sample corresponds to the informal observations of the staff and students. It is, however, difficult to speculate about the actual percentages of Italian born students in the CUNY system. The gender distribution within each category appears fairly evenly balanced with a slightly greater percentage of females represented in the first two generations.

Grade Point Average

Students were asked to indicate their grade point averages on the biographical information sheet. Figure 3 presents a picture of this self-reported distribution of grades reflecting no major difference between the genders. The total percentages given in Table 1 indicate that over 58% of the students are maintaining an average of 3.00 or above. This differs very little from the GPA distribution in the Blumberg and Lavin (1985) sample. Using slightly different parameters for their self-reported distribution of GPAs, they reported that 60% of their sample of Italian-American students reported academic averages in the "above average" category.

FIGURE 3. *Sample Data, GPA by Gender (N=204)*

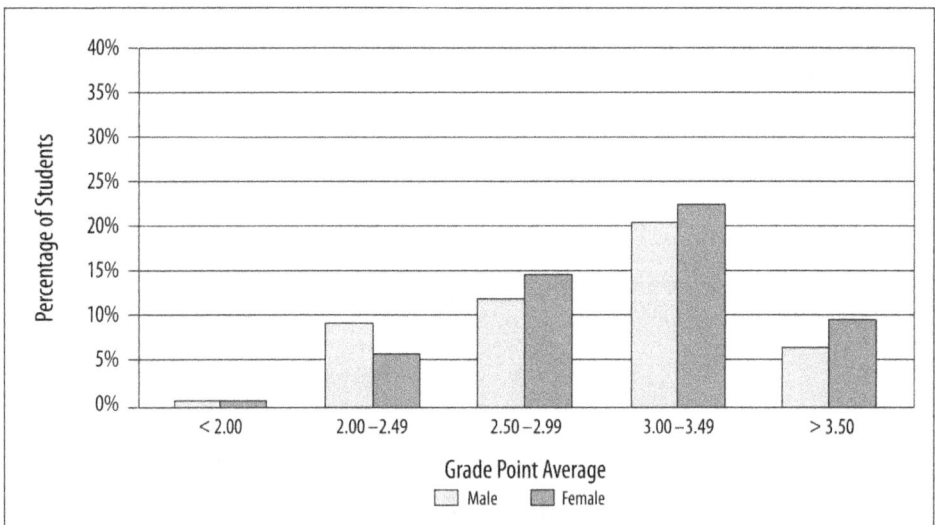

Year in College

The sample contains almost an equal amount of students in each of the four categories. The graph in Figure 4 reflects a relatively balanced representation of males and females from each undergraduate level. The only noticeable difference is in the freshman subsample where the females have about a 5% majority.

FIGURE 4. *Sample Data, Gender by Year in College*

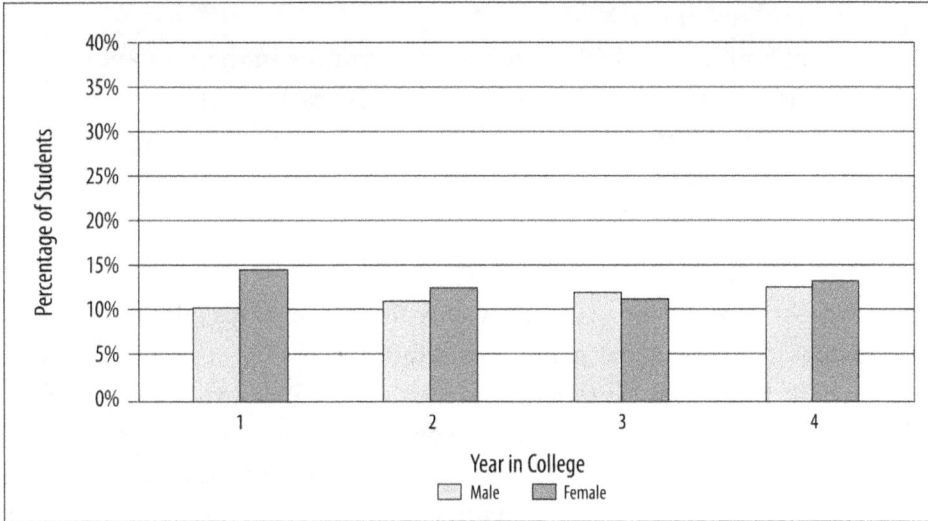

FIGURE 5. *Gender by major*

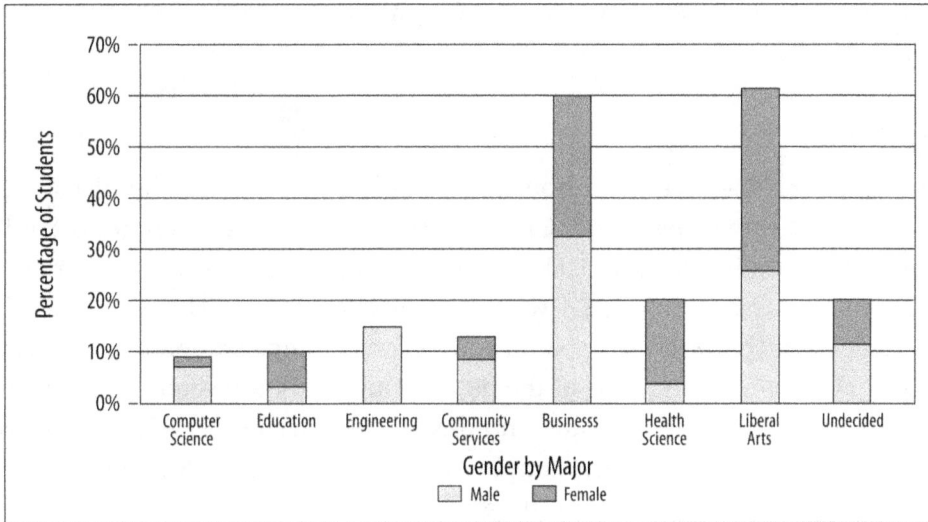

College Major

Table 1 includes the breakdown of this sample into the seven major courses of study offered in the CUNY system. The preponderance of majors were in liberal arts and business which generally reflects the choice patterns of the Italian-American students who responded to the CUNY surveys conducted by Mazitti (1981) and Castiglione (1982). Some 10%

reported being undecided about their major but the large majority in this group were freshmen.

Figure 5 indicates that the gender preferences in these categories were evenly distributed in liberal arts and business but reflected traditional gender specific choices in the areas of education, engineering, and health sciences (i.e., nursing).

College Type

Almost 75% of this sample was from the senior colleges of CUNY. This does not reflect the general distribution of Italian Americans at the university found by Blumberg and Lavin (1985). However, there was a large enough subsample (N=58) of community college students to make comparisons with the senior college subsample. An analysis of the data from these two subsamples measured in this profile revealed no significant differences on any of the variables measured (i.e., locus of control, values, etc.). Nevertheless, inferences concerning the total population of Italian-American students should be guarded vis-à-vis community college students.

Income

The income level data from this sample appears normally distributed across the categories listed. Close to 70% of the students reported family incomes ranging from $20,000 to $40,000. The median income reported in Blumberg and Lavin (1985) was about $10,000 lower. This was clearly a function of the larger number of community college students in that sample. However, an analysis of the data in this study revealed no significant relationship between income and any of the variables profiled. With regard to income level, any sample of students from CUNY would be attenuated in this category resulting in the lack of significant findings.

Representativeness of Sample

How accurately does this sample reflect the profile of the entire population of Italian-American students at CUNY? Without actual population demographics on this group, this is a difficult question to answer. We know that sample has been drawn from almost all of the colleges in the university and the high return rate and data collection methods kept any self-selection process to a minimum. We also know that the demographics resemble the larger and probably more representative sample of Blumberg and Lavin (1985) in the important areas of gender and grade point average breakdown. It does, however, appear to over represent the senior college population making inferences to the community college population more suspect. Consequently, generalizations based on the data should be guarded because they are subject to the kind of error that any sample representing slightly over 1% of the population can generate.

THEORETICAL FOUNDATION

The theoretical underpinning for the selection of the variables profiled in this study is provided for by the expectancy-valence approach to understanding and predicting achievement motivation and goal seeking behavior. Expectancy-Valence theory has its origins in the classical learning experiments of the Gestalt psychologists Lewin (1938) and Tolman (1951) and in early social learning theory (Rotter, 1955). It now enjoys wide acceptance and empirical support not only in educational psychology (Atkinson and Feather, 1966; Atkinson and Raynor, 1974) but also among organizational psychologists (Vroom, 1964; Lawler, 1973). It is basically an interactionist approach to motivation that involves both person factors and situation factors in attempting to explain the degree of effort that anyone will exert to achieve specific goals in any given situation. For our purposes, the "anyone" refers to Italian-American students and the "goals" are the various outcomes of a college experience that includes learning (an intrinsic reward), a feeling of accomplishment, performance (i.e., grades), a diploma, social recognition, social contacts and a career (i.e., a good job). In its simplest formulation, the theory postulates that individuals will apply their skills and energy to any given task (e.g., studying) if they believe that they can succeed at it, perceive that they will be rewarded for succeeding and anticipate being satisfied by any rewards that ensue from their success. The former set of perceptions or beliefs are called *expectancies* and the latter set of anticipated satisfactions we called *valences.*

Figure 6 summarizes the basic components of this approach to motivation and behavior. Thus, for example, a student who has a low regard for his academic ability may avoid enrolling for even moderately difficult courses because he fears failure or feels that he will not have the energy to meet the demands of study (i.e., first level expectancy). In another example, if a student perceives that her efforts in any given course will not be graded fairly (i.e., second level expectancy) by the instructor, her motivation to prepare for the course examinations will be less than enthusiastic. With regard to career choice, some students who garner little satisfaction from learning itself (i.e., valence) may not select certain liberal arts majors because they don't perceive a relationship between that course of study and obtaining a "good job" after college, which is the primary reason why they entered college. There are many other examples that could apply. In short, in order for students to be motivated to learn and achieve, they must perceive a relationship between their behavior and the outcomes of their behavior and, most of all, must value these outcomes.

FIGURE 6. *Expectancy-Valence Theory*

MOTIVATION
=
FIRST LEVEL EXPECTANCY
"If I apply my energy and skills to this endeavor, what are my expectations for completing it successfully?"
X
SECOND LEVEL EXPECTANCY
"If I achieve a successful outcome, what are my expectations for being rewarded?"
X
VALENCE
"What value do I place on the rewards I receive?"

In some way, the three variables profiled in this study—i.e., locus of control, values and stress—have a direct or indirect impact on the beliefs and perceptions outlined in Expectancy-Valence theory, thereby providing a source of valuable information about the general achievement motivation profile of Italian Americans in this educational setting.

RESEARCH INSTRUMENTS
Locus of Control and the IPC Scale

If students do not feel a general sense of personal control over the events in their lives, their expectancies for success in school, in particular, and life, in general, will be greatly diminished. What internal resources they attribute their success or failure to is also an important ingredient in the equation. If their perceptions of self-efficacy are low and they assign too much to "effort" in their success stories and to "lack of ability" in their failure outcomes, their expectations for future achievements will be lowered (Bandura, 1977; Feather, 1975; Weiner, 1972). Furthermore, If they believe that any rewards for their life's efforts are distributed capriciously or subject to whims and whimsies of "powerful others" or devices of "the system," then their willingness to utilize their inner resources and/or exert the effort needed to succeed will be continually colored by these externalized attributions. Thus, an assessment of the locus of control and attributional dynamics of Italian-American students is included in this profile to provide some insight into their feelings of self-efficacy and sense of personal control over the events in their lives. A research review on the locus of control construct is presented in Part 3 of this report along with the locus of control profile of the Italian-American sample.

Locus of control is such an important construct that more than thirty scales have been developed to measure it (Nowicki and Duke, 1984). Locus of control is assessed in this study by the IPC Scale devised by Hanna Levenson (1972). It is one of the older and better developed locus of control scales and has generated a great deal of research in several areas. Subjects are asked to indicate their level of agreement or disagreement with a series of general attitude statements tapping their beliefs about the operations of three dimensions of control in their lives — personal control, control by powerful others and chance. Beliefs in personal control are measured by the I Scale (e.g., "Whether or not I get to be a leader depends mostly on my ability"). The P Scale measures the extent to which people believe that their lives are control by powerful others (e.g., "I feel that what happens in my life is chiefly determined by powerful people"). The C Scale is concerned with beliefs in control by chance (e.g., "I have often found that what is going to happen, will happen"). The range of possible scores on each scale is from 0–48. Levenson (1981), however, cautions that high scores and low scores in any one of the three scales only indicate a valence of belief in the locus of control source designated by that particular scale. For example, a low score on the I Scale does not necessarily imply that the person strongly believes in external sources of control. Empirically, a subject could score high or low on all three scales but rarely has a profile been found.

Levenson (1981) provides reliability and validity data on the IPC Scale in her article in the Lefcourt series on the locus of control construct. Internal consistency correlations, split-half reliabilities and test-retest reliabilities have been reported as moderately high and validity estimates have been measured as sufficiently positive especially when concurrently related to other variables measuring the same construct. More importantly, unlike other locus of control scales, the IPC items have not been found to be contaminated by social desirability (Levenson 1972).

An Attribution Index

In the later locus of control literature, a great deal of discussion and research has centered around the attribution of specific internal and external resources and their relationship to generalized expectancies for success and failure (Weiner, 1972). With the expectation that Italian-American college students would present a general profile of internality (i.e., high I Scale scores) a focus of interest in this study is to what specific internal resources—i.e., effort or ability—these students attribute their past successes and failures in school. For example, do they feel that they have succeeded in the past because they "try hard" or because they have the general intelligence to do well with a minimum amount of effort? Moreover, if they have not done well in a specific academic endeavor (e.g., an exam), do they tend to attribute it to a lack of skill on their part or simply because they have not studied enough? Perhaps it is simply a matter of luck? The answer to these questions would actually be in the form of a ratio between three factors (i.e., ability, effort and luck) and would have obvious implications for their future expectancies for success and failure in school. A research review on the attribution concept itself is also presented in Part 3 of this report along with the attribution profile of the Italian-American sample.

Two questions were added to the biographical information form to assess the relationship of these three attributions—i.e., ability, effort and luck—for this sample and provide a sort of attribution index (cf. Appendix B). Students were simply asked to rate these three factors in order of importance in an academic success situation and an academic failure situation. Even though the questions are very specific, the brevity of this index effects its reliability and any results that ensue should be viewed as pilot findings with implications for further research. There is a longer and more reliable instrument to assess attribution that could have been utilized (Lefcourt, 1981) but it is newly constructed and data on validity is scarce. More importantly, however, it would have lengthened the research packet beyond reasonable time limits for completion in one sitting. This would have seriously hampered data collection and reduced sample size.

Values and the Scale of Values

In a recent article on student motivation by Brophy (1983), he complains that most existing approaches to classroom motivation place too much emphasis on the "expectancy" factor in Expectancy-Valence theory while relatively ignoring the "valence" concept. What a student values in his or her educational milieu is just as important as whether he or she expects to succeed. For example, a student who enjoys learning as an end in itself might be quite motivated to apply herself in an elective course that has little direct relationship to her major course of studies and career aspirations. On the other hand, any contemporary college professor would consider you "naive" if you assumed that every student who applies for entrance to college truly values the pursuit of learning and a sense of accomplishment. There are many other value orientations that interact with each other and enter into the formula for understanding the short term and long term goals of college students in an educational setting. Thus, the assessment of values is a necessary inclusion in any profile of college students. A more thorough review of the research on the values construct itself is presented in Part 4 of this report along with the values profile of this sample.

The instrument used to assess values in this study is the Scale of Values developed by Milton Rokeach (1973). This inventory provides a simple method for measuring the values construct and is widely cited in the literature as one of most valid, relatively culture-free approaches to values assessment in adults (Buros, 1985). The survey has been used to provide data on national samples of Americans in 1968 (Rokeach, 1973) and again in 1971 (Rokeach, 1979). The scale consists of two sets of 18 alphabetically arranged values along with brief defining phrases in parentheses. The first set consists of terminal values or end states and the second list are labeled instrumental values or modes of behavior. Respondents are asked to rank each set of eighteen in order of importance.

In this study, we have used Form G of the Rokeach Value Survey (RVS), which has replaced all previous forms. The only difference in this new form of the test is the addition of two new values to replace two from the previous forms. For empirical reasons (personal communication with the publisher), the value "happiness" has been replaced by "health" in the terminal value list and the value "cheerful" has been replaced by the value "loyal" in the instrumental value list. It is important to note this when comparisons are made with earlier studies in this area.

Test-retest reliabilities were computed for each of the values considered separately as well as for the total value system. The correlations ran from moderately high to high for samples ranging from seventh grade level to college and non-college adults (Rokeach, 1973). Rokeach also reports that his scale has established reasonably high validity because of its sensitivity to differences between groups from different cultures, institutions and life experiences. Moreover, social desirability and "order effects" were not found to be contaminating factors when interpreting results.

Stress And The Personal Problems Checklist (PPC)

Expectancy-Valence theory makes the assumption that the beliefs and perceptions of the individual are reasonably rational expectations and that the behavior of the motivated student or worker is purposeful. It is fairly obvious that this would not be the case when undue stress is an intervening factor. Norman Feather (1982), one of the major proponents of Expectancy-Valence theory, admits that the approach is limited by a reliance on conscious intentions and rational thought processes. He writes

> Expectancy-value models might validly be applied to behaviors where the ego is in control and where secondary process thinking and conscious intentions dominate purposeful action. But where unconscious wishes strive for fulfillment and where primary process thinking is strongly in evidence, these models may be less appropriate (p. 399).

In a chronic or traumatic stress situation, a student's normal intentions, aspirations, values and behavior are all in some way changed or distorted by the anxiety and depression that often accompany this state. In simple language, it is difficult to analyze the motivation of a student or predict how he or she will behave when personal or family problems are interfering with everyday functioning. Thus, an analysis of the more frequent stressors of students is a necessary component in any psychoeducational profile. A review of the research on the dynamics of stress and its relationship to performance and decision making in college students will be summarized in Part 5 of this report along with a stress profile.

Most standardized instruments that are designed to measure stress in students are either very clinically oriented (e.g., Beck's Depression Inventory or the MMPI) or are modeled after the Homes-Rahe Life Events Scale (cf. Linden, 1984; Goodman, S., et al. 1984). The former approach is not compatible with the basic objectives of this study and the latter model focuses only on episodic stress. The only approach that can give a comprehensive picture of both the chronic and episodic stress profile of students is a problems checklist. The most renowned of these, the Mooney Problem Checklist, was considered to be too lengthy and somewhat outdated for use in this study. A similar but briefer problems checklist has recently been developed by Joseph Schinka at Psychological Assessment Resources (cf. 1984 PAR Catalogue) and has been adopted for inclusion in this study. The Personal Problems Checklist for Adults (PPC) is a structured inventory that provides a quick profile of an individual's presenting problems and can be quite useful in determining the major stressors of any specific group of people. It contains 208 individual items that are grouped into 13 categories in the following major problems areas: social, appearance, vocational, family and home, school, finances, religion, emotions, sex, legal, health and habits, attitudes and crises. Students are asked to place a checkmark next to those problems that they are presently facing and circle the most serious. An analysis of the raw data, however, revealed that the students generally ignored the instructions regarding the distinction between circles and checkmarks with the intention of simply indicating problems. As a result, when the checklists were scored, both circled and checked problems were given equal weight.

Schinka (1986) provides no data on reliability and empirical validity for this instrument but does outline a systematic approach to item selection using several panels of expert judges (i.e., content validity). He also advises against drawing inferences from any summary data (i.e., total scores). However, there is some precedent for using total numbers of stressors checked as a rough indicator of overall stress levels (cf. Holmes-Rahe, 1967, Husaini and Neff, 1980).

Although a lack of construct validity on the PPC is an admitted liability, the usefulness and comprehensiveness of the data that it provides and the more common problems of students is concordant with the action orientation of this research project. It enables us to target specific problem areas among Italian Americans at CUNY and design the appropriate counseling strategies and programs to reduce the stress levels of these students.

STATISTICAL METHODS

Because the primary purpose of this project is to develop a psychoeducational profile of the Italian-American student at CUNY, a variety of descriptive statistical techniques are utilized to describe this sample. These include the appropriate measures of central tendency, variability and correlation that best describe and summarize the results. In addition, several inferential statistical methods are utilized to assess differences among and between various subsamples (e.g., gender). These include both the parametric and non-parametric statistical techniques that best assess the type of data (i.e., ordinal, interval, etc.) and distribution involved. A more precise presentation of the statistical strategies used in this study is included in Appendix A.

THE INTERVIEWS

In an attempt to get behind the numbers and to provide some qualitative information on this sample, 31 students were interviewed either individually or in groups. They included male and female students from the various generational categories. No attempt, however, was made to obtain a representative sample or even subsample of Italian-American students, thereby precluding any inferences from the information gathered. The individual interviews were conducted by this researcher and several of the counselors from the Italian American Institute utilizing a semi-structured interview format (cf. Appendix C and D). The group interviews took the form of focus groups and were conducted after the quantitative data had been gathered and statistically analyzed.

In both the group and individual interviews, discussion was focused on the variables profiled in this study (e.g., motivation, personal control, values, stress, etc.). Where possible, students were asked to comment or elaborate on some of the quantitative findings in order to provide us with some insight into the dynamics underlying the quantitative results. References to these interviews are made throughout discussion sections of this report to provide some possible explanations for the findings or some implications for future research but are in no way to be considered valid or reliable data about the sample.

PART 3: LOCUS OF CONTROL
REVIEW OF THE RESEARCH

The locus of control construct is perhaps one of the most heavily researched concepts in psychology today. According to the February 1982 issue of *Current Contents*, Rotter's 1966 monograph outlining the concept had been cited over 2,735 times in the literature. Julian Rotter (1954) first developed the construct within the framework of his social learning theory. He purported that one of the major variables affecting human behavior is an individual's perception of control over the reinforcements in his or her life. In the original 1966 monograph, Rotter proposed that people who have an *internal* locus of control orientation tend to attribute the successes and failures in their life to their own characteristics or behavior. On the other hand, he postulated that those who have an *external* locus of control orientation perceive that their actions and subsequent reinforcements are determined by such potent outside forces as luck, fate or powerful others.

In order to assess this dimension of personality, Rotter (1966) developed the I-E Scale—the original locus of control scale. Rotter postulated that a person scoring high on the internal scale is more likely to be a high achiever, more influential and more active in mastering his or her environment. The profileration of research that followed using his scale and similar scales (including the IPC Scale) have not only generally supported his original contentions but have gone well beyond them. In addition to its postulated relationship with achievement behavior, locus of control has also been found to be related to such diverse concepts as alcoholism (Donovan and O'Leary, 1978), cultural background (Dyal, 1984), recovery from illness (Levenson, 1981), marital adjustment (Doherty, 1983), career choice (Burroughs, 1984), obesity (Thomason, 1983) and stress (Husaini and Neff, 1980). Of particular concern in this study is its relationship to achievement orientation, career decision-making and cultural differences.

Locus of Control (LOC) and Achievement

Bar-Tel and Bar-Zohar (1977) reviewed 36 studies that examined the relationship between locus of control and academic achievement. Of these studies, 31 reported a positive relationship between internalism and measures of achievement. This relationship held constant regardless of the instrument used to assess locus of control. Both Ramanaiah, Ribich and Schmeck (1975) and Prociuk and Breen (1974), using the IPC Scale, found that internal students had better study habits and more positive educational attitudes than externally oriented students.

It should be noted, however, that this relationship between LOC and achievement has not always been consistent and not without paradox

(Lefcourt, 1976). For example, Dyal (1984) reviewed the research and concluded that the strong relationship between internality and success in school was more consistent for males than for females. In her summary of the research on gender and achievement, Levenson (1981) concluded that for females some aspects of externality may be facilitative. This appears to be especially true for the external belief in powerful others. In the Prociuk and Breen (1974) study, they reported that the female students in their study who had higher Powerful Others scores on the IPC Scale achieved better than those females who had higher scores on the Chance Scale. Internality, however, was still the highest predictor of achievement for both sexes.

Locus of Control (LOC) and Career Planning

Most of the studies that have examined the relationship between locus of control and career planning have not attempted to incorporate the LOC concept into a broader theory of career development but tried to identify simple correlations between LOC and activities associated with planning and choosing a career (O'Brien, 1984). In a nationwide study, Valecha (1972) found that for White subjects only, internals tended to seek positions that require higher skill requirements and greater personal autonomy. Maracek and Frasch (1977) report that external women spend less time in career planning, are less committed to their careers, and felt less inclined to violate gender-role stereotypes in their career choices. Similarly, Gable, Thompson and Glanstein (1976) reported a significant relationship between internality and vocational maturity in college women.

Of particular interest to the career counselor is the vocationally undecided student. In a recent study, Cellini and Kantorowski (1984) reported that both males and female college students with an internal locus of control were significantly more decided about their majors than those with an external locus of control. In an earlier study (Osipow et al., 1980), it was also reported that vocational undecidedness was related to internality but only for high ability subjects.

In general, Rotter's original contention that internality and life achievement are related seems to be borne out. If the bottom line is actual job success, there are several cross-sectional studies to establish that internals tend to attain higher occupations than do externals (Hammer and Vardi, 1981; Pandey and Tewary, 1979; Valecha, 1972). They are truly masters of their fate in a society that values decisiveness and personal control.

Locus of Control (LOC) and Cultural Background

As has been the case with other heavily researched personality variables, the locus of control research turned its attention to cross-cultural comparisons. One of the earliest and most controversial studies utilizing this variable was the survey research on US minorities cited in the Coleman Report (Coleman et al., 1966). Included in the sample were the minority groups found in great numbers in the CUNY system — i.e., Blacks, Puerto Ricans and Orientals. Each of the minority groups surveyed were found to be more external than their White counterparts.

A great deal of locus of control research has focused its attention on American Blacks since the Coleman report. Dyal (1984) cites 12 of 18 studies that generally support the Coleman data regarding the externality of Blacks in America. These results led Lefcourt (1966) to conclude that groups with minimal social and economic power either by class or race tend to be more external. With the exception of Asian students (cf. Bond and Tornatzty, 1973; Mahler, 1974) this conclusion about minority group externalism does not appear to hold true in college samples. Dyal cites several studies on Hispanics that lend no support or contrary support for so-called Hispanic fatalism in college samples. In most of the studies using the IPC Scale as a measure of LOC (cf. Levenson, 1981), the mean internalism scores of Black and Hispanic students were almost identical to those found in the White undergraduate samples.

Of particular interest are two studies on LOC conducted at a CUNY community college using the IPC Scale with samples made up primarily of minority group college students (Beck, 1979; Avrimedes, 1986). Although neither study was designed to examine intraethnic or intercultural comparisons, the means for their minority samples are noticeably similar to the general IPC profile for White undergraduate samples. It appears that, regardless of ethnic or racial background, those young people from lower and middle class homes who make a decision to enter the City University come with a feeling of personal control over their lives and careers.

It is no surprise that there has been no research in the locus of control literature on Italians Americans or even European Italians. The reputed fatalism of the early peasant immigrants might have some vestiges of culture-of-origin impact on later generations of Italians but this is unlikely in view of the modern quest for social mobility in industrialized societies. The closest thing to any kind of recent empirical research interest on personal control among Italians can be found in the Crispino (1980) study of ethnic groups. As part of an extensive survey of Bridgeport Italians, Crispino explored the relationship between a sense of fatalism and social class, ethnicity and generation. He did find that some level of resignation to fate is maintained across the generations of Italian Americans, although at decreasing levels in later generations. It must be noted, however, that Crispino's was not primarily a college sample and that education and social class were the major determinants of whether a person feels a sense of personal control over their lives. Thus, there is no reason to expect that Italian Americans, regardless of generational level, who appear to be achieving at better than satisfactory levels in college, would present a more external profile then the American college population in general.

Gender Differences

In the earlier section on achievement, the interaction between gender and LOC was discussed especially with regard to control by powerful others. In general, the LOC profiles for male and female college students seem consistently similar across the recent research on college students (Levenson, 1981). There does, however, seem to be some interaction of ethnicity and gender (Dyal, 1984). For example, in one study (Roueche and Mink, 1976), female Black college students appeared more external than the male students while the inverse was true for Hispanics. This interaction of gender and external attributions for Black females has been found in other studies (Zytoskee, Strickland and Watson, 1971). The internality of Hispanic females was also further confirmed in a study of Mexican business students, (Cole and Cole, 1977). Similar to the Rouche and Mink finding on Black students, Japanese-American college women were found to be more external than Japanese males (Mahler, 1974). Dyal (1984) discusses the interaction of gender and LOC variables among a myriad of other national and international ethnic groups in his article. Thus, it is clear that, although the results have not been consistent, a review of the research strongly supports the need for further exploration of the interaction of gender, ethnicity and LOC variables.

Without any database on Italian Americans, in general, it is difficult to speculate or hypothesize about any gender differences. However, the conclusions reached in the Cole and Cole (1977) study on gender differences and LOC among Mexican college students, economically disadvantaged American college students and advantaged American college students may shed some light on what we can expect in an Italian-American sample. They found that females in the disadvantaged samples in both countries to be more internal on the P and C Scales (i.e., lower scores) of Levenson's scale than males, while the results from the advantaged sample showed no gender differences. As a result, they proposed that "persons taking actions at self-improvement, in cultural contexts where such action is counternormative should be more internal in locus of control when contrasted with persons for whom such actions are not counternormative" (p. 21). Thus, if we can consider that it is "counternormative" for Italian-American women in New York City to enroll for and succeed in college, then we might expect similar internal orientation among the Italian-American women in this sample.

Locus of Control (LOC) and Attribution

While the LOC general categories of internal and external seem to explain outcomes that have occurred in the past, it appears that the more specific attributions of responsibility for success and failure seem to be better predictors of motivational behavior in the future (Sandler et al., 1983). In simpler language, we seem to get our beliefs about internal and external sources of control from past experience; how we incorporate that past experience and view future expectancies for success and failure in any endeavor is related to more specific LOC attributions. Borrowing from Heider's (1958) original theory of attribution, Weiner (1972, 1974) has reformulated LOC theory in an attributional framework. He breaks down internal and external loci of control into more specific stable and unstable personal characteristics. Thus, internals can attribute their success and failures in the past to the more stable personal characteristic of *ability* or to the more unstable characteristic of personal *effort*, which of course has a greater control factor. Externals, on the other hand, can attribute the outcomes in their lives to the more unstable or variable environmental characteristic of blind fate or *luck* or the more unstable environmental characteristic of *task difficulty*. Weiner describes a strong achievement profile as one in which the person attributes success to internal causes (i.e., ability and effort) and failure to an internal and unstable cause (i.e., lack of effort). He goes on to associate the fear of failure to a pattern of attribution that tends to attribute success to the more external causes and failure to the unstable internal cause (i.e., lack of ability).

Thus, a success oriented student feels that he or she can simply put out more effort to succeed while the "fear of failure" student does not feel that more effort "can do any good." In his summary of the research on attribution, Gregory (1981) cites empirical support for Weiner's hypotheses but concludes that the relationship between attribution and achievement behavior is not as strong as Weiner contended.

The research on attribution and achievement is not nearly as conclusive or comprehensive as the research on the relationship between locus of control and achievement. There also appears to be no significant cross-cultural research on attribution and achievement behavior. There has, however, been some research on gender differences and attribution in achievement scenarios. Both Dweck and Bush (1976) and Lefcourt (1981) have found that females were more apt to attribute school related failures to lack of ability than males; males tended to attribute failures more to lack of effort. Lefcourt, for a variety of empirical reasons, concludes that this data requires replication before its reliability can be assumed. Thus, it would be premature to predict a similar gender difference in attribution in this study of Italian-American students, especially in light of the brief index of attribution utilized. It would seem, however, that the profile of achieving college women, in general, might reflect a greater emphasis on effort than ability than the men in view of some of the past research on achievement and self-esteem in women (Stacey, Beraud and Daniels, 1974; Horner, 1968).

A LOCUS OF CONTROL PROFILE

As expected, the general LOC profile for this Italian-American student sample is an internal one. In Table 2, the means and standard deviations for the I, P, and C Scales we presented along with the composite results (weighted means) from 9 college studies cited in Levenson's (1981) article on the IPC Scale. Also presented in Table 2 for comparison purposes are the composite results from two studies using CUNY students conducted by Beck (1979) and Avrimedes (1986). In the CUNY samples, a majority of students were from the various minority groups within the university (i.e., Black, Hispanic, Asian, etc.). The results indicate that the LOC profile remains remarkably consistent across samples of college students. More importantly, for our interest, Italian-American college students are not culturally unique or different in presenting a generally internal profile.

TABLE 2. *Means and Standard Deviations on the IPC Scale: Italian-American Samples vs. Comparison Groups of College Students*

	NUMBER	I		P		C	
		MEAN	SD	MEAN	SD	MEAN	SD
ITALIAN-AMERICAN SAMPLE							
Perrone (1986)	217	35.36	(6.22)	18.29	(8.80)	18.30	(8.49)
NORMATIVE SAMPLE							
Levenson (1981)	2,798	34.89	-	19.78	-	18.79	-
CUNY SAMPLES							
Beck (1979) and Avrimedes (1986)	438	35.73	-	19.14	-	18.65	-

It is important to note that we are reporting averages and that the externalism scores on the P and C Scales vary from student to student. Figure 7 presents a breakdown of the sample into "pure internals" (i.e., high internal score; average or low external scores), "shared controllers" (i.e., internal score approximately equal to one or both external scales), and "pure externals" (i.e., one or both external scales higher than the internal scale). The data clearly reveals that only 8% of the sample (18 students) could be classified as pure externals – i.e., students with extreme beliefs in the influence of powerful others or fate in their lives. A larger number of students present a profile of shared control, a pattern considered by some researchers to be a more reality-oriented, less stressful, belief system (Janoff-Bulman and Brickman, 1982). "Shared controllers" are those individuals who generally have a sense of personal control over most outcomes in their lives but give external factors their due and refuse to accept responsibility for those aspects of their lives that are impossible to control. However, the evidence in a study using a similar breakdown (Prociuk and Breen, 1974) is that as far as college grades are concerned, "pure internals" are the best achievers of the three groups.

The interviews reflected this pattern of personal control evident in the survey data and tend to attribute this to family reinforcement. When asked to discuss the advantages of being raised in an Italian-American family, both men and women cited the feeling of high self-esteem and personal responsibility that was instilled in them by their parents and grandparents. One student said that the one thing both her parents and grandparents stressed was that "above all, I should feel good about myself." The decision to attend college for all was encouraged and stressed by the family for both men and women, contrary to the anti-education stereotype sometimes identified with Italian-American families. With regard to career choices, the students were almost unanimous in reporting that they were under no pressure to conform to any parental expectations, expressed or implicit. A characteristic response in this area was "my parents felt that whatever I wanted was OK with them." Many of the women who were interviewed did, however, make a distinction between personal control in their vocational life and parental control in their affiliative life (i.e., dating, marriage, etc.). To some, this appeared to be a constant source of stress and consternation.

FIGURE 7. *Locus of Control Types*

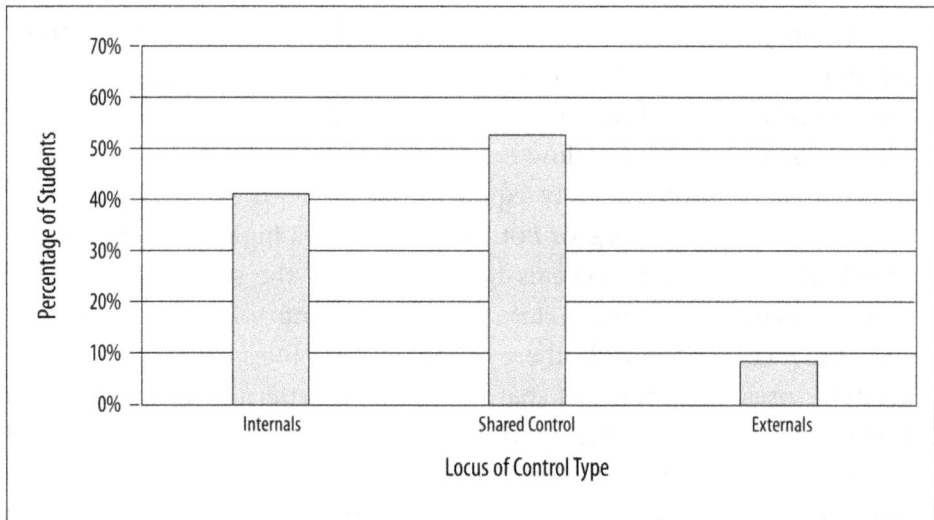

Gender and Generational Differences

Table 3 lists the mean IPC scores for men and women and the three generations of students in this sample. It is clear that there were no significant generational differences found, confirming the expectation that those students who choose to attend college have the same internal orientation regardless of the nature and extent of their contact with American society. The tendency toward fatalism found in the earlier generations of Italians in the Crispino (1980) study was not evident in this college sample.

TABLE 3. *Locus of Control Means and SDs: Gender and Generational Breakdown*

	I		P		C	
	MEAN	SD	MEAN	SD	MEAN	SD
GENERATION						
1	35.08	6.44	20.27	10.20	19.89	10.16
2	34.87	6.81	17.21	8.26	17.99	8.01
3	35.73	5.82	18.50	8.77	18.14	8.42
GENDER						
Male	34.84	6.25	19.72*	8.78	19.05	8.58
Female	35.82	6.18	17.01*	8.65	17.64	8.39

*Significantly different at the .05 level (cf. Appendix A for statistical methodology).

What is revealing in Table 3 is the significant difference between the mean scores for men and women in a direction favoring greater internality in the women on the Powerful Others dimension. It appears that the Cole and Cole (1977) results on college women in Mexico and disadvantaged college women in the US have been replicated for Italian-American women in this New York City sample. If there is validity to their hypothesis that this occurs when the pursuit of higher education is counternormative in any group, it would suggest that these young women who project such a well-defined career orientation may also entertain some acceptance (perhaps unconsciously) of the traditional stereotype that this is not the role intended for them as women. When queried about the "family vs. career dilemma" facing many contemporary career women, one student said "I'm aware of that but I try not to think about it now." The ambivalence about this issue and strategy of "putting off the worrying until later" was generally characteristic of most of the women interviewed on this issue.

An added note, vis-à-vis these gender differences: in two separate studies (MacDonald, 1971; Reimanis, 1971), a relationship was established between maternal behavior and locus of control orientation in men and women. Men who were helped and taught by their mothers were found to be significantly more internal than women who saw their mothers as protective. These results led Reimanis (1971) to speculate that when the home environment is somewhat rejecting, the daughter may be forced to be more independent to satisfy her needs. In view of the results of this study on gender differences, it would be interesting to examine the interaction of parental style and locus of control among Italian-American men and women.

Attribution Profile

Table 4 includes the mean ratings assigned to the two attribution questions included in the biographical information sheet. As expected, the students' general attribution profile reflects the same internal orientation found in the IPC results. It is clear from the data on success attributions, that these students, as a group, feel that they have succeeded in college primarily because of their internal resources of "effort" and "ability," giving almost equal weight to each. In the failure scenario, outcomes are attributed almost solely to the unstable, variable attribution of "lack of effort." "Luck," as expected, plays a small role (10%) in either of the outcome possibilities. This is the classic "success profile" outlined by Weiner (1972, 1974) and discussed earlier in this section. It reflects a general pattern of high academic self-esteem coupled with an awareness that if failure does occur, more effort will turn that outcome into a success story in the future.

TABLE 4. *Mean Attribution Ratings for Success and Failure Outcomes: Male and Female Italian-American Students Combined*

SUCCESS OUTCOME (Question #7)	FAILURE OUTCOME (Question #8)
Effort = 44.64 (%)	Lack of effort = 60.60 (%)
Ability = 47.18 (%)	Lack of ability = 29.40 (%)
Luck = 7.92 (%)	Luck = 10.02 (%)

The gender differences found in the attribution profile further enhance our understanding of the potentially high achieving Italian-American woman represented in this sample. Although the results on female students generally parallel the strong achievement profile found in the male subsample, there appears to be a major difference in their internal success attributions. Table 5 shows that the women in this sample attribute significantly more of their success in school to effort and less to ability than their male counterparts. This replicates a relationship established by Bar-Tal and Frieze (1973) who found that high achievement-motivated females tend to make maximal use of effort as a cause factor in explaining success. In their sample of women, they reported this only as a non-significant trend. In this sample of Italian-American women, the trend was significant. It also replicates the findings of Stacey, et al. (1974) and Horner (1968), whose research on academic self-esteem in women shows them to be less confident of their ability and more reliant on their effort in learning situations.

TABLE 5. *Mean Attribution Ratings for Success and Failure Outcomes: Italian-American Males vs. Females*

	SUCCESS OUTCOMES			FAILURE OUTCOMES		
	EFFORT	ABILITY	LUCK	LACK OF EFFORT	LACK OF ABILITY	LUCK
MALES	40.84 (%)*	50.59 (%)**	8.33 (%)	58.85 (%)	30.14 (%)	11.01 (%)
FEMALES	48.11 (%)*	44.34 (%)**	7.54 (%)	62.20 (%)	28.72 (%)	9.12 (%)

*Significantly different at the .01 level (cf. Appendix A for statistical methodology).
**Significantly different at the .05 level (cf. Appendix A for statistical methodology).

If Weiner (1972) is correct about the relationship between attribution and future behavior in achievement situations, many of the Italian-American women in this sample feel that they have to try harder than men in order to succeed in both their educational and career pursuits. On the one hand, this orientation toward greater effort will more than likely result in a greater record of achievement (e.g., higher grades, promotions, etc.) for these women. What is also quite possible, however, is that a constant focus on effort might result in more fatigue and greater stress levels for these women as the demands of school and career persist and/or increase. In one of the interviews a female undergraduate said "I would never fail a course for lack of effort. I'd stay up all night to get everything right." Many clinicians and counselors have speculated that the "fear of success" syndrome initially identified only in women (Horner, 1968) and later in both men and women (Tresemer, 1977) might be attributed to this overemphasis on effort for success coupled with a fear that "they will run out of energy."

When informed of these attributional gender differences in the interviews, the female students have generally acknowledged their validity. Two possible explanations for this phenomenon emerged from the interview records. Several students suggested that, even though they have the ability, women feel that they must try harder than men because of their awareness of the inequities in the treatment of women in American society. The implication is that they perceive that they will be evaluated on more stringent standards than men. One student offered a variation on this theme. She felt that she was under pressure to succeed because of any failure on her part would reflect on other women. Whether these feelings had anything to do with the fact that they were Italian American or not was not clear and requires further exploration.

Summary

In general, the Italian-American students in this sample present what might be considered a "healthy" locus of control profile as far as achievement motivation is concerned. They feel that they have personal control and responsibility for most of the outcomes in their academic and vocational lives. They project the profile of the modern Italian-American student offered by Krase (1983). They are serious about their education, have confidence in their academic ability, make their own decisions regarding school and career, and feel supported by their parents in their educational pursuits. Italian-American women, although more similar to than different from men in most areas, appear to project a more internal, effort-oriented approach to accomplishing their educational and vocational goals. This obviously has implications for counseling in a gender context as well as a cultural context and will hopefully generate further research on this issue.

It is also clear that these findings have implications for the counseling and development of those young Italian Americans who may not fit this profile—especially those Italian-American high school students and community college students who, though academically and intellectually qualified, do not aspire to the same higher educational goals as most of the students in this sample.

PART 4: VALUES

REVIEW OF THE RESEARCH

Interest in the study and measurement of human values extends across several disciplines and professions. Philosophers have explored their relationship to moral behavior while anthropologists and sociologists have examined their role in the comparative analyses of various cultures and societies—past and present. This list can be expanded to include political scientists, theologians, historians, educators and of course, psychologists. Like locus of control, the study of values has its roots in social psychology with the classic work of researchers like Allport (1935) and Kluckhohn (1951). More recently, the psychologist most often quoted and identified with the concept of values is Milton Rokeach. He provides us with a definition of values that highlights their centrality and stability as cognitive systems:

> A value is an enduring belief that a specific mode of conduct or end-state of existence is personally or socially preferable to an opposite or converse mode of conduct or end-state of existence (Rokeach, 1973, p. 5).

He views values as relatively stable and general structures that transcend time and situations and lie at the base of our beliefs, attitudes, needs and motivation (Rokeach, 1968, 1973, 1979). Rokeach agrees with Kluckholn (1951) that they are socially shared conceptions of what is or is not desirable and with Williams (1971) that they serve as standards or criteria for what is acceptable behavior.

In his definition, Rokeach specifies that values can refer either to modes of conduct or end-states—i.e., means or ends. With this in mind, he outlines two sets of values or value systems. *Terminal values* refer to end-states of existence and include values like *a comfortable life, salvation, equality* and *health*. They would be roughly equivalent to long term goals or aspirations in a student's career plan. Rokeach outlines two kinds of terminal values; those having a *personal* orientation (e.g., inner harmony, self-respect, etc.) and those having a *social* orientation (i.e., world of beauty, equality, etc.) The set of values referring to modes of conduct are called *instrumental values* and include values like *ambitious, loyal, honest* and *clean*. These values are those ideal behaviors and personality characteristics that people "ought" to have in order to accomplish their goals in life. Rokeach again distinguishes between two subsets of values in this category. Some instrumental values have a *moral* orientation (e.g., clean, loyal, honest, etc.); others are more related to *competency* (e.g., logical, intellectual, capable, etc.).

In any research, values may be treated as either dependent or independent variables. Some studies have examined the conditions that generate the development of value systems in individuals and groups. They explore the various cultural, institutional and personal forms that act upon the individual and influence the selection of what value orientations have greater priority in life (cf. Feather, 1975; Rokeach, 1973, 1979). As independent variables, values have been studied vis-à-vis their impact on a variety of factors that include educational and occupational choice

(Rokeach, 1973; Feather, 1975); gender differences (Rokeach, 1973, 1979) deviant behavior (Berman, 1973), lifestyles (Vinson, Scott and Lamont, 1977); traditional and non-traditional sex roles (Ball-Rokeach, 1976); school impact (Newcomb, et al., 1967; Feather, 1975); and educational adjustment (Feather, 1975; Matteson, 1975). It is their relationship to career decision-making, educational adjustment and cultural impact that are most relevant in this profile.

Career Decision Making

Holland (1959) in his theory of vocational planning highlights the need for an evaluation of values priorities in determining life goals and identifying a career environment that best suits the personality of a searching college student. Similarly, The National Institute of Education (NIE) defines career awareness as an interaction among values, preferences, skills and self-concept (Wise, Charner and Randour, 1976). Every experienced career counselor is familiar with the critical role a student's value system plays in making choices about life and career. An assessment of values figures prominently even in the various computer software packages developed as adjuncts to career counseling services offered at many high schools and colleges.

The specific relationship between values and occupational or career choice has been examined in several studies. Rokeach (1973) cites a number of such studies in presenting the values profiles of such diverse occupational groups as university professors, policemen, service station attendants, salesmen, priests, business executives, scientists and artists. The profiles differed in many ways leading Rokeach to conclude that different subsets of values are predictive (though not perfectly) of certain occupational roles and choices. Similarily, Harrington and O'Shea (1982) found that certain values are associated with particular career clusters in a logical direction. For example, editors valued creativity; managers valued leadership; computer programmers preferred working with their mind and nurses tended to value working with people.

An extensive study (N=531) on educational choice and values was conducted by Feather and Collins (1974) at Mitchell College in New South Wales. In this study of first year students, Feather compared the values rankings on the Rokeach Value Survey (RVS) with a student's choice of major at the college. He found that students in business administration ranked a *comfortable life, social recognition,* and being *ambitious* as much more important than did those students in teacher education and general studies. Teacher education students and general studies (roughly equivalent to liberal arts) students assigned more importance to *a world at peace, mature love, true friendship,* being *honest* and being *loving* than did students in business administration.

Although the major objective of this study was to develop a values profile of Italian-American students, the data collected does lend itself to an exploration of the relationship between values and educational choice for liberal arts and business majors (the size of the subsamples in these two categories was sufficient for an analysis). If the relationship between values and major holds true for this CUNY sample, results similar to the Mitchell College study can be expected.

Educational Adjustment

There has been some research examining the relationship between values and adjustment to a particular educational environment. Essentially, this kind of study would examine the hypothesis that a student's personal value system affects whether he or she is (or will be) more comfortable attending a school that stresses similar values and uncomfortable at one that emphasizes different values. In two separate studies (Feather, 1975; Matteson, 1975) this "values-fit hypothesis" was established. In a study on close to 3000 high school students, Feather found a positive relationship between happiness ratings and degree of similarity between personal values and school values. In the Matteson study, a link was established between satisfaction in graduate school and degree of similarity between student and professorial value orientations. This values-fit concept has logical implications for achievement motivation and achievement itself, although no empirical relationship has been established.

With the values-fit hypothesis in mind, the values profile of this Italian-American student sample is compared to the national values profile for college faculty to establish an educational comfort index for the group.

Cultural and Ethnic Differences

Most of the cross-cultural and interethnic comparisons of value systems that have been conducted have used the RVS. One of the advantages of the scale is that it is relatively culture-free and lends itself to these kinds of comparisons (Buros, 1985). The RVS has provided meaningful and comparative data on samples tested in Canada (Rokeach, 1973); Israel (Rim, 1970); South Vietnam (Penner and Anh, 1977); South Australia (Feather, 1975); and West Germany (Schneider, 1977). In America, Rokeach (1973) compared the values profiles of Black Americans and White Americans and found significant differences on 7 of the 36 values. In a more recent study at CUNY (Roman, 1986), a values profile of Hispanic students at Kingsborough Community College was developed.

The literature on Italian-American values focuses primarily on their orientation toward family (Tomasi and Engles, 1970; Gambino, 1973, 1974; Barzini, 1965) and work (Papajohn and Speigel, 1975). Although there have been no studies using the RVS, there have been some values surveys conducted on Italians. In a 1968 study, Femminella found a relationship between ethnicity and values orientation among Italians on Long Island. Conversely, Crispino (1980) in his study of the assimilation of Italians in Bridgeport found little evidence to support a differentiation of values on a strictly ethnic basis. With regard to Italian-American students, both the Krase (1983) and Blumberg and Lavin (1985) survey data indicated that Italian-American students were job-oriented and viewed education from a career-based perspective. In the Blumberg and Lavin study, Italians in the senior colleges seemed more vocationally oriented than any of the other groups surveyed (p. 38).

There is no question that Italians, as a group, are both culturally and structurally assimilated into American society. Crispino (1980) makes a strong argument (based on his evidence) for the straight-line theory of assimilation with regard to Italian Americans. His results indicate that both education level and social class are greater determinants of attitudes and values than ethnicity—especially for later generation Italian Americans. Thus, the values profile for this sample, made up of primarily second and third generation Italian Americans, should reflect the values profile of the general community of students in this area. Moreover, there is good reason to speculate that the values orientation of those few aspiring college students who have emigrated from a modern, industrialized Italy, would likewise parallel the values orientation of their peers at CUNY.

Gender Differences

In *The Sociology of Gender*, Davidson and Gordon (1979) cite several studies in an extended discussion of parental and social class influence on

the values systems of men and women in contemporary American society. By way of summary, they conclude that while the valued characteristics for both boys and girls are similar, parents—especially working class
parents—expect their boys to be masculine and their girls to be feminine.
These differences due to the socialization of sex-role expectations have
been replicated in the national survey conducted in 1968 and 1971 (reported in Rokeach, 1973, 1979) and the Feather (1975) studies on college
students. In general, these investigators have found that men place more
emphasis on values concerned with achievement and intellectual pursuits, while women assigned more importance to values concerned with
love, affiliation and the family.

A review of the literature on value shifts in American society since the
Rokeach surveys would lead us to believe that these gender differences
may not completely hold true for a sample of college students in 1986.
Moreover, the reputed gender similarities among Italian men and women
vis-à-vis family orientation and emotionality (Rotunno and McGoldrick,
1982) might also account for fewer traditional sex-role differences in an
Italian-American values profile. Even with the clearly defined, sex-role
differentiations in the early immigrant families, Davidson and Gordon
(1979) remind, us that the alleged "submissiveness" of the Italian immigrant woman was situationally determined. In many situations, these
women were clearly in control and were expected to be quite task-
oriented and extraordinarily vocal and aggressive.

A VALUES PROFILE

Table 6 lists the terminal and instrumental rankings for the sample.
Composite rank orders are presented first, followed by numerals in parentheses that represent the median ranking for that particular value. It is
clear from these rankings that the Italian-American students in this sample tend to place greater importance on personal, interpersonal and family values rather than social, political, intellectual or religious values.
They do share the traditional American values for honesty, ambition, responsibility, good health and comfortable living but appear to care little
for national issues like national security, the environment and social
equality. When queried in the interviews about their values and long-
term goals in life, both men and women, with very few exceptions, related themes of family, home, comfortable living and most of all, personal

happiness. They related very moderate "success stories" with regard to career even among those who aspired to the professions. They appeared to view career strictly as a means to achieve the personal and family growth they value so much.

TABLE 6. *Terminal and Instrumental Value Medians and Composite Rank Orders for Italian-American Students*

TERMINAL VALUES*		INSTRUMENTAL VALUES*	
A comfortable life	4 (7.2)	Ambitious	4 (7.3)
An exciting life	10 (8.8)	Broadminded	10 (10.0)
A sense of accomplishment	8 (8.2)	Capable	7 (9.1)
A world at peace	13 (11.5)	Clean	15 (11.8)
A world of beauty	16 (15.0)	Courageous	13 (11.1)
Equality	15 (13.4)	Forgiving	11 (10.5)
Family security	3 (6.2)	Helpful	8 (9.4)
Freedom	7 (8.1)	Honest	1 (4.4)
Health	1 (3.1)	Imaginative	17 (12.5)
Inner harmony	9 (8.4)	Independent	6 (8.3)
Mature love	6 (8.0)	Intellectual	9 (10.0)
National security	18 (15.5)	Logical	16 (11.8)
Pleasure	11 (9.5)	Loving	3 (5.2)
Salvation	17 (15.3)	Loyal	5 (7.6)
Self-respect	2 (5.6)	Obedient	18 (15.1)
Social recognition	14 (11.7)	Polite	14 (11.3)
True friendship	5 (7.4)	Responsible	2 (4.7)
Wisdom	12 (9.6)	Self-controlled	12 (11.0)

*Form G of the RVS.

A profile of their predominant political ideology is reflected in the "equality-freedom" disparity in their general profile—i.e., they rank freedom higher than equality (cf. Table 6). In Rokeach's two-value model of politics (1973), the 70% of American college students who fall into this "equality-freedom" type tend to be less politically sophisticated, unclear about their political identity, and less politically active.

Also revealing in this profile are the values assigned to the lower extremes in each set—i.e., *salvation* and *obedience*. The low priority assigned to *salvation* would seem to indicate a lack of religiosity in an ethnic group traditionally identified with a strong adherence to Catholicism. This appears to run counter to Lenski's (1963) and Crispino's (1980) findings of increasing religiosity in later generation ethnics. One possible explanation for this result was offered by a young student in a focus group interview.

She explained that salvation for her was associated with old age and death, two concepts that were remote for her at this stage of her life. If this result is, in fact, related to a present-time orientation rather than a lack of religiosity, we might see this value take on increasing importance in any research with the older age groups.

The low rank assigned to *obedience* also seems counterindicative in a group of students so openly devoted and committed to their families. This was discussed in several interviews and the explanations given usually centered around the reputed counterdependency of Italians as a group. It is, however, more likely associated with the dynamics of their developmental stage and their general sense of internalism. Support for the latter comes from the data. Internalism on the IPC Scale was found to be significantly correlated in a positive direction with obedience rankings (cf. Table 7). Because lower ranks denote higher importance on the RVS, the more internal their locus of control the lower they value obedience.

TABLE 7. *Significant Correlations Between LOC Variables and Personal Values*

LOC VARIABLE	PERSONAL VALUE	r^*	p
Internal	Social recognition	.19	.01
	Imaginative	−.21	.01
	Obedient	.19	.01
	Polite	.18	.01
Powerful choice	Equality	.21	.01
Chance	Health	−.19	.01

*Positive correlations indicate lower value preferences and vice-versa.

Comparisons with Other Groups

How culturally unique is this values profile? The competitive data and similarity indices presented in Tables 8 and 9 provide some information in this regard. The similarity index is simply a Spearman rank-order correlation between the values rankings from two separate samples. It was suggested and utilized by Feather (1975) to compare value rankings across studies. As it is with all correlations, the closer the correlation approximates "+1" the greater the relationship or degree of similarity between the two sets of values.

TABLE 8. *Terminal Composite Rank Orders and Similarity Indices for Italian-American (Italian) Sample, NORC College Sample, Non-Italian CUNY Sample, and Hispanic CUNY Sample*

TERMINAL VALUES	ITALIAN SAMPLE	NORC SAMPLE*	NON-ITALIAN CUNY SAMPLE	HISPANIC CUNY SAMPLE**
A comfortable life	4	13	7	4
An exciting life	10	16	9	5
A sense of accomplishment	8	5	11	8
A world at peace	13	2	15	11
A world of beauty	16	15	17	12
Equality	15	8	14	16
Family security	3	1	3	13
Freedom	7	3	4	10
Health	1	***	1	***
Inner harmony	9	9	10	18
Mature love	6	11	8	6
National security	18	12	18	9
Pleasure	11	18	12	14
Salvation	17	14	16	7
Self-respect	2	6	2	17
Social recognition	14	17	13	3
True friendship	5	7	6	1
Wisdom	12	4	5	15

GROUPS COMPARED	SIMILARITY INDEX
Italians vs. NORC sample	.41
Italians vs. non-Italians	.91****
Italians vs. Hispanics	.03****

*Rokeach (1969) used Form D of RVS.   ***Form D of RVS did not include this value.
**Roman (1986) used Form D of RVS.   ****Index calculated on 17 values ranked by both studies.

The NORC sample (cf. Tables 8 and 9) is a national sample of college students surveyed in 1968 and reported in Rokeach (1973). The composite rankings and similarity indices for the two samples suggest only a moderate relationship (.41 and .66). There are large differences between the two samples on the importance given to several values. Italians in this sample appear to assign greater priority to a *comfortable life, an exciting life, pleasure, mature love, loving,* and *self-respect* and less priority to *a world at peace, equality, freedom, wisdom, broadminded, courageous, and self-controlled.* Furthermore, the similarity indices suggest that there are greater similarities in the instrumental values of the two samples than their terminal values. These results, however, are more than likely attributable to the value shifts in the population since the 1968 NORC survey. Rokeach (1973) in a later study provides empirical support for these shifts over only a three-year period. Unfortunately, the 1968 survey provides the only reliable database available on American college students.

TABLE 9. *Instrumental Composite Rank Orders and Similarity Indices for Italian-American (Italian) Sample, NORC College Sample, Non-Italian CUNY Sample, and Hispanic CUNY Sample*

INSTRUMENTAL VALUE	ITALIAN SAMPLE	NORC SAMPLE*	CUNY SAMPLE	HISPANIC CUNY SAMPLE**
Ambitious	4	4	4	13
Broadminded	10	3	8	15
Capable	7	10	7	10
Clean	15	17	17	18
Courageous	13	5	10	6
Forgiving	11	12	12	2
Helpful	8	7	11	3
Honest	1	1	1	5
Imaginative	17	15	16	9
Independent	6	9	3	11
Intellectual	9	8	6	17
Logical	16	11	13	16
Loving	3	13	5	13
Loyal	5	***	9	***
Obedient	18	18	18	1
Polite	14	16	15	12
Responsible	2	2	2	8
Self-controlled	12	6	14	4

GROUPS COMPARED	SIMILARITY INDEX
Italians vs. NORC sample	.66
Italians vs. non-Italians	.91****
Italians vs. Hispanics	.01****

*Rokeach (1969) used Form D of RVS.   ***Form D of RVS did not include this value.
**Roman (1986) used Form D of RVS.   ****Index calculated on 17 values ranked by both studies.

For this reason, the RVS was administered to non-Italian students in several undergraduate classes at one of the CUNY senior colleges to provide more recent and more local group data for comparison. This sample (N=84) is included for comparison purposes only and is by no means presented as representative of the CUNY student population. However, the results here are revealing and tend to support the expectation that the Italian-American student profile is not a culturally unique one. The values rankings for the two samples are notably similar—almost identical—and the similarity index for both the terminal and instrumental value sets is high (r=.91 and .91 respectively). There appears to be only one notable difference. Italians seem to place less value on *wisdom* than the non-Italian sample. It must be noted here that these comparisons are exploratory and that no valid inferences can be drawn from them.

A recent doctoral dissertation provides us with an opportunity to compare this Italian-American sample with another large ethnic group in CUNY — Hispanics. Roman (1986) at Kingsborough Community College surveyed the values of 304 students enrolled in the Bilingual Program, using a Spanish translation of Form D of the RVS. The results presented in Table 8 reveal a clear pattern of cultural differences between these two groups. One of the most revealing disparities is in the degree of importance the two groups assign to *obedience, salvation, self-respect, social recognition, family security* and *loving*. This has obvious implications for personal counselors, career counselors and student activities professionals. It would be interesting and useful to compare the values profiles of other sizeable ethnic and racial groups at CUNY.

Gender Differences

As expected, there are no significant generational differences found in this sample (results not presented). However, there were significant gender differences but not nearly as many as found among American adults in the NORC survey and not all in an expected direction. In the data presented in Table 10, men rank *ambition, a comfortable life, an exciting life, pleasure and obedience* significantly higher than women. Women rank *equality, inner harmony, self-respect, forgiving, honest and loving* significantly higher than men. Male value preferences appear to favor the traditional American profile of the upwardly mobile, ambitious, action-oriented business executive. They are also more pleasure seeking, maintaining the double standard so often noted in American society. Women, on the other hand, appear to prefer the more introversive, humanistic values related to inner peace, personal happiness and social justice.

TABLE 10. *Terminal and Instrumental Composite Rank Orders and Value Medians for Italian-American Male and Female Students*

TERMINAL VALUE	MEN	WOMEN	p*
A comfortable life	2 (5.7)	8 (8.2)	.001
An exciting life	7 (7.7)	11 (9.7)	.001
A sense of accomplishment	9 (9.0)	4 (6.9)	
A world at peace	14 (11.7)	12 (10.5)	
A world of beauty	16 (14.7)	16 (15.1)	
Equality	15 (14.2)	15 (12.5)	.01
Family security	3 (5.8)	3 (5.6)	
Freedom	8 (8.9)	7 (7.8)	
Health	1 (3.0)	1 (3.2)	
Inner harmony	11 (9.8)	6 (7.8)	.01
Mature love	6 (7.6)	9 (8.3)	
National security	17 (14.8)	18 (15.8)	
Pleasure	10 (9.1)	13 (11.4)	.001
Salvation	18 (15.3)	17 (15.4)	
Self-respect	4 (6.6)	2 (4.7)	.01
Social recognition	13 (11.4)	14 (11.9)	
True friendship	5 (7.3)	5 (7.5)	
Terminal Value similarity index= .86			

INSTRUMENTAL VALUE	MEN	WOMEN	p*
Ambitious	1 (5.1)	6 (8.6)	.01
Broadminded	11 (10.4)	10 (9.7)	
Capable	5 (8.4)	8 (9.6)	
Clean	13 (11.0)	16 (12.2)	
Courageous	12 (10.7)	14 (11.6)	
Forgiving	16 (11.8)	7 (8.9)	.01
Helpful	7 (9.1)	9 (9.7)	
Honest	3 (6.0)	1 (3.2)	.01
Imaginative	14 (11.6)	17 (13.0)	
Independent	4 (8.9)	4 (7.9)	
Intellectual	9 (9.8)	11 (9.9)	
Logical	17 (11.8)	15 (11.7)	
Loving	4 (6.1)	2 (4.5)	.01
Loyal	8 (9.3)	5 (8.0)	
Obedient	18 (14.4)	18 (16.2)	.01
Polite	15 (11.7)	12 (10.6)	
Responsible	2 (5.2)	3 (5.2)	
Self-Controlled	10 (10.4)	13 (11.6)	
Instrumental Value similarity index= .80			

*Cf. Appendix A for statistical methodology.

These are values usually associated with the helping and teaching professions. In view of the reality that many of these Italian-American women share the same corporate job aspirations as the men, one begins to wonder about their future adjustment and satisfaction in corporate environments that may force them to abandon or deny their basic value orientations. Relevant to this, Astin (1978) found that college women were more likely than college men to choose careers that were relevant to their intrinsic interests and gave them an opportunity to express their identity.

Although there are demonstrated differences, men and women in this sample exhibit similarities on 25 of the 36 values. Moreover, the gender similarities index is quite high for both terminal and instrumental values (.86 and .80 respectively). In the NORC sample, there were similarities on only 16 of the 36 values surveyed, indicating that the differences between men and women are narrowing as women strive for social, economic and personal equality in the American system. Even in the areas of difference, Italian-American women still rank success oriented values like *ambition* and *a comfortable life* in the top 50th percentile of their rankings and Italian-American men show high regard for values like *loving, loyal, self-respect* and *true friendship*. This certainly supports the Davidson and Gordon (1979) contention that the value differences among Italian-American men and women are not as wide as might be expected from what has been written and assumed about their role in the family and culture.

Not to be overlooked is the significant gender difference found for the value of *obedience*. This difference was not found in either the 1968 nor the 1971 NORC sample and is probably ethnically related. Although the composite ranking for this value is identical for both men and women in the Italian-American sample (cf. Table 10), women rank it consistently lower than men. An examination of the raw data reveals that only 4 of the 115 female students surveyed ranked it higher than 10. This seems to support the hypothesis made earlier with regard to locus of control, that the achieving women in this sample appear to be making a statement about their freedom from the control of others and are presenting a profile of counterdependency (possibly inflated) as a result. When queried about this in the interviews a characteristic response for the female students was "I love my family but I make my own decisions."

Values and Educational Choice

Table 11 lists the values that are found to be significantly related to choice of major for liberal arts and business students only. Business majors favor *a comfortable life, family security* and *loyalty* more than liberal arts students. The preference of *comfortable living* as a life goal seems logical and was one of the values significantly preferred by the business students in other studies (Feather, 1975; Brawer, 1973). It is difficult to speculate about *family security* as a preference except to attribute this to perhaps a more traditional, conservative orientation for aspirants to the world of business. The only significant preference for the liberal arts majors was for *a world of beauty.* This preference for aesthetics and a world view also appears logically associated with students interested in the liberal arts and also confirms the finding in the Feather (1975) study. What is more revealing are the lack of differences in values orientation found among these majors. In the Mitchell College study there were differences on 9 of the 36 values profiled.

TABLE 11. *Significantly Different Value Medians for Italian-American Business and Liberal Arts Students*

	BUSINESS	LIBERAL ARTS	
VALUE	MAJORS (N=63)	MAJORS (N=63)	p*
A comfortable life	6.7	9.1	.01
A world of beauty	14.4	12.7	.01
Family security	6.3	7.8	.05

*Cf. Appendix A for statistical methodology.

It would require further research to examine whether the career decision-making process for Italian-American students (and CUNY students in general) involves any kind of reflection or clarification of values on their part. Certainly, the responses given in the interviews to questions related to career choice suggest that personal values play a small part in the process. When asked why they chose their particular major, most students either gave vague, non-specific reasons or made their selection based on job market realities and personal skill proficiency. For example, this quote from a male student: "I'm majoring in finance because I have always been good in math and there are jobs there."

TABLE 12. *Terminal Composite Rank Orders and Similarity Indices for Italian-American Students and Faculty From Four Academic Fields*

TERMINAL VALUE	ITALIANS	BUSINESS*	BIOLOGICAL SCIENCES*	PHYSICAL SCIENCES*	SOCIAL SCIENCES*
A comfortable life	4	13	16	15	15
An exciting life	10	9	8	7	8
A sense of accomplishment	8	3	1	1	1
A world at peace	13	6	6	9	7
A world of beauty	16	14	12	11	12
Equality	15	7	7	8	3
Family security	3	1	4	4	5
Freedom	7	2	5	2	6
Health	1	**	**	**	**
Inner harmony	9	8	9	6	9
Mature love	6	11	13	10	10
National security	18	17	15	17	17
Pleasure	11	15	17	16	16
Salvation	17	18	18	18	18
Self-respect	2	4	2	3	2
Social recognition	14	16	14	14	14
True friendship	5	12	10	12	11
Wisdom	12	5	3	5	4

GROUPS COMPARED	SIMILARITY INDEX
Italians vs. business faculty	.58***
Italians vs. biological sciences faculty	.41***
Italians vs. physical sciences faculty	.51***
Italians vs. social sciences faculty	.42***

*Rokeach (1979) used Form D of RVS.   ***Index calculated on 17 values ranked in both studies.
**This value is not ranked in Form D.

Values and Educational Adjustment

Tables 12 and 13 compare the composite rankings for this sample with the values profile of 212 faculty members from four general disciplines at Michigan State University and Wayne State University (Rokeach, 1973). Rokeach contends that this data can be considered a rough approximation of what academic values in the United States are like. It can also serve as a comparative group to help identify what the similarities and differences between student and faculty value orientations at CUNY might be. The moderate similarity index values obtained (cf. Tables 12 and 13) are an expected result considering the age, socioeconomic and status differences between the two groups compared. Both faculty and students do share the American values for honesty, family, self-respect and responsibility. What is revealing, however, are their differences in values related to academic study and achievement. The rankings assigned to the values in Tables 12 and 13 reflect the students' generally low regard for intellectuality, wisdom, logical thinking and a sense of accomplishment so revered by their professors. There is reason to speculate that these differences would hold true if comparisons were made with the CUNY faculty itself.

TABLE 13. *Instrumental Composite Rank Orders and Similarity Indices for Italian-American Students and Faculty From Four Academic Fields*

TERMINAL VALUE	ITALIANS	BUSINESS*	BIOLOGICAL SCIENCES*	PHYSICAL SCIENCES*	SOCIAL SCIENCES*
Ambitious	4	8	6	11	11
Broadminded	10	6	9	2	1
Capable	7	3	5	3	3
Clean	15	17	17	17	17
Courageous	13	7	4	6	9
Forgiving	11	14	12	12	13
Helpful	8	11	11	10	10
Honest	1	1	1	1	2
Imaginative	17	10	8	5	5
Independent	6	9	10	9	7
Intellectual	9	4	3	4	4
Logical	16	5	7	8	8
Loving	3	13	15	13	12
Loyal	5	**	**	**	**
Obedient	18	18	18	18	18
Polite	14	16	16	16	16
Responsible	2	2	2	7	6
Self-controlled	12	12	13	14	14

GROUPS COMPARED	SIMILARITY INDEX
Italians vs. business faculty	.54***
Italians vs. biological sciences faculty	.51***
Italians vs. physical sciences faculty	.38***
Italians vs. social sciences faculty	.44***

*Rokeach (1979) used Form D of RVS.   ***Index calculated on 17 values ranked in both studies.
**This value is not ranked in Form D.

If the Matteson (1975) and Feather (1975) conclusions (cf. Educational Adjustment section of this report) are valid with regard to the relationship between student values and their level of satisfaction and adjustment in college, this finding raises some concern about the situation at CUNY. It must be noted here that the Italian-American profile is not necessarily a culturally unique one at CUNY and that this values-fit discrepancy probably applies to many student groups in the university. It is certainly worth further study because of its obvious implications for retention, faculty-student relations and intellectual quality of life on the various campuses.

Summary

In general, the Italian-American students in this sample share the values of American society in general. They respect honesty, responsibility, independence, good health, family stability, ambition, loyalty, self-integrity and comfortable living. They seem to favor values related to family, personal growth and interpersonal relations and place low priority on values related to societal, political and religious issues. There is some reason to believe from this study that this profile is not culturally unique and mirrors the profile of the general student body at CUNY and probably other local colleges as well. Conclusions about comparisons with the national student population are difficult to make because of the lack of a recent reliable database.

Although there are some significant and revealing gender differences, men and women appear more similar than different in their values orientations. This is a change from the past and probably reflects the changes in the socialization of women in the last decade. What may be culture-specific is the apparent counterdependency of this Italian-American sample of women reflecting their strong internal control orientation and achievement drive.

The findings also reveal a relationship between educational choice and values orientation for this sample and a possible disparity between student values and the values of professors in academically relevant areas. These results have several implications for the career counseling and academic development of CUNY students, in general, as well as the Italian-American students who are the focal group of this study.

PART 5: STRESS
REVIEW OF THE RESEARCH

Stress and burnout among contemporary college students are validated phenomena (Meier and Schmeck, 1985). Arthur Chickering (1969) contends that it is developmentally normal for college students to face a number of personal problems but in recent years, studies indicate that a significant portion of college students experience psychological and psychosocial stress (Heppner and Neal, 1983). In his book, entitled *Campus Shock*, about college students in the '70s, journalist Lansing Lamont (1979) interviewed counseling directors. They reported 40–50% increases in patient visits to university mental health clinics at colleges like Cornell, Yale, Harvard and Columbia. Similarily, Ohlsen (1983) reports that at some college campuses as many as 50% of the student population avail themselves of the counseling services in one academic year.

The specific nature of the problems reported has also been examined in the counseling literature. In a 1984 study, Mathiasen surveyed eleven campus counseling directors who utilized a variety of assessment instruments to study the major reporting symptomatology of their student clients. Depression, anxiety and general stress headed the list. In a 1982 survey of 1,000 college students, Barnard and Barnard found that 20% of the respondents reported having made suicidal threats or attempts precipitated by stressors related to dating, relationships and friends. Only 7% of these students reported academic pressures as major stressors. Students, in general, however, do list academic stress as the source of many of their problems (Houston, 1971).

In a very recent survey of student problems using methodology similar to the one used in this study, Archer and Lamnin (1985) asked close to 900 students to list their major personal stressors. The major stressors listed were intimate relationships, parental conflict and expectations, finances, interpersonal conflict, peer acceptance and pressure, meeting other students, future career plans, not enough free time, adjustment to unexpected change, appearance, and job. It is reasonable to assume that Italian-American students would include several of these problems in their personal stress lists.

Stress and Achievement

Even though college life itself has been established as a source of stress in students, the deleterious effects of stress on academic adjustment and performance has also long been established in the educational and psychological literature. Every college offers some form of personal counseling services for that reason. Recent studies continue to confirm this relationship in direct and indirect ways. Chronic and episodic stress in college students has recently been found to lead to depression (Sarason, et al., 1978), binge drinking (Rabow and Neuman, 1983), poor study skills (Gadzella and Williamson, 1984); ineffective problem solving skills (Nezu, 1985), vocational indecisiveness (Khan, 1983); and math anxiety (Betz, 1978). In the Sarason study (1978) he found a direct relationship between stressful life experiences and grade point average in college. Similarily, Ovcharchyn and colleagues (1981) found that students with stress resistant personalities (i.e., Type B) placed a greater importance on academic success and actually achieved higher grade point averages than stress-prone students (i.e., Type A personalities).

Although this study is not designed to examine the relationship between stress and academic performance among Italian-American students, this research review is presented to highlight the relevance and educational value of developing a stress profile of these students so that counseling services and strategies can be targeted.

Gender Differences

In general, surveys have established that women in the United States have somewhat poorer mental health than men. Using a psychological symptom checklist, Warheit and colleagues (1976) report that women respondents attain significantly higher scores than male respondents. Women also appear to have a higher rate of anxiety neuroses and depression (Dohrenwend and Dohrenwend, 1976). On the college campus, counseling centers consistently report that female students have a higher usage of services than male students (Ohlsen, 1983). Kramer, Berger and Miller (1974) also found this trend for the usage of counseling services outside the college campus. They suggest that women may be more likely to acknowledge adjustment problems while men might have more difficulty asking for help.

Some recent research has focused on the nature of the different problems and stressors listed by male and female students. In their study of stress, depression and cognitive distortion, Sowa and Lustman (1984) reported significant gender differences among college students. Although men reported more stressful life experiences in this study, women rated the impact of stressors more severely and had higher depression. In the Archer and Lamnin study (1985) cited earlier, only a few significant gender differences were found in the personal stress lists of college men and women. Women reported significantly more concern with personal appearance than men. Men listed meeting new students and peer acceptance more often than women.

In view of these research results, similar gender differences with regard to both the nature and extent of stress are expected in this profile of Italian-American college students.

Italians and Stress

A review of the literature revealed that there has been no recent research on stress and the Italian-American college student. There has, however, been some clinical research conducted on Italian Americans in general. Studies have found that Italians, when compared with other ethnic groups, tended to be less prone to go for treatment of mental health problems (Rabkin and Struening, 1976); drop out of treatment more frequently (Sugarman, 1975); express more emotionality and hostility under stress (Greeley and McCreedy, 1975; Zborowski, 1969); have lower thresholds for physical and emotional distress and a greater need for immediate relief (Twaddle, 1969; Croog, 1961); somatasize their problems more often (Ragucci, 1981); and have a higher rate of affective disorders than thought disorders (Roberts and Myers, 1954). However, the relationship between ethnic origin and low stress resistance was not found among younger Italian-American subjects in a recent study at the Harvard Medical School (Knoopmen, et al., 1984).

Without any recent research at all on stress and Italian-American college students, it is difficult to project whether their stress profile will differ markedly from that of their non-Italian peers in CUNY and other colleges. The earlier clinical findings on Italian adults did uncover several ethnic correlates of stress, but this 1986 sample of second and third generation college students is too far removed, in many ways, from those earlier samples to make any reasonable hypotheses.

Stress and Locus of Control

There appears to be overwhelming evidence that a sense of perceived control is beneficial to physical and emotional health (Reid, 1984; Lefcourt, 1983). Lefcourt (1972) goes so for as to suggest that the development of internal locus of control in patients should be a desired goal of psychotherapy. Rotter (1975), however, has pointed out that "there must be a limit on personal control" (p. 60). Similarily, Wong and Sproule (1984) argue and cite evidence to support their hypothesis that the relationship between stress and internality is curvilinear — i.e., individuals who are extremely high or low in internality are more stress prone than people who have a greater belief in shared control. They contend that those individuals whose sense of control exceeds realistic bounds will suffer more trauma when the inevitable and uncontrollable episodic stressors (e.g., accidents, death in the family, etc.) occur in their lives.

There is also strong supporting evidence for the relationship between externality and stress proneness (cf. O'Brien, 1984). Morelli, et al. (1979) established a relationship between chance control on the IPC Scale and neuroticism in college students. Furthermore, Hiroto (1974) and Dweck and Repucci (1973) both report empirical evidence to support the relationship between learned helplessness and externality.

Although it is not one of the primary goals of this study to examine the relationship between locus of control and stress in this sample of ethnic college students, the data collected does allow some exploration of this issue. The findings have implications for developing counseling strategies to reduce stress in these students.

A STRESS PROFILE

The gender differences in this profile were so great that any attempt to present composite results for this sample would be misleading. Thus, the personal stress lists for males and females are presented and discussed separately. Tables 14 and 15 contain the top ranked stressors for males and females computed from their personal problem checklists (PPC). The rankings were determined by the frequency (i.e., percentage of students responding) with which the problems were reported by each group. Only those problems that were checked by one-third or more of the males or females profiled were included in this list.

The last column in each table contains the corresponding PPC rankings of a comparison sample of non-Italian CUNY students (N=218). To obtain these comparative rankings, the PPC was distributed to students in several classes at two separate CUNY colleges. Although the sample is large, it should not be considered necessarily representative of the non-Italian student population at CUNY. Furthermore, because of the differences in the way in which the data was collected for Italians and non-Italians, only the comparative ranks are represented for the non-Italian group and no statistical comparisons are made between the two groups. This non-Italian data is to be treated as if it were from a separate study.

The Male Profile

Table 14 contains the top ranked stressors for the males in this sample. In general, their problems are related to job, school, finances and recreation. Job and finances are closely linked in this profile and also in their responses to questions about this in the interviews. There is no reason to believe that they earn any more or less than other students but among these young Italians, work is highly valued as a source of making money and maintaining financial independence. Related to this, a recent international survey of work motivation reported that European Italians, unlike Americans, rate working for a good salary higher than working for a feeling of self-accomplishment (Inglehart, 1982). This apparently is also true for Italian Americans and probably accounts for their concerns in this area. These attitudes linking work, pay and independence, unfortunately, may also cause some of these students to overload themselves and coupled with the usual and expected academic concerns and pressures of achievement oriented students, create a source of distress for them. Counselors have often observed this as the precipitating cause for "dropping out," academic failure, or stress-related physical and psychological effects.

In several of the interviews with these young men, they themselves show an awareness of this issue and express the need for recreation and "rest breaks" from both school and work. Some manage their time well enough to satisfy this need, in some instances through their participation in the activities of the Italian club at their college. A few, however, seem helpless or unwilling to change their situation. In a study at the University of Kentucky (Weiner and Hunt, 1983) students were asked (hypothetically) if they would forego a 10% pay increase for additional leisure time. In general, they favored a leisure orientation. A similar question was asked in some of our interviews and the characteristic responses favored a work rather than a leisure orientation. One student, who was already overloaded, said he would take on more hours if paid well. This has implications for both the curricular and vocational counseling of these students.

TABLE 14. *Major Stressors on the PPC, Italian-American Male Students vs. CUNY Non-Italian Male Students*

	ITALIAN (N=101)		NON-ITALIAN (N=81)
PROBLEM	RANK	PERCENTAGE	RANK
Not having good study habits	1	56%	1
Not getting enough exercise	2	47%	2
Not making enough money	2	47%	3
Need a vacation	3	41%	6
Having difficulty concentrating	4	34%	9
Wasting money	4	34%	10
Job not paying enough	4	34%	9
Being afraid of sexual diseases	4	34%	7
Not having a good place to study	4	34%	12
Depending on others for financial support	5	33%	10
Getting bad grades	6	33%	10

How unique is this stress profile for male Italians at CUNY? The data from the non-Italian sample (N=81) generates a very similar stress list for non-Italians (cf. Table 14). They seemed to share some of the same academic, financial and job related concerns as the Italian students. The shared concern about sexual diseases is probably related to the recent media attention on that issue. Non-Italians do, however, seem less concerned about financial dependence, suggesting that the "work for pay for financial independence" relationship may be ethnically correlated. Certainly, this exploratory finding would suggest more controlled research on this relationship.

What may also be revealing are the problems that are found in the non-Italian list that are not as prevalent for Italians. An analysis of the raw data from their PPC Scales reveals that non-Italians frequently cited problems with sleeping habits, shyness, not having a job, privacy at home and budgeting. "Shyness" was not included in the Italian list because it did not meet the 33% frequency criterion but close to 30% of the Italian males reported a problem in this area, suggesting a high prevalence of interpersonal anxiety among male students in general. Further study of the ethnic correlates of these stressors would provide invaluable information for those counselors who believe in "counseling in a cultural context."

Female Stress Profile

The data from Table 15 and Table 16 indicates that the gender differences in this sample are great. First of all, women have reported a significantly larger number of total problems on the PPC when compared to men. They have also indicated significantly greater difficulty in the PPC problem areas related to appearance, vocational adjustment, family/home issues, emotional adjustment, health habits and perception of crises (cf. Table 15). Although the PPC lacks construct validity, their total scores can be a considered a rough approximation of perceived stress in these young women.

TABLE 15. *Major Stressors on the PPC, Italian-American Female Students vs. CUNY Non-Italian Female Students*

	ITALIAN (N=101)		NON-ITALIAN (N=137)
PROBLEM	RANK	PERCENTAGE	RANK
Not getting enough exercise	1	63%	2
Not making enough money	2	55%	5
Not having good study habits	3	54%	1
Needing a vacation	4	50%	3
Feeling anxious or uptight	5	47%	16
Feeling depressed or sad	5	47%	7
Being overweight	5	47%	19
Getting bad grades	6	43%	6
Feeling lonely	6	43%	17
Eating too much	7	42%	23
Having trouble concentrating	3	37%	10
Wasting money	8	37%	17
Job not paying enough	9	36%	10
Not being able to relax	9	36%	22
Parents interfering with decisions	10	35%	18
Having the same thoughts over and over again	10	35%	21

These gender differences with regard to stress are not unexpected (cf. Review of the Research in this section). At the very least, the findings suggest that these Italian-American women, like women in general, may be more likely to acknowledge adjustment problems while men might deny the need for help or have more difficulty asking for it (Kramer, Berger and Miller, 1974). At the very worst, this provides some evidence that the achieving Italian-American woman at CUNY is under greater general stress than her male counterpart.

TABLE 16. *Significant Gender Difference on the PPC Among Italian-American Students*

	MALES	FEMALES	
PPC PROBLEMS	f	f	p*
Not getting enough exercise	46.5%	63.4%	.05
Feeling anxious and uptight	30.6%	47.0%	.05
Feeling depressed or sad	27.7%	47.0%	.01
Being overweight	19.8%	47.0%	.001
Feeling lonely	19.8%	47.0%	.001
Eating too much	17.8%	48.0%	.001
PPC CATEGORIES	MEAN***	MEAN***	p**
Social	2.53	3.63	.01
Appearance	1.01	1.58	.01
Family/home	2.04	3.18	.01
Emotional	3.06	4.61	.01
Health habits	2.73	3.39	.05
Total number of problems checked	23.05	29.54	.01

*For statistical methodology cf. Appendix A.
**For statistical methodology cf. Appendix A.
***i.e., mean number of problems checked in each category.

The gender differences listed in Table 16 highlight that men and women in this sample differ not only with regard to the extent of their stress but also to the specific nature of their major stressors. Women do share some of the academic, vocational and financial concerns of their male peers but greater numbers of them report stressors related to depression, anxiety, loneliness, a concern for weight, and overeating. What is more revealing is that between 40 and 50% of these young women admitted that these were personal problems for them (cf. Table 15). Even allowing for some significant sampling error, it is alarming to consider the number of Italian-American women in the general CUNY student population who may be experiencing the same feelings of anxiety, loneliness and depression. This finding alone supports a greater need for effective counseling services and focused student service programs for these women.

The high frequency of problems related to overeating and being overweight appears not only gender related but possibly ethnically related (cf. Table 15). A number of non-Italian women did report "problems with eating" in their checklists but concern for eating too much and being overweight do not occur with nearly the frequency that it does in the Italian sample. Several recent articles in the counseling literature have called attention to the issue of weight consciousness and compulsive eating in college women (Kagan and Squires, 1984; Hooker and Convisser, 1983). Some have discussed these issues out of concern for the increasing prevalence of bulimia in college women (Boskind-Lodahl, 1976). Compulsive eating, however, is not necessarily related to bulimia (Kagan and Squires, 1984). Thus, concerns for weight and overeating among the Italian-American women in this sample should not be construed as evidence of a high incidence of eating disorders in this particular ethnic group. The Anorexia and Bulimia Association (in a personal communication) reported that there have been no studies on the possible ethnic or racial correlates of these disorders.

There has, however, been a relationship established between emotional stress (i.e., depression) and bulimia in women (Hooker and Convisser, 1983). Researchers at the Harvard Medical School have recently reported biochemical similarities between the two psychiatric disorders and have used anti-depressant medication with success in treating bulimia (Ely, 1983). The high incidence (50%) of reported feelings of depression in Italian-American women coupled with their concern for overeating would certainly warrant further research on the relationship between these two reported stressors.

The interviews with the female students do provide some insight into these results on stress. Although most of the women queried about feelings of depression denied that this was a problem for them, several were willing to discuss issues related to eating and weight. A few, who were not themselves overweight, said that they simply did not feel good about themselves when they gained a little weight and admitted being under constant pressure to maintain their weight and appearance. They attributed their concern for this to their awareness of the importance of a "good appearance" both socially and vocationally.

Both males and females interviewed on this issue agreed that this problem might be culturally related. With only a few exceptions, they reported that it is traditional for Italians to eat a great deal and enjoy it. In their own homes, they are urged to "fill" their plates or, in some cases, have their plates "filled" for them. In either scenario, there are usually large amounts of tasteful food set before them and "seconds" are not an exception but the general rule. Crispino (1980) focuses on the traditional importance of food and cooking skills among Italians and includes it as one of the dependent variables in his analysis of their assimilation in this country.

It is important to note that there were exceptions to this "cultural eating pressure" reported by some of the third generation women interviewed. In their cases, they reported that their mothers actually monitored their diets and expressed concern for the appearance and fitness of their daughters. Some of these second generation mothers were working women and weight conscious themselves.

Noticeably absent in the stress profiles of Italian-American women were concerns for social competence and problems with parents. Shyness and parent problems were listed among the top stressors in the non-Italian female profiles. Several (Italians) did, however, complain about feeling lonely and about parental interference with their decisions. The interview data does shed some light on the issue of parental interference. Although almost every woman interviewed felt that they had complete freedom in planning their vocational and educational future, they did express concern about parental controls on their affiliative lives. Some of the complaints were mild but several reported this as an area of constant stress for them.

In general, Italian-American women present a complex stress profile in this study that provides us with important information about their needs and concerns. On the other hand, this exploratory data appears to raise more questions then it answers. Hopefully, it will open the door to further research.

Stress and Locus of Control

As expected, there was a relationship established in this study between locus of control and stress but like other results in this area, it is gender related. Tables 17 and 18 present the results of a correlational analysis of relationship between locus of control scores and the total number of stressors reported by the male and female students in this sample. The results clearly indicate that feelings of personal control are related to this "rough" approximation of overall stress but for women only. Specifically, internalism for the female subsample was negatively correlated with total PPC scores while the two external measures were positively correlated with them. The multiple correlations between all three LOC variables and stress were highly significant with the most weight attributed to internalism as an independent predictor. This finding could mean many things. It could suggest that it is important for women to feel "in control" in order for them to be free of stress in their lives. It could further indicate that internal women, in fact, have greater control over the potential stressors in their lives and thus are less stress prone. It is also possible that internal women have a greater capacity for denial and will not admit as readily to personal problems. It may even simply be a "response set" for externals to check off more problems on a problems checklist but this is counter indicated by the fact that the differences were not found for male externals. This also raises some questions about whether this is a culturally unique scenario or whether it is solely gender related. In any event, it certainly appears that feelings of personal control mean "different things" for men and women as far as personal stress is concerned.

TABLE 17. *Regression Analysis of the Relationship Between LOC Variables and Stress Among Male Italian-American Students*

	r	p
Internal LOC x PPC total	–.07	-
Powerful Others LOC x PPC total	–.02	-
Chance LOC x PPC total	.01	-
RIPC x PPC total = .083 R^2 = .007 F ratio = .222		
p = .880 not significant		

TABLE 18. *Regression Analysis of the Relationship Between LOC Variables and Stress Among Female Italian-American Students*

	r	p
Internal LOC x PPC total	–.21	.05
Powerful others LOC x PPC total	–.12	-
Chance LOC x PPC total	.17	.01
RIPC x PPC total = .323 R^2 = .104 F ratio = 4.32		
p = .007 significant at .01 level		

Beta weights for female LOC variables: Internal = –.675; Powerful Others = .317; Chance = .356

In interpreting this finding, it is important to reiterate the exploratory nature of this study and the lack of construct and predictive validity of the PPC Scale, especially when using total number of problems as a measure of overall stress. The gender differences, however, are quite significant and warrant further research exploration with instruments better suited as measures of overall stress. The PPC has adequately served its purpose in this study by providing a comprehensive picture of the needs and problems of an Italian-American student sample.

Summary

In general, the stress profile of the students in this sample is a complex one that requires further study especially with regard to gender differences and its relationship to locus of control. It does, however, provide us with enough information about the nature and extent of specific problems to make some recommendations vis-à-vis counseling services and strategies (cf. Part 6 of this report). Men, in general, report problems centered around academic and vocational adjustment. Women appear to share these concerns but report greater numbers of problems than men especially in the areas of emotional adjustment and concern for appearance.

PART 6: IMPLICATIONS AND APPLICATIONS

> The values of individual achievement, planning for the future, and striving to improve his status in the American social system were irrelevant. The law that forced him to send his children to school when they could be working to contribute to the family finances was viewed as an intrusion to be resisted as long as possible. Even children were expected to contribute financially to the family. The child who found himself drawn into the middle-class value system of his teachers and developed strong achievement drives found little support for these aspirations at home. Career ambitions were shunned if they seemed to risk alienation from the family and loss of a broad base of social support provided by the extended family unit (Papajohn and Speigel, 1975, p. 105).

This description of the impact of the first generation Italian family on the achievement motivation and independence of its children finds its antithesis in the profile of the Italian American that emerges from both the quantitative and qualitative data in this study. These young people feel in personal control over their lives and the decisions that have an impact on their educational and vocational futures. They feel generally supported by their families in this regard. Furthermore, they seem confident that they have both the energy and ability to succeed in higher education. They seem to share the traditional American middle-class values for health, ambition, sense of responsibility, family, accomplishment and comfortable living but they also place great emphasis an the individual values of personal growth, affiliation and inner harmony over sociopolitical, intellectual and religious values. They seem to be encountering some of the same economic, academic and emotional problems as most college students but do appear to exhibit some culturally unique patterns in their stress profiles. The findings with regard to these students seem to be independent of the generational status of their families but do have differing implications for their socialization and personal growth as achieving men and women in American society.

Although, in many ways, the psychoeducational profile of these students reflects the profile of CUNY students in general, the results of this exploratory research do provide us with information about some of the special needs and concerns of Italian Americans at CUNY and suggest some specific action strategies that are designed to improve and enhance counseling and student development services for them in the future.

COUNSELING IN A GENDER CONTEXT

The most consistently significant findings across the variables examined in this study are related to gender. Although the men and women in this sample are more alike than different in their general achievement and stress profiles, their differences highlight the importance of counseling in a "gender context" as well as in a "cultural context." The profile of the achieving Italian-American woman is different in some significant ways from that of the achieving Italian-American male with regard to personal control and attribution. They feel that they have to be in greater control and must try harder to succeed. They also appear more determined to resist pressures from outside influences when making decisions about their educational and vocational futures. They place greater emphasis on inner peace and self-integrity than men and less emphasis on materialistic and pleasure related values. They may be under greater stress than their male counterparts and it is quite possible that some of this is related to their strong achievement orientation coupled with the awareness that what they are doing may be non-traditional or counternormative for them as Italian-American women. Their stress profile is certainly different with regard to the specific nature of their stressors. In view of these results, the following recommendations for action are offered:

(1) A more focused and intensive research project should be initiated to further examine and clarify the differences between Italian-American men and women at CUNY. It should include an intensive interview process with a larger and more representative sample that includes questions, related to issues of control, attribution and stress and their relationship to ethnicity, cultural patterns and socialization practices. There should also be some research inquiry into the nature of stress for these students using a more standardized measure of stress and/or one of the more recently developed measure of well-being (cf. Schlosser and Sheeley, 1985)

(2) Program developers, teachers and individual counselors committed to the development of Italian-American men and women at CUNY should increase their sensitivity to these findings and other identified gender differences. This can be accomplished through mini-conferences similar to the workshops on the contemporary Italian-American woman presented by the Italian American Institute in its 1985-86 workshop series at CUNY. There should be similar presentations focused on the men as well. Other vehicles might include human relations training workshops for professional counselors and teachers with gender and ethnicity as the major theme. The ethnotherapy model might provide a workable format for such group experiences with students and professionals alike. This group approach was originally developed for blacks by Cobbs (1972) and later adapted for other ethnic groups by Judith Klein, Joseph Giordano and others at the Institute on Pluralism and Identity of the American Jewish Committee. Ethnotherapy sessions with Italian adults and students were demonstrated at a recent CUNY workshop (cf. Sirey, Patti, and Mann [1985] for a description and evaluation of the group process and its outcomes.)

(3) A series of focus groups dealing with gender differences should be scheduled for Italian-American students at the different CUNY campuses. Their major objective should be to raise their level of awareness about and sensitivity to gender issues especially in relationship to academic achievement and interpersonal relations. The grouping in these sessions should be both homogeneous and heterogeneous with regard to gender.

(4) These results on gender differences imply that the campus presence of adequate and appropriate role models of the achieving Italian-American man and woman is important to the vocational and personal growth and

the maturity of these students. This has been an issue with other ethnic and racial groups at CUNY and applies to Italian Americans as well. This can be done by increasing student's contact with successful Italian-American and native Italian professionals and/or business executives through student activities programming. Of course, the most effective way of enhancing this role modeling process is to increase out-of-class contact between students and members of the Italian-American faculty and staff at the various colleges of CUNY and to encourage the active recruiting of young Italian-American professionals to come to work at the university.

COUNSELING FOR INTERNALITY

Although most of the students in this sample projected profiles of internal or shared control with an internal orientation (cf. Figure 7 in Part 3 of this report), there was a minority of students (8%) who were clearly external in orientation. Extrapolated to the general population, this would apply to a sizeable number of students who feel that they have very little personal control over their lives. In view of the relationship established between achievement, stress and personal control in the general literature and between stress and personal control with the female subsample in this study, student development research programs and services should focus some attention on the identification and counseling of these students. In view of the generally strong internal orientation of both Italian and non-Italian students at CUNY, these externally oriented young people may be experiencing even greater problems socializing and competing with their control oriented peers.

There have been a number of articles in the counseling and psychological literature suggesting approaches to counseling that have as their objective the modification of the locus of control orientation of students from external to internal (Duckworth, 1983; Harris, 1983). One of the more promising approaches is suggested and discussed by Husa (1982) utilizing what he calls "rational self-counseling" as a primary stress prevention technique designed to help students learn to be more internal.

Some caution should be taken, however, before any active counseling strategies are employed to increase a student's LOC profile from external to internal. Levenson (1982) has some reservations about the wisdom of training for internality. She feels that some degree of defensive externality (i.e., powerful others orientation) is facilitative and somewhat reality oriented in the sociopolitical and achievement areas. However, she does emphasize the importance of increased personal responsibility in the personal health area and appears to support educational counseling to increase internality in externals facing health problems. The recommendation here is really focused on those "pure externals" (i.e., chance orientation) who feel powerless "in the face of" the forces of fate and luck in their lives.

THE MEANING OF WORK

The high value that Italians place on work and financial independence is well documented in the literature and is further confirmed in this sample of students. The possibility that this cultural value orientation may be a source of stress for some of these students also emerges from this profile. We know that Italians, more then any other ethnic or racial group at CUNY, cite school time employment as a major source of support for them (Manzitti, 1983). Blumberg and Lavin (1985) also report that Italian Americans in the community colleges were more likely to be working part-time than minorities or other whites. There is evidence that employment has negative effects on success in college (Brewer, 1973). The possibility that many of these students overload themselves is reflected in the many concerns they report about work, finances, money management and a need for relaxation in their stress profiles and interviews (cf. Part 5 of this report).

Castiglione (1982) provides some excellent illustrations of what probably happens with many of these students:

(1) A student who has been working 35 hours per week becomes aware that his school work is suffering because of his inability to devote sufficient time in study or preparation. As a consequence, the student takes less demanding courses the next semester. This action results in an upturn in the student's GPA even though the number of work hours has not changed. The student has compensated for the diminution in study time by taking courses that do not require very much study time.
(2) Another student quits a part-time job in order to take several difficult required courses. His/her average for the semester is B– (pp. 57 and 58).

Even though the student described in first of these examples has successfully coped with his "overload" situation, it is likely that he has done so not without some stress and fatigue and certainly with a "drop" in GPA for the over loaded semester.

Furthermore, not all of these students resolve these situations as quickly and easily as these illustrations imply, especially those students with more external LOC orientations.

The approach to counseling recommended here is both an educational one and a preventive one. Student workshops and small group experiences should be developed and centered around themes related to the meaning and value of work and its relationship to academic achievement and curricular planning. Another effective vehicle for discussing this issue is through career education courses and workshops. Incorporated into these workshops and courses should be a training module on time management for students. Relevant to this, there is an instructor's manual available for counselors and teachers planning to conduct time management workshops for college students (Perrone and Swires, 1985).

EDUCATIONAL ADJUSTMENT

It is more than likely that the CUNY faculty values profile reflects the profile of college faculty throughout the nation. In view of this, there appears to be a "values-gap" between students and faculty at CUNY in areas related to intellectual and academic interest (cf. Part 4 of this report). This certainly reflects the complaints of many faculty members and administrators about the lack of academic orientation and intellectual curiosity among students in general. Although this situation may not be necessarily ethnically or racially correlated, the results of this study suggest that this "values-gap" exists between many Italian-American students and their professors. Krase (1983), in his survey of Italian-American students at CUNY found that many of them, although doing well academically, felt alienated at school and did not participate in on-campus activities because they perceived the general atmosphere to be cold and impersonal. Krase attributes this educational discomfort in Italian students to the perceived dissonance between their campus experiences and the high value they place on personalness and intimacy. In Part 4 of this report, there is a discussion of the possible impact of this situation on their educational adjustment and achievement.

Although we are, in this report, primarily concerned with Italian Americans, we should focus our efforts as counselors and teachers to, in some way, mediate between the academic priorities of the university faculty and the strong vocational needs and values of its student population. The most effective way to accomplish this is through increased out-of-classroom contact between students and faculty. One recent study (Cangemi, 1980) established that increased interaction between faculty and students on the college campus reduced attrition rates of students with educational adjustment problems.

Faculty, in these situations, would serve as academic role models or mentors to students. Because of the leadership and enthusiasm of John Gardner at the University of South Carolina, the faculty-mentor concept has been proven effective in enhancing retention among college freshmen and has been incorporated into many freshman orientation programs throughout the nation (cf. Fidler, 1979). The annual "Freshman Year Experience" conference sponsored by the University of South Carolina is strongly recommended for those CUNY professionals interested in developing this concept at their college.

Through theme centered workshops and small group experiences, counselors working with Italian-American students can address the issue of their educational adjustment and encourage them to clarify and examine their personal values vis-à-vis their concordance with their own academic goals and aspirations. In a special issue of the APGA Journal dedicated to values and the counselor, Rokeach and Regan (1980) outline an approach to counseling using values confrontation as a strategy to make students more aware of the inconsistencies within their values systems and between their values and their educational aspirations and career choices. In the article, they suggest that the RVS, used in this study, be administered to students who come to counseling with presenting problems related to values conflict and ambiguity.

Conversely, counselors can also work as change agents at their various institutions to help personalize the college atmosphere and encourage more meaningful faculty-student interaction on-campus and off-campus. Krase (1983) writes, "In order to feel at home in the college environment it is important and necessary for students to find things there with which they are familiar and which they bring back and make part of their family and neighborhood life"(p. 9).

STRESS MANAGEMENT

Increased concern about stress among college students, in general, is discussed and documented in Part 5 of this report. The stress profile of

Italian-American students that emerges from the data in this survey justifies professional concern for this ethnic group — especially among female students. Although we cannot conclude from this study that Italians undergo more stress than any other student group, it is clear from the sample data that large numbers of them are reporting concerns that need the attention of professional counselors and other student development personnel. To be specific, when 40–50% of a sample surveyed admit to being anxious, depressed, lonely and/or worried (based on the female data), there should be a focused effort to examine the causes (i.e., research) and intervene to reduce the level of stress for these students.

Although the traditional focus and mission of college counseling services has been reactive and therapeutic, more and more counseling centers are shifting their attention to proactive and preventive counseling strategies and models, stressing their educational rather than supportive mission in the university. Thus, the recommendation here is twofold:

(1) Counselors assigned to work with Italian-American students should enhance their skills in crisis intervention therapy and stress management counseling with college students. This can be accomplished through in-service training, professional workshops and/or continuing education experiences. Incorporated into these training experiences should be some discussion or information related to the cultural correlates of stress.

(2) Counselors and psychologists on-campus should design and conduct stress management workshops for Italian-American students with a special focus on some of the issues and problems identified in this study. One area that appears to need attention is the relationship of sociocultural eating patterns in families to stress, another is concern for appearance and weight control among achieving Italian-American women. There are several models and strategies for dealing with these issues in recent counseling literature (Kagan, 1984; Hooker, and Convisser, 1983; Lichtenstein and Sherman, 1983). Furthermore, an excellent generalized stress management model that would be useful to counselors interested in designing workshop experience can be found in an article by Stevens and Pfost (1984). They recommend that there should be eight components to any stress management workshop for college students: assessment; information about stress; relaxation training; cognitive restructuring; problem solving; time management; nutritional counseling; and exercise planning.

ETHNIC STUDIES

Although one of the repeated themes of this report has been the lack of psychological and educational research on Italian-American students, the reality is that there has been very little recent research of this nature on many other of the diverse ethnic and racial groups that attend the university. Derald Sue (1981) admits that even the great numbers of published materials on the larger racial minority groups have been "fragmented and/or myopic" (p. xi).

CUNY publicly prides itself in providing a quality higher education experience for the various and diverse ethnic and racial groups that reside in the New York community. In the process of conducting this research and preparing this report on Italians, it became obvious that we could use needs analysis data of this sort on the Asians, Blacks, Hispanics, Greeks, Vietnamese, Jews, Irish and any other group that attend the university in sizable numbers. Similarily, we need more sociocultural, sociopolitical and historical information on these groups if we are to serve their special educational and human resource needs.

There has been a call in the literature for a greater focus on ethnic studies and research in the university setting (Brown, 1979; Hernandez, 1977; Banks; 1975). This is one more "call" for a greater university commitment to encouraging a better cultural understanding of our student population and making this information an integral part of the academic curriculum. The research should be both applied and theoretical; exploratory and focused; descriptive and inferential. Relevant to this, the study and development of Italian studies in the university is the proposed research focus of Richard Gambino, the recipient of the 1986–87 Faculty Fellowship sponsored by the Italian American Institute at CUNY.

References

Alba, R. D. (1981). "The Twilight of Ethnicity Among American Catholics of European Ancestry." *Annals*, 454 (March), 86–97.

Alba, R. D. (1985). *Italian Americans: Into the Twilight of Ethnicity*. Englewood Cliffs, NJ: Prentice Hall.

Allport, G. (1985). "Attitudes." In C. Murchison (Ed.), *Handbook of Social Psychology*. Worcester, MA: Clark University Press.

Archer, J. and Lamnin, A. (1985). "An Investigation of Personal and Academic Stressors on College Campuses." *Journal of College Student Personnel*, 26(3), 210–215.

Astin, H. S. (1978). "Women and Work." In J. Sherman and F. Denmark (Eds.), *Psychology of Women: Future Directions and Research*. New York: Psychological Dimensions.

Atkinson, J. W. and Feather, N. T., Eds. (1966). *A Theory of Achievement Motivation*. New York: John Wiley and Sons.

Atkinson, J. W. and Raynor, J. O., Eds. (1974). *Motivation and Achievement*. Washington: Winston.

Avrimedes, W. (1986). "The Effect of Counseling Style on the Academic Achievement of High-risk College Freshmen with Different Locus of Control Orientation." Unpublished doctoral dissertation, New York University.

Ball-Rokeach, S. J. (1976). Receptivity to Sexual Equality. *Pacific Sociological Review*, 19, 519–540.

Bandura, A. (1977). "Self Efficacy: Toward a Unifying Theory of Behavioral Change." *Psychological Review*, 84, 919–999.

Banks, J. A. (1975). *Teaching Strategies for Ethnic Studies*. Rockleigh, NJ: Allyn and Bacon, Inc.

Bar-Tal, D. and Frieze, I. (1973). "Achievement Motivation and Gender as Determinants of Attributions for Success and Failure." Unpublished manuscript, University of Pittsburgh.

Bar-Tal, D. and Bar-Zohar, Y. (1977). "The Relationship Between Perception of Locus of Control and Academic Achievement: Review and Some Educational Implications." *Contemporary Education Psychology*, 2, 181–199.

Barzini, L. (1965). *The Italians*. New York: Bantam Books.

Beek, P. (1979). "Locus of Control and Task Instruction Effects Upon Creative Problem Solving." Unpublished doctoral dissertation, Fordham University.

Berman, E. (1973). "The Development and Dynamics of Multiple Personality." Unpublished doctoral dissertation, University of Chicago.

Bernard, J. L. and Bernard, M. L. (1982). "Factors Related to Suicidal Behavior Among College Students and the Impact of Institutional Response." *Journal of College Student Personnel*, 23, 409–413.

Betz, N. E. (1978). "Prevalence, Distribution and Correlates of Math Anxiety in College Students." *Journal of Counseling Psychology*, 25, 441–448.

Blumberg, A. and Lavin, D. E. (1985). "Italian-American Students at the City University of New York: A Socioeconomic and Educational Profile." Unpublished report, City University of New York, Office of Institutional Research and Analysis and the Italian American Institute.

Bond, M. H. and Tornatzky, L. G. (1973). "Locus of Control in Students from Japan and the United States: Dimensions and Levels of Response." *Psychologia*, 16, 209–213.

Boskind-Lodahl, M. (1976). "Cinderella's Step Sisters: A Feminist Perspective on Anorexia Nervosa and Bulimia." *Signs: Journal of Women in Culture and Society*, 2, 342–356.

Brawer, F. B. (1973). *New Perspectives on Personality Development in College Students*. San Francisco: Jossey-Bass.

Brophy, J. (1983). "Conceptualizing Student Motivation." *Educational Psychologist*, 18(3), 200–215.

Brown, P. K. (1979). "The 1980s: Decade for Ethnic Studies?" *The History Teacher*, 12 (3), 359–371.

Buros, O. A. (1985). *The Ninth Mental Measurements Yearbook*. Highland Park, NJ: Gryphon Press.

Burroughs, L. V. (1984). "Careers, Contingencies and Locus of Control among White College Women." *Sex Roles*, 11(3-4), 289–302.

Campisi, P. J. (1948). "Ethnic Family Patterns: The Italian Family in the United States." *American Journal of Sociology*, 28, 443–449.

Cangemi, J. P. (1980). "Some Observations Concerning Interpersonal Relations on the College Campus and Declining Enrollment." *Journal of Instructional Psychology*, 7(2), 50–52.

Canino, G. and Canino, I. (1980). "The Impact of Stress on the Puerto Rican Immigrant: Some Treatment Considerations." *American Journal of Orthopsychiatry*, 50(3), 232–238.

Castiglione, L. (1982). "A Demographic Study of Italian-American College Students Attending the City University of New York." Unpublished report, Italian American Institute, City University of New York.

Cellini, J. V. and Kantorowski, L. A. (1984). "Locus of Control and Career Decidedness: Some Methodological Issues." *Psychological Reports*, 55(2), 613–614.

Chickering, A. (1969). *Education and Identity*. San Francisco: Jossey-Bass.

Child, I. (1943). *Italian or American*. New Haven: Yale University Press.

Clark, K. (1947). *Dark Ghetto*. New York: Harper and Row.

Cobbs, P. (1972). "Ethnotherapy in Groups." In L. Soloman and B. Berson (Eds.), *New Perspectives on Encounter Groups*. San Francisco: Jossey-Bass.

Cole, D. L. and Cole S. (1977). "Counternormative Behavior and Locus of Control." *Journal of Social Psychology*, 101, 21–28.

Coleman, J. S., Campbell, E. O., Hohson, C. V., McPartland, J., Mood, A. M., Weinfeld, F. D. and York, R.L. (1966). "Equality of Educational Opportunity." Washington DC: Government Printing Office.

Cordasco, F. and LaGumina, S. J. (1972). *Italians in the United States. A Bibliography of Reports, Texts, Critical Studies and Related Material*. New York: Oriole Press.

Covello, L. (1967). *The Social Background of the Italo-American School Child*. Leiden, Netherlands: E.J. Brill.

Crispino, J. (1980). *The Assimilation of Ethnic Groups: The Italian Case*. New York: Center for Migration Studies.

Croog, S. H. (1961). "Ethnic Origins and Responses to Health Questionnaires." *Human Organization*, 20, 61–69.

Davidson, L. and Gordon, L. K. (1979). *The Sociology of Gender*. Chicago: Rand McNally College Publishing Co.

Deutsch, M. (1960). "Minority Group and Class Status as Related to Social and Personality Factors in Scholastic Achievement." *Society for Applied Anthropology Monograph*, No. 2.

Doherty, W. A. (1983). "Locus of Control and Marital Interaction." In H. M. Lefcourt (Ed.), *Research with the Locus of Control Construct, Vol. II: Developments and Social Problems*. New York: Academic Press.

Dohrenwend, B. P. and Dohrenwend, B. S. (1976). "Sex Differences and Psychiatric Disorders." *American Journal of Sociology*, 62, 294-302.

Donovan, D. M. and O'Leary, M. R. (1978). "The Drinking Related Locus of Control Scale: Reliability, Factor Structure and Validity." *Journal of Studies on Alcohol*, 39, 759–784.

Duckworth, D. H. (1983). "Evaluation of a Program for Increasing the Effectiveness of Personal Problem Solving." *British Journal of Psychology*, 74(1), 119–127.

Dweck, C. S. and Repucci, N. D. (1973). "Learned Helplessness and Reinforcement Responsibility in Children." *Journal of Personality and Social Psychology*, 25, 109–116.

Dweck, C. S. and Bush, E. S. (1976). "Sex Differences in Learned Helplessness: (1) Differential debilitation with Peer and Adult Evaluators." *Developmental Psychology*, 12, 147–156.

Dyal, J. A. (1984). "Cross-Cultural Research with the Locus of Control Scale." In H.M. Lefcourt (Ed.), *Research with the Locus of Control Construct. Vol. 3: Extensions and Limitations*. New York: Academic Press.

Egelman, W. (1982a). "Family Values and Educational Attainment: Intergenerational Change Among Italian Americans." Paper presented at annual meeting of the Eastern Sociological Society, Philadelphia, Pennsylvania.

Egelman, W. (1982b). "Italian-American Educational Attainment: An Introductory Analysis Utilizing; Recent Current Population Survey Data." Paper presented at annual meeting of the American Italian Historical Association, St. John's University, Jamaica, NY.

Egelman, W. and Salvo, J. (1984). "Italian Americans in New York City: A Demographic Overview." Paper presented at annual meeting of the American Italian Historical Association, Washington DC.

Ely, E. (1983). "Rx for Bulimia." *Harvard Magazine*, 86(2), 53–56.

Epstein, H. (1979) *Children of the Holocaust*. New York: G. P. Putnam.

Feather, N. T. (1975). *Values in Education and Society*. New York: Free Press.

Feather, N. T. (1982). "Expectancy-Value Approaches: Present Status and Future Directions." In N. T. Feather (Ed.), *Expectations and Actions: Expectancy-Value Models in Psychology*, (pp. 395–415). Hillsdale, New Jersey: Lawrence Erlbaum Associates.

Feather, N. T. and Collins, J. M. (1974). "Differences in Attitudes and Values of Students in Relation to Program of Study at a College of Advanced Education." *Australian Journal of Education*, 18, 16-29.

Feminella, F. X. (1968). "Ethnicity and Ego Identity." Unpublished doctoral dissertation, New York University.

Fidler, P. P. (1979). "Research Summary: University 101." Unpublished report, Division of Student Affairs, University of South Carolina.

Gable, R. K., Thompson, D. L. and Glanstein, P. J. (1976). "Perceptions of Personal Control and Conformity of Vocational Choices as Correlates of Vocational Development." *Journal of Vocational Behavior*, 8, 259–267.

Gadzella, B. and Williamson, J. D. (1984). "Study Skills, Self-Concept and Academic Achievement." *Psychological Reports*, 54(3), 923–929.

Gambino, R. (1973). "La Famiglia: Four Generations of Italian Americans." In J.A. Ryan (Ed.), *White Ethnics: Life in Working Class America*. Englewood Cliffs, NJ: Prentice-Hall.

Gambino, R. (1974). *Blood of My Blood: The Dilemma of Italian Americans*. New York: Doubleday.

Gans, H. J. (1962). *The Urban Villagers*. New York: The Free Press.

Giordano, G. P. and Giordano, J. (1977). *The Ethno-Cultural Factor in Mental Health*. New York: Institute on Pluralism and Group Identity of the American Jewish Committee.

Glazer, N. and Moynihan, D. P. (1970). *Beyond the Melting Pot*. Cambridge: MIT Press.

Goodman, S., et al. (1984). "On Going to the Counselor: Contributions of Life Stress and Social Supports to the Decision to Seek Psychological Counseling." *Journal of Counseling Psychology*, 31, 306–313.

Greeley, A. M. (1974). *Ethnicity in the United States*. New York: John Wiley and Sons.

Greeley, A. M. (1977). *The American Catholic: A School Portrait*. New York: Basic Books.

Greeley, A. M. and McCready, W. (1975). "The Transmission of Cultural Heritages: The Case of Irish and Italians." In N. Glazer and D. P. Moynihan (Eds.), *Ethnicity: Theory and Experience*. Cambridge: Harvard University Press.

Gregory, W. L. (1981). "Expectancies for Controllability, Performance, Attributions and Behavior." In H.M. Lefcourt (Ed.), *Research with the locus of Control Construct, Vol. 1: Asssessment Methods*. New York: Academic Press.

Hammer, J. H. and Vardi, Y. (1981). "Locus of Control and Career Self-Management Among Non-Supervisory Employees in Industrial Settings." *Journal of Vocational Behavior*, 18, 13–29.

Harrington, T. F. and O'Shea, A. J. (1982). *Manual for Harrington-O'Shea Career Decision Making System*. Circle Pines, MN: American Guidance Service.

Harris, R. M. (1983). "Changing Women's Self-Perceptions: Impact of a Psychology of Women Course." *Psychology Reports*, 52(l), 314.

Heider, F. (1958). *The Psychology of Interpersonal Relations*. New York: Wiley.

Heppner, P. P. and Neal, B. W. (1983). "Holding Up the Mirror: Research on the Roles and Functions of Counseling Centers in Higher Education." *The Counseling Psychologist*, 11 (l), 81–98.

Hernandez, N. G. (1977). "Another Look at Multicultural Education Today." *Journal of Research and Development in Education*. 11(1), 4–9

Hiroto, D. S. (1974). "Learned Helplessness and Locus of Control." *Journal of Experimental Psychology*, 102, 187–193.

Holland, J. L. (1959). "A Theory of Vocational Choice." *Journal of Counseling Psychology*, 6, 35–45.

Holmes, T. H. and Rahe, R. H. (1967). "The Social Readjustment Rating Scale." *Journal of Psychosomatic Research*, 11, 213–218.

Hooker, D. and Convisser, E. (1983). "Women's Eating Problems: An Analysis of a Coping Mechanism." *The Personnel and Guidance Journal*, 62(4), 236–239.

Horner, M. (1968). "Sex Differences in Achievement Motivation and Performance in Competitive and Non-Competitive Situations." Unpublished doctoral dissertation, University of Michigan.

Houston, B. K. (1971). "Sources, Effects, and Individual Vulnerability of Psychological Problems for College Sudents." *Journal of Counseling Psychology*, 18 (2), 157–165.

Husa, H. (1982). "The Effects of Rational Self-Counseling on College Students' Locus of Control." *Journal of College Student Personnel*, 23(4), 304–307.

Husaini, B. A. and Neff, J. A. (1980). "Characteristics of Life Events and Psychiatric Impairment." *Journal of Nervous and Mental Diseases*, 168, 159–166.

Ianni, P. A. and, Ianni E. (1972). *A Family Business: Kinship and Social Control in Organized Crime*. New York: Russell Sage.

Inglehart, R. (1982). "Changing Values in Japan and the West." *Comparative Political Studies*, 14(4), 44–47.

Janoff-Bulman, R. and Brickman, P. (1982). "Expectation and What People Learn from Failure." In N. T. Feather (Ed.), *Expectations and Actions: Expectancy-Value Models in Psychology*. Hillsdale, NJ: Erlbaum.

Kagan, D. M. and Squires, R. L. (1984). "Compulsive Eating, Dieting, Stress and Hostility Among College Students." *Journal of College Student Personnel*, 25(3), 213–220.

Khan, S. R. (1983). "A Study of the Influence of Tension on Educational and Vocational Aspirations." *Indian Psychological Review*, 24(4), 20–24.

Kluckholn, C. (1951). "Values and Value Orientation in the Theory of Action." In T. Parsons and E. A. Sils (Eds.), *Toward a General Theory of Action*. Cambridge: Harvard University Press.

Kohn, M. and Schooler, C. (1973). "Occupational Experience and Psychological Functioning: An Assessment of Reciprocal Effects." *American Sociological Review*, 38, 97–118.

Koopman, C., Eisenthal, S. and Sroeckle, J. D. (1984). "Ethnicity in the Reported Pain, Emotional Distress and Requests of Medical Outpatients." *Social Science and Medicine*, 18(6), 487–490.

Kramer, H. C., Berger, F. and Miller, G. (1974). "Student Concerns and Sources of Assistance." *Journal of College Student Personnel*, 15(5), 389–393.

Krase, J. (1983). "Educational Attainment and Educational Values: Italian-American Generations." Revision of paper presented at the American Italian Historical Association XV Conference, "Italian Americans Through the Generations: The First 100 Years." October 29–31, 1982, St. John's University, Jamaica, NY.

Lamont, L. (1979). *Campus Shock: A Firsthand Report on College Life Today*. New York: E.P. Dutton.

Lawler III, E. E., (1973). *Motivation in Work Organizations*. Monterey, California: Brooks/Cole.

Lefcourt, H. M. (1966). "Internal-External Control of Reinforcement: A Review." *Psychological Bulletin*, 65, 206–220.

Lefcourt, H. M. (1976). *Locus of Control: Current Theories and Research*. Hillsdale, NJ: Erlbaum.

Lefcourt, H. M. (1981). "The Construction and Development of the Multidimensional- Multiattributional Causality Scales." In H. M. Lefcourt (Ed.), *Research with the Locus of Control Construct, Vol. I: Assessment Methods*. New York: Academic Press.

Lefcourt, H. M. (1983). "The Locus of Control as a Moderator Variable: Stress." In H.M. Lefcourt (Ed.), *Research with the Locus of Control Construct, Vol. II: Developments and Social Problems*. New York: Academic Press.

Lenski, G. (1963). *The Religious Factor*. Garden City, NY: Anchor Books.

Levenson, H. (1972). "Distinctions within the Concept of Internal-External Locus of Control. Development of a New Scale." *Proceedings of the 80th annual convention of the American Psychological Association*, 261–262.

Levenson, H. (1981). "Differentiating among Internality, Powerful Others and Chance." In H.M. Lefcourt (Ed.), *Research with the Locus of Control Construct, Vol. I: Assessment Methods*. New York: Academic Press.

Lewin, K. (1938). *The Conceptual Representation and the Measurement of Psychological Forces*. Durham, North Carolina: Duke University Press.

Lichentstein, B. and Sherman, R. A. (1983). "Self-Management Versus Formal Treatment in Efforts at Weight Control." Paper presented at annual meeting of the Western Psychological Association, San Francisco, California.

Linden, W. (1984). "Development and Initial Validation of a Life Event Scale for Students." *Canadian Counselor*, 18(3), 106–110.

Lopreato, J. (1970). *Italian Americans*. New York: Random House.

MacDonald, A. P. (1971). "Internal-External Locus of Control: Parental Antecedents." *Journal of Consulting and Clinical Psychology*, 37, 141–147.

Mahler, I. (1974). "A Comparative Study of Locus of Control." *Psychologia*, 17, 135–139.

Manzitti, E. T. (1983). "Research on Ancestral Groups among the CUNY Graduates." Paper presented at spring conference "The Italian-American Experience in Education," Staten Island, New York.

Maracek, J. and Frasch, C. (1977). "Locus of Control and College Women's Role Expectations." *Journal of Counseling Psychology*, 24, 132–136.

Mathiasen, A. E. (1984). "Attitudes and Needs of the College Student Client." *Journal of College Student Personnel*, 25(3), 274–275.

Matteson, H. R, (1975). "Satisfaction and Dissonance Between Professors' and Students' Value Orientations." *College Student Journal*, 9(3), 258–267.

McGoldrick, M. and Pearce, J. K. (1981). "Family Therapy with Irish-Americans." *Family Process*, 20, 223–244.

McGoldrick, M., Pearce, J. K. and Giordano, J., (Eds.). (1982). *Ethnicity and Family Therapy*. New York: Guilford Press.

Meier, S. T., and Schmeck, R. R. (1985). "The Burned-Out College Student: A Descriptive Profile." *Journal of College Student Personnel*, 26, 63–69.

Mintz, N. and Schwartz, D. (1976). "Urban Ecology and Psychosis: Community Factors in the Incidence of Schizophrenia and Manic Depressive Psychosis Among Italians in Greater Boston." *International Journal of Social Psychology*, 10(2), 101–118.

Morelli, G., Krotinger, H. and Moore, S. (1979). "Neuroticism and Levenson's Locus of Control Scale." *Psychological Reports*, 44, 153–154.

Murphy, H. B. M. (1978). "European Cultural Offshoots in the New World: Differences in their Mental Hospitalization Patterns: Part 1. British, French and Italian influences." *Social Psychiatry*, 13, 1–9.

Newcomb, T. M., Koenig, K., Flacks, R., and Warwick, D. (1967). *Persistence and Change: Bennington College and Its Students after Twenty-Five Years*. New York: Wiley.

Nezu, A. M. (1985). "Differences in Distress Between Effective and Ineffective Counseling." *Journal of Counseling Psychology*, 32, 135–138.

Nowicki, S. and Duke, M. P. (1983). "The Nowicki-Strickland Life Span Locus of Control Scales: Construct Validation." In Lefcourt (Ed.), *Research with the Locus of Control Construct, Vol. II: Developments and Social Problems*. New York: Academic Press.

O'Brien, G. E. (1984). "Locus of Control, Work and Retirement." In H.M. Lefcourt (Ed.), *Research with the Locus of Control Construct, Vol. III: Extension and Limitations*. New York: Academic Press.

Ohlsen, M. M. (1983). *Introduction to Counseling*. Itasca, Illinois: F. E. Peacock Publishers, Inc.

Osipow, S. H., Carney, C. G. Winer, J. L., Yanico, B., and Koschier, M. (1980). *The Career Decision Scale*, (3rd Rev.). Columbus, Ohio; Marathon Consulting and Press.

Ovcharchyn, C. A., Johnson, H. H. and Petzel, T. P. (1981). "'Type A Behavior, Academic Aspirations, and Academic Success." *Journal of Personality*, 49, 3–13.

Pandey, J. and Tewary, N. B. (1979). "Locus of Control and Achievement Values of Entrepreneurs." *Journal of Occupational Psychology*, 52, 107–111.

Papajohn, J. and Spiegel, J. (1975). *Transactions in Families*. San Francisco: Jossey-Bass.

Penner, L. A. and Anh, T. (1977). "A Comparison of American and Vietnamese Systems." *Journal of Social Psychology*, 101, 187–204.

Perrone, J. and Swires, M. (1985). *Time Management: A Manual for Teachers and Counselors.* ERIC/CAPS, University of Michigan.

Prociuk, T. J. and Breen, L. J. (1974). "Locus of Control, Study Habits and Attitudes and College Academic Performance." *Journal of Psychology,* 88, 91–95.

Rabkin, J. and Struening, E. (1976). "Ethnicity, Social Class and Mental Illness in New York City: A Social Area Analysis of Five Ethnic Groups." (Working Paper No. 17). New York: Institute on Pluralism and Group Identity.

Rabow, J. and Neuman, C. A. (1983). "Saturday Night Live: Chronicity of Alcohol Consumption Among College Students." University of California Alcohol Research Center, "Psychological Approaches to Alcoholism" symposium, Los Angeles, California.

Ragucci, A. T. (1981). "Italian Americans." In A. Hargood (Ed.), *Ethnicity and Medical Care.* Cambridge: Harvard University Press.

Ramaniah, N. V., Ribich, F. D. and Schmeck, R. R. (1975). "Internal-External Control of Reinforcement as a Determinant of Study Habits and Academic Attitudes." *Journal of Research in Personality,* 9.

Reid, D. W. (1984). "Participatory Control and the Chronic Illness Adjustment Process." In H.M. Lefcourt (Ed.), *Research with the Locus of Control Construct, Vol. III: Extensions and Limitations.* New York: Academic Press.

Reimanis, G. (1971). "Effects of Experimental IE Modification Techniques and Home Environmental Variables in IE." Paper presented at annual meeting of the American Psychological Association, Washington DC.

Rim, Y. (1970). "Values and Attitudes." *Personality,* 1, 175–187.

Roberts, B. and Myers, J. K. (1954). "Religion, National Origin, Immigration and Mental Illness." *American Journal of Psychiatry,* 110, 759–764.

Rokeach, M. (1968). *Beliefs, Attitudes and Values.* San Francisco: Jossey-Bass.

Rokeach, M. (1973). *The Nature of Human Values.* New York: Free Press.

Rokeach, M. (1979). *Understanding Human Values.* New York: Free Press.

Rokeach, M. and Regan, J. F. (1980). "The Role of Values in the Counseling Situation." *The Personnel and Guidance Journal,* 58(9), 576–583.

Roman, J. T. (1986) "Value Systems among Hispanic Students in a Community College in the City University of New York." Unpublished doctoral dissertation, New York University.

Rotter, J. B. (1954). *Social Learning and Clinical Psychology.* Englewood Cliffs, NJ: Prentice-Hall.

Rotter, J. B. (1966). "Generalized Expectancies of Internal Versus External Control of Reinforcement." *Psychological Monographs,* 80, (1, Whole No. 609).

Rotter, J. B. (1975). "Some Problems and Misconceptions Related to the Construct of Internal Versus External Control of Reinforcement." *Journal of Consulting and Clinical Psychology,* 43(1), 56–67.

Roueche, J. E. and Mink, O. G. (1976). "Impact of Instruction and Counseling on Higher Risk Youth." Final Report, National Institute of Mental Health Grant R01MH22590.

Rotunno, M. and McGoldrick, M. (1982). "Italian Families." In M. McGoldrick, J. Pearce and J. Giordano (Eds.), *Ethnicity and Family Therapy.* New York: Guilford Press.

Ruiz, R. A., Padilla, A. M. and Alvarez, R. (1978). "Issues in the Counseling of Spanish Speaking/Surnamed Clients: Recommendations for Therapeutic Services." In G.R. Walz and F. Benjamin (Eds.), *Transcultural Counseling: Needs, Programs and Techniques.* New York: Human Sciences Press.

Sandler. I., Reese, F., Spencer, L. and Harpin, P. (1983). "Person X Environment Interaction and Locus of Control: Laboratory, Therapy, and Classroom Studies." In H. M. Lefcourt (Ed.), *Research with the Locus of Control Construct, Vol. II: Developments and Social Problems.* New York: Academic Press.

Sarason, I. G., Johnson, J. H. and Siegel, J. M. (1978). "Assessing the Impact of Life Changes: Development of the Life Experience Survey." *Journal of Consulting and Clinical Psychology.* 46, 932–946.

Schinka, J. (1986). "Interorganizational Memorandum to Staff at Psychological Assessment Resources Regarding the Public Dissemination of Information on the Personal Problems Checklist."

Schlosser, M. B. and Sheeley, L. (1985). "Subjective Well-Being and the Stress Process." Paper presented at the 93rd Annual Convention of the American Psychological Association, Los Angeles, California.

Schneider, M. (1977). *Ein Empirischer Beitrag zur Wettheorie von Rokeach im Bereich Politischer Einstellungen und Politischen Verhaltens*. Bonn: Rheinische Friedrich-Wilhelms-Universitat Presse.

Sirey, A. R., Patti, A. and Mann, L. (1985). *Ethnotherapy: An Exploration of Italian-American Identity*. New York: National Institute for Psychotherapies, Inc.

Sowa, C. J., and Lustman, P. J. (1984). "Gender Differences in Rating Stressful Events, Depression and Depressive Cognition." *Journal of Clinical Psychology*, 40(6), 1334–1337.

Stacey, J., Beraud, S. and Daniels, J. (Eds.). (1974). *And Jill Came Tumbling After: Sexism in American Education*. New York: Dell Press.

Stevens, M. J. and Pfost, K. S. (1984). "Stress management interventions." *Journal of College Student Personnel*, 25(3), 269–270.

Sue, D. W. (1981). *Counseling the Culturally Different: Theory and Practice*. New York: John Wiley and Sons.

Sue, S., Sue, D. W., and Sue, D. (1975). "Asian Americans as a Minority Group." *American Psychologist*, 30, 906–910.

Sugarman, B. (1975). "Dropout Patterns in a Therapeutic Community: Behavior that does not Correlate with Social Background and Some Implications for Motivation." *Corrective and Social Psychiatry and Journal of Behavior Technology Methods and Therapy*, 21(3), 2–6.

Thomason, J. A. (1983). "Multidimensional Assessment of Locus of Control and Obesity." *Psychological Reports*, 153 J (Part 2), 1083–1086.

Tolman, E. C. (1951). *Behavior and Psychological Man*. Berkeley: University of California Press.

Tomasi, L. F. (1972). *The Italian-American Family*. New York: Center for Migration Studies.

Tomasi, S. M., and Engles, M. H. (Eds.) (1970). *The Italian Experience in the United States*. New York: Center for Migration Studies.

Tresemer, D. (1977). *Fear of Success*. New York: Plenum Press.

Twaddle, A. C. (1969). "Decisions and Sick Role Variations." *Journal of Health and Social Behavior*, 10, 105–115.

Valecha, A. G. K. (1972). "Construct Validation of Internal-External Locus of Control Reinforcement Related to Work-Related Variables." Proceedings of the 80th annual convention of the American Psychological Association, 7, 455–456.

Vecoli, R. J. (1978). "The coming of age of the Italian Americans: 1945–1974." *Ethnicity*, 15, 119–147.

Vinson, D. E., Scott, J. E. and Lamont, L. M. (1977). "The Role of Personal Values in Marketing and Consumer Behavior." *Journal of Marketing*, 41, 44–50.

Vroom, V. H. (1964). *Work and Motivation*. New York: John Wiley and Sons.

Warheit, G., Holzer III, C., Bell, R. and Arey, S. (1976). "Sex, Marital Status and Mental Health." *Social Forces*, 55, 459–470.

Weiner, A. I. and Hunt, S. L. (1983). "Work and Leisure Orientations among University Students: Implications for College and University Counselors." *The Personnel and Guidance Journal*, 61(9), 538–541.

Weiner, B. (1972). *Theories of Motivation: From Mechanism to Cognition*. Chicago: Markham.

Weiner, B. (1974). *Achievement Motivation and Attribution Theory*. Morristown, NJ: General Learning.

Williams, R. M. (1971). "Change and Stability in Values and Values System." In B. Barber and A. Inkeles (Eds.), *Stability and Social Change*. Boston: Little, Brown.

Wise, R., Charner, I. and Randour, M. L. (1976). "A Conceptual Framework for Career Awareness in Career Decision Making." *The Counseling Psychologist*, 6(3) 47–53.

Wong, T. P. and Sproule, C. F. (1984). "An Attribution Analysis of the Locus of Control Construct and the Trent Attribution Profile." In H. M. Lefcourt (Ed.), *Research with the Locus of Control Construct, Vol. III: Extensions and Limitations.* New York: Academic Press.

Zborowski, M. (1969). *People in Pain.* San Francisco: Jossey-Bass.

Zytoskee, A., Strickland, B. R. and Watson, J. (1971). "Delay of Gratification and Internal Versus External Control among Adolescents of Low Socioeconomic Status." *Developmental Psychology, 4,* 93–98.

APPENDIX A
STATISTICAL ANALYSES

PAGE 167: TABLE 3

Three separate two-way analyses of variance were used to determine the effects of gender (independent variable) and generation levels (independent variable) on the three IPC measures of locus of control (dependent variables). The only significant F ratio was found between the gender main effects variable and the Powerful Others LOC measure. Because gender is a dichotomous variable, no post-hoc comparisons were necessary. The results are presented in Table 1A.

TABLE 1A. *ANOVA Table: Gender x Generation x Powerful Others LOC*

		POWERFUL OTHERS LOC		
SOURCE	df	MS	F	p
Gender (A)	1	388.7502	5.110	.0233
Generation (B)	2	91.8266	1.207	.3008
AxB	2	35.7841	.470	.6313
Error	211	16052.2100	-	-

PAGE 169: TABLE 5

Six separate one-way analyses of variance were used to determine the relationship between gender (independent variable) and attribution (dependent variables) on the three measures of attribution for the success condition and the failure condition. Significant F ratios were found between the gender main effects variable and both the effort and the ability attribution ratings in the success condition. No post-hoc comparisons were necessary. The significant results are presented in Table 2A.

TABLE 2A. *ANOVA Tables: Gender x Effort Attribution for Success, Gender x Ability Attribution for Success*

		EFFORT ATTRIBUTION		
SOURCE	df	MS	F	p
Gender	1	2799.9130	6.472	.0098
Error	210	415.2801		

		ABILITY ATTRIBUTION		
SOURCE	df	MS	F	p
Gender	1	1868.0000	4.26	.0376
Error	210	437.8174		

PAGE 181: TABLE 10

The data was analyzed using two different statistical methods. Similar results were obtained regarding significant findings. Two-way analyses of variance were employed to determine the effects of gender and generation on the values rankings of this sample. In a statistical strategy justified and suggested by Feather (1975, p. 23–25) in his research with the Scale of Values, the rank scores were transformed to normalized scores so that a two-way ANOVA could be used on the data. Significant effects were found for the main effects of gender on 11 values. No post-hoc comparisons were necessary.

The Kruskak-Wallis ANOVA by ranks method was also used to assess the effects of gender on the value rankings of this sample with no transformation of the ordinal data necessary. Significant gender effects results were confirmed for the same values obtained in the two-way ANOVAs. The results of the Kruskak-Wallis analyses are summarized in Table 3A.

TABLE 3A. *Summary of Significant ANOVA Results for Values Rankings: Gender x Generation*

DEPENDENT VARIABLE (VALUE)	df	H RATIO	p
A comfortable life	1	11.110	.0012
An exciting life	1	10.892	.0014
Equality	1	7.763	.0055
Inner harmony	1	7.894	.0052
Pleasure	1	11.233	.0012
Self-respect	1	10.440	.0016
Ambitious	1	8.709	.0035
Forgiving	1	6.664	.0096
Honest	1	9.618	.0023
Loving	1	6.751	.0092
Obedient	1	8.295	.0043

PAGE 183: TABLE 11

The Kruskak-Wallis ANOVA by ranks method was employed to determine the relationship between major choice (independent variable) and values (dependent variable). Significant results are summarized in Table 4A.

TABLE 4A. *Significant ANOVA Results: Major Choice by Values*

DEPENDENT VARIABLE (VALUE)	df	H RATIO	p
A comfortable life	1	8.150	.004
A world of beauty	1	7.192	.007
Family security	1	3.627	.053

PAGE 194: TABLE 16

Gender differences on the PPC problem frequencies were determined by employing Z tests for the significance of difference between proportions. The significant Z values are listed in Table 5A.

To test the gender differences for the PPC category means and the PPC total mean, one-way analyses of variances were employed using gender as the independent variable and the total number of problems checked in each category and on the entire checklist as the dependent variables. The significant F ratios are listed in Table 6A.

TABLE 5A. *Significant Z Ratios: Gender x PPC Problems*

PPC PROBLEM	Z RATIO	p
Not getting enough exercise	2.29	.05
Feeling anxious or uptight	2.29	.05
Feeling depressed or sad	2.71	.01
Being overweight	4.21	.001
Feeling lonely	3.38	.001
Eating too much	3.52	.001

TABLE 6A. *Significant F Ratios: Gender x PPC Categories and Total*

PPC CATEGORY	F RATIO	p
Social	8.720	.0038
Appearance	11.544	.0012
Family/home	6.516	.0110
Emotional	9.373	.0029
Health habits	4.314	.0366
PPC total	7.398	.0071

References

Hayes, W. L. (1969). *Statistics*. New York: Holt.

Pedhazur, E. L. (1982). *Multiple Regression in Behavioral Research*. New York: Holt, Rinehart, and Winston.

Bruning, J. L. and Kintz, B. L. (1968). *Computational Handbook of Statistics*. Glenview, Illinois: Scott, Foresman and Company.

APPENDIX B

INFORMATION AND INSTRUCTIONS

There are over 17,000 Italian-American students attending City University and yet we know very little about your needs and concerns as students. The purpose of this research project is to identify these major areas of need so that we can develop programs and services to assist you in making your educational experience in CUNY a rewarding and fulfilling one. To do this we need your cooperation and ask you to complete the Background Information section below and the three brief surveys enclosed. All of this should take about 45 minutes to complete. It is important that you return the envelope with the completed materials enclosed to the counselor or teacher who distributed them to you. On your campus this individual is: _____ in room _____ . If for some reason, you cannot contact this individual, please contact us and we will arrange to pick up the materials. Please be open and candid in responding to the surveys. No names are requested and all results will be reported as group statistics. We appreciate your assistance. Your participation in this project will benefit you and your peers throughout CUNY in the form of improved counseling and academic services for Italian-American students.

BACKGROUND INFORMATION

Please answer the following questions about yourself and your family by checking (✓) or writing in the appropriate response:

1. Your sex: ☐ Male ☐ Female

2. Your age _____

3. Which CUNY college are you presently attending? _____

4. What is your current standing in college? ☐ Freshman ☐ Sophomore ☐ Junior ☐ Senior

5. What is your major or intended major (if you are undecided write undecided) _____

6. What is your cumulative grade point index? (F=0 to A=4.00) _____

7. If you receive a good grade in a course or exam, what percentage of your success
   would you attribute to luck ____%; academic ability ____%; effort ____%. (should total 100%)

8. If you were to receive a poor grade in an exam or course, what percentage of your performance
   would you attribute to luck ____%; lack of ability ____%; lack of effort ____% (should total 100%)

9. What is your father's ethnic background? ☐ Italian ☐ Other
   What is your mother's ethnic background? ☐ Italian ☐ Other
   Where were you born?   ☐ US ☐ Italy ☐ Other
   Where was your father born?   ☐ US ☐ Italy ☐ Other
   Where was your mother born?   ☐ US ☐ Italy ☐ Other
   Where was your father's father born?   ☐ US ☐ Italy ☐ Other
   Where was your father's mother born?   ☐ US ☐ Italy ☐ Other
   Where was your mother's father born?   ☐ US ☐ Italy ☐ Other
   Where was your mother's mother born?   ☐ US ☐ Italy ☐ Other

10. What is the gross annual income of your household?
    ☐ under $10,000   ☐ $10,000–$20,000   ☐ $20,000–$30,000
    ☐ $30,000–$40,000   ☐ $40,000–$75,000   ☐ over $75,000

APPENDIX C

INTERVIEW FORMAT (100% Italian Parentage)

STEP 1: The interviewee is given information about the exact purpose and nature of the study and the potential utilization of data from the interview. He/she is told that all data will be reported as group data and that his/her anonymity will be preserved. He/she is also given assurances that no excerpt from the audiotape or videotape of the interview will be included in any media presentation for public viewing unless the interviewee first reviews the excerpt and approves (in writing) its inclusion in the final product.

STEP 2: The interviewee is given a Consent Agreement Form and a Background Information sheet to complete before the interview.

STEP 3: THE INTERVIEW

ETHNICITY:

1. Tell me about yourself? Your family, where you grew up? Your hobbies and interests? Anything you think is important to know about you?
2A. How do you identify yourself ethnically? What do you call yourself: Italian, Italian American, American? (*order will vary in each interview*)
2B. Why? Is there any reason why you prefer one more than the others, *or* is there any reason why you don't have any preferences?
3. What is it like for a man/woman growing up in an Italian-American family? Was it harder or easier because of your gender? Were you treated any differently than your brothers or sisters?
4A. What about your close friends? Are most of them Italian or non-Italian?
4B. Men? Women? 4C. Can you think of any reasons for your preferences?
5. Imagine that a friend of yours is describing you to a person who has never met an Italian American, what would your friend say is Italian about you?
6. What are some of the strengths you have received from being raised in an Italian-American (Italian) family and culture? What are some of the good things about growing up Italian?
7. What do you think are some of the problems you have encountered from growing up in an Italian-American family?
8. Do you belong to the Italian club at your college? Why/why not?

ACHIEVEMENT, MOTIVATION, CAREER CHOICE, LEVEL OF ASPIRATION:
9. Let's talk about school. 9A. Why did you decide to go to college?
9B. Was it your decision alone or were you influenced by someone else? Who? Explain?
9C. Why did you decide to go to _____ College? Why not a private college?
9D. (*For community college students only*) Why not a senior (four year) college?
10. (*For students with a clear preference for "effort" or "ability" on items 7–8 on Background Information sheet*):
10A. In question #7 on the Background Information sheet you attributed most of your success in school to effort/ability. Why not more to ___ than to ___ ? Let's talk about it? (*open-ended probing here*)
10B. In question #8 on the sheet, you attribute failure mainly to? Why? (*probing continues*)
11. (*For "decided" students only*):
11A. You said that you were majoring in _____ . What do you plan to do with it?
11B. How did you come to decide on _____ ? Ever consider anything else? What seems attractive about _____ ? If something better came along would you change your mind?

(For "undecided" students only):

11C. I see here that you are undecided about your major: _____ . Can we talk about why?
(open-ended, unstructured probing here)

12A. Most parents have plans for their children, things they'd like them to do or go into. Did yours have any plans like that?

12B. How do your folks feel about your plans now?

STRESS:

13. Students complain a lot about being overloaded and under stress. What are some of the things that hassle you or create stress for you these days? Anything else? Discuss study results if available.

14A. If you have a problem that is bothering you, who do you talk to about it? Your parents? A close friend? A priest?

14B. Why? _____ Why not? _____

14C. If you had a serious personal problem, would you go to a counselor with it? In school? Outside of school? Why? _____ Why not? _____

VALUES, GOALS:

15. Where do you want to be 5 years from now? What kind of job? What level? Earnings? Where would you like to live? Apartment? House? Married? Children?

16. Where do you want to be 10 years from now?

17A. What's the most important thing for you in life? What do you value most? Your priority in life?

17B. What else? Discuss study results if available. _____

STEP 4: DEBRIEFING

1. Do you want to talk about anything else?

2. Can I answer any questions for you about the interview or the study?

3. Remember that the information you have given me will be kept anonymous. I assure you that if I decide to use any excerpts of the tape for a media presentation, I will let you review it first and get your permission to include it (or not).

APPENDIX D

INTERVIEW FORMAT (Mixed Parentage)

STEP 1: The interviewee is given information about the exact purpose and nature of the study and the potential utilization of data from the interview. He/she is told that all data will be reported as group data and that his/her anonymity will be preserved. He/she is also given assurances that no excerpt from the audiotape or videotape of the interview will be included in any media presentation for public viewing unless the interviewee first reviews the excerpt and approves (in writing) its inclusion in the final product.

STEP 2: The interviewee is given a Consent Agreement form and a Background Information sheet to complete before the interview.

STEP 3: THE INTERVIEW

ETHNICITY:

1. Tell me about yourself? Your family, where you grew up? Your hobbies and interests? Anything you think is important to know about you?

2A. I see from your info sheet that your mother/father is Irish. Which parent do you identify yourself with ethnically? Do you call yourself, Italian American, Irish American, American, etc.

B. Is there any reason why you prefer one more than the other? Is there any reason why you don't have any preference?

3A. What about your close friends? Are most of them Italian or non-Italian?

3B. Men? Women? 3C. Can you think of any reasons for your preferences?

4. Imagine that a friend of yours is describing you to a person who has never met an Italian American, what would your friend say is Italian about you?

5. What are some of the good things about being raised in a family with parents from different ethnic backgrounds?

6. What do you think are some of the problems you have encountered from growing up in this kind of family?

7. Do you belong to the Italian club at your college? Why/why not?

ACHIEVEMENT, MOTIVATION, CAREER CHOICE, LEVEL OF ASPIRATION:

8. Let's talk about school. 8A. Why did you decide to go to college?

8B. Was it your decision alone or were you influenced by someone else? Who? Explain?

8C. Why did you decide to go to _____ College? Why not a private college?

8D. (*For community college students only*) Why not a senior (four year) college?

9. (*For students with a clear preference for "effort" or ability" on items 7–8 on Background Information sheet*):

9A. In question #7 on the Background Information sheet you attributed most of your success in school to effort/ability. Why not more to ___ than to ___ ? Let's talk about it? (*open-ended probing here*)

9B. In question #8 on the sheet, you attribute failure mainly to? Why? (*probing continues*)

10. (*For "decided" students only*):

10A. You said that you were majoring in _____ . What do you plan to do with it?

10B. How did you come to decide on_____? Ever consider anything else? What seems attractive about _____? If something better came along would you change our mind? (*For "undecided" students only*):

10C. You said here that you are undecided about your major: _____ . Can we talk about why? (*open-ended, unstructured probing here*)

11A. Most parents have plans for their children, things they'd like them to do or go into. Did yours have any plans like that?

11B. How do your folks feel about your plans now?

STRESS:

12. Students complain a lot about being overloaded and under stress. What are some of the things that hassle you or create stress for you these days? Anything else? Discuss study results if available.

13. If you have a problem that is bothering you who do you talk to about it? Your parents? A close friend? A priest? 13B. Why or why not?

13C. If you had a serious personal problem, would to go to a counselor with it? In school? Outside of school? Why or why not?

VALUES, GOALS:

14. Where do you want to be 5 years from now? What kind of job? What level? Earnings? Where would you like live? Apartment? House? Married? Children?

15. Where do want to be 10 years from now?

16A. What's the most important thing for you in life? What do you value most? Your priority in life?

16B. What else? Discuss study results if available.

STEP 4: DEBRIEFING

1. Do you want to talk about anything else?

2. Can I answer any questions for you about the interview? About the study?

3. Remember that the information you have given me will be kept anonymous. I assure you that if I decide to use any excerpts of the tape for a media presentation I will let you review it first and get your permission to include it (or not).

APPENDIX E

ITALIAN AMERICAN RESEARCH PROJECT AT CUNY

CONSENT AGREEMENT FORM

I am familiar with the purposes and goals of this research project sponsored by the Italian Institute and agree to participate in this audio/video taped interview with the understanding that any information or data gathered from it will be presented in such a way as to preserve my anonymity. I am aware that I can discontinue the interview at any time and that my participation in the interview will not affect my academic standing at CUNY in any way. If any excerpts from the tape of this interview are selected for inclusion in a media presentation for public viewing, I have been given assurances that I will have an opportunity to review the segment(s) selected *before* inclusion and give my approval (or disapproval) of its use in the final presentation.

Name of student: _____ Date: _____

College: _____ Student's signature: _____

Family vs. Career: A Dilemma for the Italian-American Woman of the '80s

GERALDINE LANZILLI BATTISTA

This paper highlights the results of a survey focusing on the conflict women face when combining career and family roles, and comparing the responses of Italian-American women to those of non-Italian-American women.

The research of Covello (1967), Gambino (1974) and many others has clearly documented that Italian Americans come from a family centered culture and have a strong sense of role expectations.

To counteract hostile forces Italians came to rely primarily on their families and on their internal resources (Rotunno and McGoldrick, 1982). The Italians developed a life style based on the family; any outside intrusion was viewed as injurious to the family and to its self-preserving way of life.

Any form of advancement—social, educational and professional—was not encouraged and, for the most part, discouraged. Since children were needed to work to help support the family, education was not practical (Covello, 1967).

Research of the '70s pointed out that Italian Americans have done well financially, but have not made much headway in executive and professional occupations (Gambino, 1974). Their financial success was achieved through skilled, semi-skilled and unskilled labor, rather than through white collar positions. This method was unlike that of the Jews, who went to great lengths to secure an education for their children; and the WASPs, who raised their children to be self-sufficient and independent (Alba, 1985; Gambino, 1974; Rotunno and McGoldrick, 1982). Seemingly, this was due to misperceptions about education that directly conflicted with American values.

Richard Alba (1985), a more recent researcher in this area, found the status of Italian Americans of the '80s to be different. He felt the Italians lagged behind WASPs chiefly because they had a lower starting point.

Their parents had less education and less prestigious occupations and they've been somewhat hindered as a result. This conclusion weakened the case of ethnicity being a barrier to attainment. In his work he went on to reassess the achievements of Italian Americans, finding little difference in their attainment and those of other major white ethnic groups. He believes that with each new generation the educational attainment will continue to rise and that these changes, and others, dilute the ethnic cultural influence and one's sense of cultural identity.

Some researchers have found supporting evidence for Alba's assimilation theory, others have not, but some researchers have found that Italian Americans have assimilated while cultural orientations still prevail. One example is the study by Dr. James Perrone (1986) of Italian-American college students at the City University of New York. He found that overall the students in his psychological profile were culturally and structurally assimilated into American society. Yet, when he interviewed students about their values and long-term goals in life, both men and women, with few exceptions, related themes of "family, home, comfortable living and most of all, personal happiness."

When Perrone asked students about their career plans and aspirations, meeting family expectations was a major consideration. For example, when he questioned these students about their values and long-term goals, he found that career was viewed "strictly as a means to achieve the personal and family growth they value so much." This was found even in students who aspired to the professions. He also observed that Italian-American undergraduate women had not yet focused on how they would manage their career and family. When Perrone questioned the women about the "family versus career dilemma" one student stated that she was aware of it but was trying not to think about it now. This ambivalence and "putting off the worrying until later" attitude was characteristic of the women he interviewed.

Several other works by Italian-American researchers clearly reveal the conflicts that Italian-American women have had in relation to traditional role expectations (Scelsa, 1986; Sirey and Valerio, 1983). Barolini (1985) considers these conflicts part of becoming an individual. She acknowledges that this is something we all must go through but that some cultures make this more difficult to achieve. She feels that this is particularly true for the Italian-American woman because throughout the generations she has been considered the core of the family and the transmitter of its traditions and values. Lurie (1986) explains that Italian-American women who seek demanding professional positions often have to cope with fears of appearing selfish or of losing their Italian identity and values.

Martorella (1980) believes that Italian-American women are less often found in high-level management positions because these jobs demand a full-time commitment. She explains that this may not be practically or psychologically possible for Italian-American women, especially those with children. Deviations from these expectations produce guilt that is uncomfortable and hard to deal with. In one of her papers Balancio (1986) wrote that the traditional background is an asset to the career-oriented women, but points out that guilt and the sense of obligation that career aspirations may cause, are destructive to the self-esteem that would lead to upward mobility. Sirey agrees and states: "Achieving often brings pangs of guilt because you're separating from your family and you're different from them" (in DeFiglio, 1986, p. 7). This realization helps to assuage the guilt. It also helps to find role models for the modern side of oneself. Martorella (1982) explains that there are disadvantages in being part of an extended family, especially for a career woman. She points out that the resulting stress increases with the establishment of a primary relationship. The ages 25–35 are viewed as most problematic because of the conflict between job and family role expectations, i.e., marriage, childbearing, where to live, etc. Women in this situation find themselves in a "double-bind," lacking alternatives and support from significant others that, in turn, can have a negative impact to their success outside the family.

Balancio (1986) explains that "as children, our experiences are filtered through a cultural apparatus which shades the meaning of incoming imagery and symbolism" (p. 5). These images affect how we view ourselves. She looks at the images of Italian-American women in the media and points out how these images may affect their perceptions of reality and self-esteem. She believes that the images of Italian-American women as earth mothers, madonnas or sex objects seriously take away from their being viewed equally. She explains that who they choose to marry, whether they pursue a career, whether they have children, the number of children they have and how they rear them, will be influenced by these images.

Others see the Italian-American background as an asset. D'Andrea (1983) believes that Italian tradition provides support to Italian women as wives and mothers through the family and religion. She states that the

Italian-American woman's role definition is made up of characteristics that provide her with a positive sense of self.

It seems that the presence and amount of conflict is influenced by many factors. Balancio (1986) and Davidson and Gordon (1979) feel that gender roles of Italian-American women today are a function of their birth cohort, social class, birth order, educational background, work experience, family traditions and community identities. It is important to understand that while working is not a new experience for these women, the direction, orientation and purpose of their work is. Through the experiences of these women, at various educational and chronological stages, we learn of the struggle with these issues, which for some are life long.

It is recognized that all women face conflicts stemming from post-industrial changes in the traditional women's role and that women for centuries have been dealing with many issues concerning their right to equal opportunities in education and their need for self fulfillment. Apart from the struggle with society, women are in conflict between the traditional values they were brought up with and the new values of equality with men (Regan and Roland, 1985; Mortimer, Hall and Hill, 1978; Hall and Hall, 1978). This conflict makes career decisions stressful.

The Industrial Revolution has been thought to have a significant impact on the status of women. It created many jobs and opportunities primarily for single women, women from working class backgrounds and those married women who had to work out of necessity. This occurrence, as well as the post-World War II baby boom, which brought about the expansion of a wider variety of educational, medical, governmental and recreational services that were also dominated by women workers, encouraged women to not only enter the work force but to remain in it (Van Dusen and Sheldon, 1976). Ferber (1982) also feels that it was at this time that the stereotype of the ideal American family began. She explains that with industrialization, work now meant employment outside the home. Therefore, the meaning for housewife was confined to caring for children, nurturing her husband, and maintaining her home.

An examination of the literature concerning women's roles and careers tells us that significant changes have occurred and that it is acceptable, and even expected, that women will marry and work and, later on, have children and continue to work. (Davidson and Gordon, 1979; Van Dusen and Sheldon, 1976). Women are now seen as significant and valuable additions to the work force. Although present childcare facilities and maternity benefits leave much to be desired, progress is being made to facilitate a woman's ability to continue to work after having children. As these situations become easier to handle, combining career and family roles might prove less stressful.

The aim of this study was to focus on career and family attitudes of women between the ages of 21–35, because marital and childbearing concerns peak during this time. Law school women were targeted because they already held bachelor's degrees and were pursuing graduate degrees in a career-oriented discipline. There is also very little research done in this area. An Italian (N=38) and non-Italian-American (N=70) sample was collected. It was hypothesized that Italian-American women would experience greater conflict because of their cultural background.

Before highlighting the results of this survey, it is important to note that since no tests of significance were conducted, the findings are to be thought of as indicators of trends and suggestions for future research, rather than representations of statistically significant differences between Italian-American and non-Italian-American women.

Overall, the data did suggest that the attitudes of both groups were similar to those which emphasize individuality and equality with men, supporting the work of Alba (1985), Perrone (1986) and others, who found that Italian Americans are structurally and culturally assimilated into American society. The data also showed some differences between the responses of the two groups.

The data indicated that 48% of the mothers of the non-Italian-American women worked while the respondents were in grade school, whereas only 26% of the mothers of the Italian-American women worked. This difference suggests that Italian-American mothers valued being home with children more than non-Italian-American mothers. It is worth noting that when combining responses regarding whether the mothers worked or worked part-time, the number of Italian-American mothers working increased to 63% and only rose 4% among the non-Italian-American mothers, totaling 52%. This suggests that work was valued, but needed to be structured around the family's schedule to enable one to meet family responsibilities and individual wishes.

The majority of the Italian-American and non-Italian-American women felt that their parents held equal roles and input in family matters. Although in questions pertaining to responsibility for running the household, 62% of the Italian-American women considered their mother's role equal to their father's role, whereas 78% of the non-Italian-American women responded that their mothers are responsible for these roles. Similar responses were found in questions regarding responsibility for the caring and rearing of the children. Sixty percent of the Italian-American women responded that their parents are equally responsible for the caring and rearing of the children, while 75% of the non-Italian-American women responded that their mothers alone were responsible for these activities. The majority of responses within both groups considered the father to be the provider and head of household, although this was found to a greater degree in non-Italian-American women's responses (67%) than the Italian-American women's responses (55%).

The Italian-American women consistently responded that their mothers and fathers held equal roles in the division of family responsibility. This included general roles, decision-making, household and child-related responsibilities in the family. When asked who the provider and head of household was, the majority of Italian-American women answered with father. The equality that is apparent in the division of responsibility among the parents of the Italian-American respondents is different from what the predominant literature has outlined as being traditionally patriarchal, but it gives credence to the work of D'Andrea (1983), who believes it seems more accurate to consider the powers within the family to be shared. Additional research is needed to pinpoint the reasons for this change. It is hard to know whether the change is perceptual or actual. For example, does running the household (cleaning, cooking) include taking care of the maintenance of the house and car (plumbing, painting, car maintenance)? Are the respondents acknowledging that powers within the family are not patriarchal or have roles changed because there is a respect for mutual career attainment and equality? If the latter is true, one might infer that family and career roles would be less stressful for the Italian-American mothers.

Respondents felt that their parents were supportive of their career/educational plans and were not uncomfortable with their decision to work outside the home. The respondents for both groups felt that it was not difficult to meet their parents' expectations. The majority also disagreed that their parents wished them to settle down and have children. The Italian-American parents were twice as likely as the non-Italian-American parents to agree that too much time was spent outside the home. However, the non-Italian-American parents were more than three times as likely as the Italian-American parents to think that respondents should settle down and have children.

It seems that attitudinal changes have taken place in parental attitudes of the Italian-American respondents in regard to education. The literature outlines education as threatening to family cohesiveness (Covello, 1967; Gambino, 1974; Mann, 1986). This was the result of the unstable historical background of Italians. The fact that Italian-American parents were more likely to feel that respondents spent too much time outside the family may imply that, for some, these traditional feelings still exist.

Family plans were still more important than career plans. This was more apparent among the responses of Italian-American women. This is consistent with other research results that emphasize family within the Italian-American culture. The majority of both groups—89% of the Italian-American women and 83% of the non-Italian-American women—agreed that they plan to have children. This percentage remained the same—83% for non-Italian-American women—in regard to their being responsible for the caring and rearing of children; whereas it decreased to 54% amongst the Italian-American women. This difference raises questions regarding whether a cultural change is implied or whether this can be regarded as additional support for equal roles in the Italian-American family. The overall support for childrearing responsibility is consistent with the work of Merriam and Hyer (1984), and Coser and Rokoff (1985), among others, who point out that women are still responsible for the majority of the household and childrearing tasks regardless of the changes in career or educational roles, and that work force participation would produce stress for these women. Regan and Roland (1985) and Mortimer, Hall and Hill (1978) agree that the increase of female participation in the work force creates conflict due to deviations from traditional gender-based roles. This seems especially so for the non-Italian-American women.

The married and non-married Italian-American and non-Italian-American women felt their spouses/partners were, or would be, supportive of their careers and would not feel threatened if they outranked or made more money than they did. Overall, the non-Italian-American women agreed with each statement less often than the Italian-American women. The non-married groups also tended to be less assured of their partners support than the married women. In regard to spouse/partner's willingness to relocate, the non-married, non-Italian-American women were the only group to agree that their partners would relocate to advance their career.

Two important findings concern respondents' comfort when combining career and family roles. The non-married, non-Italian-American women reported 24% more often than the Italian-American women that their career/educational activities added stress to relationships with their partners. The results previously mentioned found that these career-oriented women adhered to more traditional domestic roles. The stress that is found is consistent with the work of Merriam and Hyer (1984) and Coser and Rokoff (1985), who found that the continuance of traditional domestic roles in career-oriented women results in increased levels of stress. This calls for educational and counseling strategies to prevent and relieve this stress.

The Italian-American women had no conflict with each role separately, or with guilt that might arise from non-fulfillment of these roles. Yet, when asked if the combination of career/educational and family roles created conflict, 71% (7 out of 10) of the Italian-American women agreed. This is particularly important since 25% (less than 3 out of ten) of the non-Italian-American women agreed. This finding supports the proposed hypothesis and is consistent with the beliefs and works of researchers who acknowledge that this combination creates more conflict for Italian-American women than for non-Italian-American women (Balancio, 1986; Barolini, 1985; Davidson and Gordon, 1979; DeFiglio, 1986; Lurie, 1986; Martorella, 1982; Perrone, 1986; Scelsa, 1986; Sirey, 1982 and Sirey and Valerio, 1983). What this survey does not provide is support for their rationale as to why this conflict exists.

Lastly, the respondents were asked whether they would seek assistance if professional counseling services were provided to help them deal with career and family issues. The majority of both groups responded negatively, which means that more creative interventions are needed to help all women deal with family and career issues. This seems particularly necessary for achieving Italian-American women, since it has been depicted in this study that 71% acknowledge conflict, as opposed to 25% of non-Italian-American women who acknowledge conflict.

These findings demand that we ask more questions which focus on why this combination creates conflict for career-oriented Italian-American women. Workable solutions need to be found. We also want to find out more about the ramifications of this conflict for Italian Americans as a group. If the conflict is prevalent among this educational caliber of women, is it prevalent among other educational levels (high school, college, working women) as well and how does it affect the achievement and aspirations of these different groups of Italian-American women? These are just some of the questions that need to be explored. Exploring them will be the first step to understanding the conflicts facing Italian-American women, and the impact that family roles and values have on their aspirations.

References

Alba, R. D. (1985). *Italian Americans: Into the Twilight of Ethnicity*. Englewood Cliffs, New Jersey: Prentice Hall, Inc.

Balancio, D. M. (1986). *Education, Social class and Italian American Women Working*. Paper presented at the National Organization of Italian-American Women conference, 1987, New York, NY.

Bardwick, J. M. (1980). "The Seasons of a Woman's Life." In D. McGuigan (Ed.), *Women's Lives: New Theory, Research and Policy* (pp. 35–37) Ann Arbor, MI: University of Michigan.

Barolini, H. (Ed.). (1985). *The Dream Book: An Anthology of Writings by Italian-American Women*. New York: Schocken Books.

Covello, L. (1967). *The Social Background of the Italo-American School Child*. Leiden, Netherlands: E. J. Brill.

D'Andrea, V. (1983). "The Ethnic Factor and Role Choices of Women: Ella Grasso and Midge Costanza, Two Firsts for American Politics." In R. V. Pane (Ed.), *Italian-Americans in the Professions* (pp. 253-264). Staten Island, New York: American Italian Historical Association.

Davidson, L. and Gordon, L. K. (1979). *The Sociology of Gender*. Chicago: Rand McNally College Publishing Co.

DeFiglio, P. (1986). "Italian-American Women: Manicotti vs. Manhattan." *Heritage*, Autumn, 6, 12.

Ferber, M.A. (1982). "Women and Work: Issues of the 1980s." *The Journal of Women in Culture and Society*, 8(2), 273-298.

Gambino, R. (1974). *Blood of My Blood*. NY: Anchor Press, Doubleday and Co., Inc.

Lewin, E. and Damrell, J. (1978). "Female Identity and Career Pathways: Post-Baccalaureate Nurses Ten Years After." *Sociology of Work and Occupations*, 5(1), 31-54.

Lurie, T. (1986). 'Italian-American Women: Old Values, New Goals." In J. Giordano, (Ed.), *The Italian-American Catalog: A Lavish and Loving Celebration and Guide to Culture, History, Neighborhoods, Family, Food and Drink* (pp. 21-24). NY: Lakeville Press.

Mann, L. (1986). "Ethnotherapy with Italian Americans: An Evaluation of Short-Term Group Explorations of Ethnic Identification and Self-Esteem." Unpublished doctoral dissertation, New York University, NY.

Martorella, R. (1982). "Italian-American Women: Strategies for Coping with Value Conflict, Family, and with Work." Paper presented at a meeting of the Italian American Institute to Foster Higher Education, New York.

Merriam, S. B. and Hyer, P., (1984). Changing Attitudes of Women Towards Family-Related Tasks in Young Adulthood. *Sex Roles*, 10(9/10), 825-835.

Perrone, J. (1986). "Italian-American Students at CUNY: A Psychoeducational Profile." Unpublished manuscript, Italian American Institute of the City University of New York.

Regan, M.C. and Roland, H. E. (1982). "Rearranging Family and Career Priorities: Professional Women and Men in the Eighties." *Journal of Marriage and Family Therapy*, 4, 985-991.

Rotunno, M. and McGoldrick, M. (1982). "Italian Families." In M. McGoldrick, J. K. Pearce, and J. Giordano (Eds.) *Ethnicity and Family Therapy* (pp. 340-363). NY: Guilford Press.

Scelsa, J. V. (1986). "Italian-American Women: Their Families and American Education, Systems in Conflict." In R. C. Caporale (Ed.), *Italian Americans Through the Generations* (pp. 169-171). Staten Island, NY: American Italian Historical Association.

Sirey, A. R. (1982). "The Achieving Italian-American Woman: Assessing Traditional Values and Changing Sex Roles." Paper presented at a meeting of the Italian American Institute to Foster Higher Education, New York.

Sirey, A. R. and Valerio, A. M. (1983). "Italian-American Women: Women in Transition." *Ethnic Groups, 4*, 177-186.

Van Dusen, R. A. and Sheldon E. B. (1976). "The Perspective." *American Psychologist*, 31(2), 106-116.

APPENDIX

BACKGROUND DATA:

In order to obtain a better understanding of individual backgrounds as they effect career and family attitudes, please provide the following information. Circle or check off your responses, or write in your response in the spaces provided.

Age _____

Martial status (circle as many as apply):

S   M   D   W   SEP   S/Partnered (defined as having a serious boyfriend or involved in some kind of long-term relationship)

Check as many as apply:

I live
- ☐ alone
- ☐ with husband
- ☐ with mother
- ☐ with friend
- ☐ with father
- ☐ with child
- ☐ with partner
- ☐ with children

I consider myself (check as many as apply, but at least one from each category):

Ethnicity	☐ White	☐ Black	☐ Hispanic	☐ Asian
	☐ American	☐ American Indian	☐ Italian American	☐ Jewish
	☐ Italian	☐ Irish	☐ Other _____	
Religion	☐ Catholic	☐ Protestant	☐ Jewish	☐ Other _____
Generation	☐ Immigrant	☐ First generation	☐ Second generation	☐ Third generation

My mother considers herself (check as many as apply, but at least one from each category):

Ethnicity	☐ White	☐ Black	☐ Hispanic	☐ Asian
	☐ American	☐ American Indian	☐ Italian American	☐ Jewish
	☐ Italian	☐ Irish	☐ Other _____	
Religion	☐ Catholic	☐ Protestant	☐ Jewish	☐ Other _____
Generation	☐ Immigrant	☐ First generation	☐ Second generation	☐ Third generation

My father considers himself (check as many as apply, but at least one from each category):

Ethnicity	☐ White	☐ Black	☐ Hispanic	☐ Asian
	☐ American	☐ American Indian	☐ Italian American	☐ Jewish
	☐ Italian	☐ Irish	☐ Other _____	
Religion	☐ Catholic	☐ Protestant	☐ Jewish	☐ Other _____
Generation	☐ Immigrant	☐ First generation	☐ Second generation	☐ Third generation

INCOME LEVEL:

A. Parents income level:

☐ under 10,000   ☐ 10,000–19,999   ☐ 20,000–29,999
☐ 30,000–39,999   ☐ 40,000–49,999   ☐ over 50,000

B. If married, your present income level:

☐ under 10,000   ☐ 10,000–19,999   ☐ 20,000–29,999
☐ 30,000–39,999   ☐ 40,000–49,999   ☐ over 50,000

C. If married, what percentage of your family income do you earn yourself?:

☐ 0%–25%   ☐ 25%–50%   ☐ 50%–75%   ☐ over 75%

EDUCATION AND OCCUPATION (circle correct number):

Level of schooling completed by mother:

Grade school: 1   2   3   4   5   6   7   8
High school: 9   10   11   12
College: 1   2   3   4
Graduate school: M.A., M.S., etc. / J.D., PH.D., M.D. etc.

Level of schooling completed by father

Grade school: 1   2   3   4   5   6   7   8
High school: 9   10   11   12
College: 1   2   3   4
Graduate school: M.A., M.S., etc. / J.D., PH.D., M.D. etc.

Level of schooling completed by partner:

Grade school: 1   2   3   4   5   6   7   8
High school: 9   10   11   12
College: 1   2   3   4
Graduate school: M.A., M.S., etc. / J.D., PH.D., M.D. etc.

Who gave you educational or career guidance in high school (check all that apply)?:

☐ Clergyman   ☐ Guidance counselor   ☐ Family   ☐ Friends   ☐ Teachers

Who gave you educational or career guidance in college (check all that apply)?:

☐ Clergyman   ☐ Guidance counselor   ☐ Family   ☐ Friends   ☐ Teachers

Occupation of mother_____
Occupation of father_____
Occupation of partner_____
Your occupation_____

Approximately how many hours per day do you spend in a career and/or educational role?:

☐ 0 to 5   ☐ 5 to 10   ☐ 10 to 15

Approximately how many hours per day do you spend in a domestic role?:

☐ 0 to 5   ☐ 5 to 10   ☐ 10 to 15

SURVEY ON CAREER AND FAMILY ATTITUDES

Instructions: Please respond to each of the following statements in terms of the extent to which each describes your general feeling on career and family issues. In responding to these statements, please keep the following in mind:

- There are no right or wrong answers or responses to these statements. This inventory is simply designed to get a description of your general feelings about career and family issues.
- Each response should be an independent judgment. That is, your response to one question should not be influenced by your response to any other questions.
- Work through these questions quickly and record your initial responses.
- Please circle the number on the right of the statement that best describes your general feeling about the question.

Use the following scale:

 5 = you *agree strongly* with the statement.
 4 = you *agree* with the statement.
 3 = the statement *does not apply* to you and your lifestyle.
 2 = you *disagree* with the statement.
 1 = you *disagree strongly* with the statement.

DOMESTIC ROLE (circle one):

5	4	3	2	1	
Strongly agree	Agree	Does not apply	Disagree	Strongly disagree	

If I could afford to I would hire domestic help to take care of my chores and/or children in order to pursue my career and/or education	5	4	3	2	1
My role as a working woman and/or student impinges excessively on my role as a mother and or wife/partner	5	4	3	2	1
I plan on having children	5	4	3	2	1
It's best to stop working when you have children	5	4	3	2	1
It's best to stay home until children start grade school	5	4	3	2	1
I am or will be responsible for the caring and rearing of the children	5	4	3	2	1
My family plans are more important than my career plans	5	4	3	2	1

If I had an important project due at work and my child was sick, I would (check one):

☐ Call a relative to come care for the child.

☐ Take the child to the babysitter, describe the illness and procedures to take if the condition worsens.

☐ Take the day off from work.

☐ Ask my spouse/partner to take the day off from work to care for the child.

☐ Undecided.

Who holds the dominant role in your parent's home?   ☐ Mother ☐ Father ☐ Equal

Who is responsible for running the household in your
parent's home?   ☐ Mother ☐ Father ☐ Equal

Who is responsible for caring and rearing the children
in your parent's home?   ☐ Mother ☐ Father ☐ Equal

My mother worked when I was in grade school: ☐ Yes   ☐ No   ☐ Part-time

Who is considered the provider and head of the household?   ☐ Mother ☐ Father ☐ Equal

Who has more say about family matters?   ☐ Mother ☐ Father ☐ Equal

CAREER ROLES (circle one):

5	4	3	2	1	
Strongly agree	Agree	Does not apply	Disagree	Strongly disagree	

My role as wife/mother/partner/daughter impinges excessively on my role as a working woman/student	5	4	3	2	1
I often feel guilty because I'm not able to be the kind of wife/mother/ partner/daughter I'd like to be	5	4	3	2	1
My career plans are more important than having a family	5	4	3	2	1
I feel my admittance to law school was luck	5	4	3	2	1
I would prefer to have a job in my neighborhood or county	5	4	3	2	1
I would live apart from my maiden family in order to pursue my career	5	4	3	2	1
The combination of career and/or educational and family responsibility creates conflict for me	5	4	3	2	1
I would seek assistance if my school/employer provided professional counseling services to help me deal with career/family issues	5	4	3	2	1
The nature of my career and/or educational disciple often conflicts with my values and role expectations	5	4	3	2	1
I feel my admittance to law school was due to my previous accomplishments	5	4	3	2	1
I feel that my career and/or educational aspirations would be easier to attain if I were of another ethnic group	5	4	3	2	1

What is the single most important thing you feel you miss in family life as a result of being a working woman and/or student? _____

RELATIONSHIPS (circle one):

5	4	3	2	1	
Strongly agree	Agree	Does not apply	Disagree	Strongly disagree	

My career/education has curtailed my opportunities to establish
  intimate relationships   5 4 3 2 1

My parents are supportive of my career and educational plans   5 4 3 2 1

My parents think I spend too much time outside the family   5 4 3 2 1

I find it difficult to meet my parent's expectations   5 4 3 2 1

My parents think I should settle down and have children   5 4 3 2 1

My parents are uncomfortable with my decision to work outside the home   5 4 3 2 1

Rank from 1-8 the importance of the following things in your life:

☐ having children ☐ responsibility to spouse/partner ☐ education   ☐ career

☐ housework ☐ responsibility to family ☐ being home with children ☐ leisure time

If you answered partnered or married, please answer the following questions.
All others indicate your responses as if you were married.

My spouse/partner participates in 50% of the domestic chores   5 4 3 2 1

I am responsible for the day-to-day operations of my household   5 4 3 2 1

My partner/spouse supports my decision to have career   5 4 3 2 1

My spouse/partner would feel threatened if I outranked him in
  occupational status and/or career accomplishments   5 4 3 2 1

My spouse/partner would feel threatened if I earned more money than he did   5 4 3 2 1

My spouse/partner would relocate to advance my career   5 4 3 2 1

My involvement in a career/educational activities has added stress to my
  relationship with my spouse/partner   5 4 3 2 1

PART THREE
Italian-American High School Students in New York City

Statistical Profile of Educational Attainment Including High School Dropout Rate Indicators for Italian-American and Other Race/Ethnic Populations: United States, New York State and New York City

JOSEPH V. SCELSA
VINCENZO MILIONE

INTRODUCTION

The graduation of high school students is a major priority of our education system[1]. Achieving the minimal proficiency of a high school diploma is critical for entering the labor market, as well as for developing specialized careers through higher post secondary education. Standards of high school graduation performance that were acceptable in the past decades no longer apply. Many students are still dropping out of high school. Within some communities the proportion of students dropping out of high school before graduation is alarmingly high.[2] These communities face a continuing pattern of low education levels since parents' educational attainment directly influences the next generation's academic achievements. Besides addressing the overall issues of the quality and quantity of the delivery of education services, individual communities can work with their members to adjust community culture and lifestyles to encourage high school retention.

Population data on high school dropout statistics when collected are very limited to racial affirmative action categories. Data stratified by ethnic class within these racial categories are not available. In order to estimate the dropout rates within a particular ethnic population a mathematical model was developed by the John D. Calandra Italian American Institute using census data and New York City Board of Education dropout statistics. The Calandra Model was initially applied to estimate Italian-American high school dropout rates as compared to the other race/ethnic populations.[3] This study reports on the distinction between the high school dropout patterns of Italian-American students compared to other race/ethnic groups.

THE CALANDRA HIGH SCHOOL DROPOUT INDICATOR MODEL

The Calandra High School Dropout Indicator Model (HSDIM) was developed by using 1980 census data and 1987–88 New York City Board of Education dropout statistics.

CENSUS POPULATION DATA

The 1980 Census of Population and Housing data was compiled for estimating population size.[4] Italian-American ethnicity data was reported based on the respondents self identification of family ancestry. This included single as well as multiple Italian-American ancestry. The other racial categories of American Indian, Asian/Pacific Islander, Black and Hispanic were reported through self-identification of racial class.

For each census respondent, the highest education grade was identified and whether the respondent completed this grade. The respondent who did not complete any grade from nine to twelve years of school is considered a potential high school dropout. In order to approximate a four year high school cohort peer group, only respondents between eighteen to twenty-one years old were included. This cohort group would have attended high school grades together from the ages of fifteen to eighteen years old in 1977 to 1980. In addition, the eighteen to twenty-one year group would also include those who may have completed their high school grades at a later age beyond eighteen years. The eighteen to twenty-one-year-old group is the best cross-sectional profile of those respondents who completed their high school education on time as well as those respondents who completed their high school education after the age of eighteen.

NEW YORK CITY BOARD OF EDUCATION DATA

The other database used in the Calandra HSDIM is data collected and summarized by the New York City Board of Education for racial minority groups and the White population[5]. The data included the number of dropouts in grades nine to twelve, and the number of students enrolled in these grades predominantly within the ages of fifteen to twenty-one.

More than 13% of the high school population is between eighteen and twenty-one.

The New York City Board of Education defines the annual dropout percentage as the number of students dropping out divided by the total number of enrolled students:

Annual Dropout Percentage =
[First-time Dropouts/Population Enrollment Base] x 100

The annual survival rate is calculated from the annual dropout percentage as follows:

Annual Survival Rate = 100% – Annual Dropout Percentage

The annual survival rate represents the probability of the high school population staying in school within each year of high school. Over the four years of high school the projected survival rate is defined as average yearly rate multiplied by itself four times.

Four Year Projected Survival Rate = [Annual Survival Rate/100] [4]

The four year projected dropout rate is then calculated by subtracting the four year projected survival rate from a 100% graduation rate:

Four Year Projected Dropout Rate = 1 – [Four Year Projected Survival Rate]

The four year projected dropout percentage is equal to the four year projected dropout rate as a decimal number times 100 for a measure of percentage.

Four Year Projected Dropout Percentage =
[Four Year Projected Dropout Rate] x 100

The Board of Education reported the four year projected dropout percentages for minority groups that include Alaskan Native/American Indian, Asian/Pacific Islander, Hispanic, and Black (non-Hispanic) students. The four year projected dropout percentage was also calculated for White (non-Hispanic) students.

MODEL CALIBRATION

The Calandra HSDIM estimates a relational correlation between the percentage that do not finish a high school grade as reported in the census data and the summary counts of high school dropouts reported by the Board of Education.

The high school grade completion (HSGC) rate of high school students in the 1977 to 1980 cohort is determined by:

$$HSGC_g = [DNF/P]_g$$

Where:

$HSGC_g$ = High school grade completion rate for ethnic group g.
P_g = Population between 18–21 years old for ethnic group g.
DNF_g = Population of 18–21 year olds who did not finish high school grade for race/ethnic group g.

Assuming a linear relation between the high school grade completion rate of each ethnic group as reported by the census and their high school dropout rate (HSDR) as reported by the New York City Board of Education, we have:

$$[HSDR]_g = A \times f[HSGC]_g + B$$

Where A and B are correlation coefficients that are estimated by regression analysis, the resultant regression model yielded the following coefficients with a goodness of fit, $R^2 = .83$:

$$[HSDR]_g = .305 \times [DNF]_g + 3.35$$

The above equation provides an estimate of between group variation in the dropout rate for ethnic group, g. The small number between group data points results in a large within group variation. The within group pattern is then adjusted by multiplying the estimated high school dropout rate for ethnic group g, belonging to racial group G, $HSDR_G$ divided by the model estimate for racial group G, $HSDR^*_G$.

$$[HSDI]_g = [HSDR]_g \times [HSDR/HSDR^*]_G$$

The high school dropout indicator (HSDI) is calculated for each race/ethnic group and compared to the Board of Education data (see Figure A). The high degree of correlation between the estimated and actual high school dropout rates enables the model to be used to project Italian-American dropout statistics. The Italian-American (IA) dropout rate is calculated by:

$$[HSDR]_{IA} = .305 \times [\% \, DNF]_{IA} + 3.35$$

Where the dropout indicator for Italian-American students within the White (W) student population is:

$$[HSDI]_{IA} = [HSDR]_{IA} \times [HSDR_w / HSDR^*_w]$$

The dropout rate for White (non-Italian-American) students (WNIA) is then:

$$[HSDR]_{WNIA} = .305 \times [\%DNF]_{WNIA} + 3.35$$

and the dropout indicator is:

$$[HSDA]_{WNIA} = [HSDR]_{WNIA} \times [HSDR_w / HSDR^*_w]$$

This model can be used to project Italian-American high school dropout patterns within the White high school community. The model implicitly captures education behavior in adjusting high school grade completion rates to high school dropout patterns (see Figure A).

FIGURE A. *New York City Board of Education Four Year Dropout Rate vs. Calandra Dropout Rate Model by Race and Ethnicity*

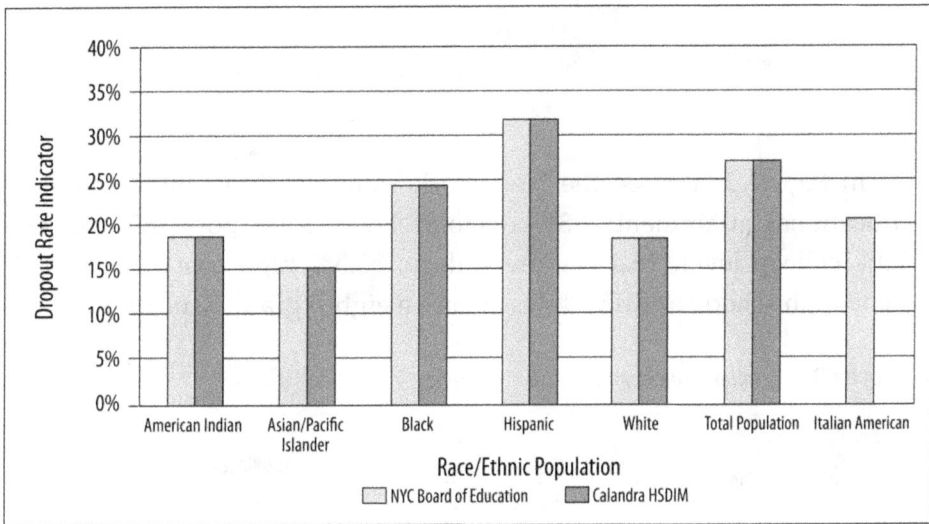

ITALIAN-AMERICAN EDUCATIONAL ATTAINMENT

Prior to presenting the results of applying the Calandra Model to estimating high school dropout rate for the Italian-American community, we present a profile of Italian-American educational attainment for those respondents twenty-one years or older. The first three illustrations—Figures 1, 2, and 3—profile the range of Italian-American educational attainment for the United States (US), New York State (NYS) and New York City (NYC), utilizing 1980 census data. In Figure 1, we present the national profile of Italian Americans: 1.5% doctoral level (8+ years of college); 6.7% post-graduate level (4–7 years of college); 6.8% college level; 18.7% some college; 35.2% high school only; 15.6% some high school; and 15.5% less than an eighth grade education.

FIGURE 1. *US Italian-American Educational Profile*

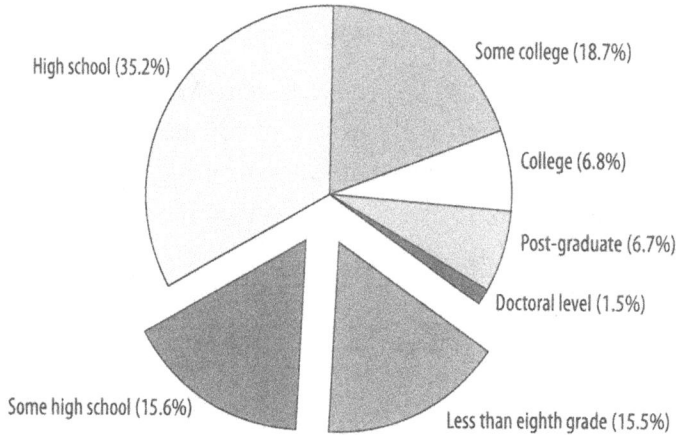

In Figure 2, we see the New York State profile of Italian-American educational attainment: 1.3% doctoral level; 5.5% post-graduate level; 6.0% college level; 16.2% some college; 35.3% high school only; 16.8% some high school; and 18.8% less than an eighth grade education.

FIGURE 2. *NYS Italian-American Educational Profile*

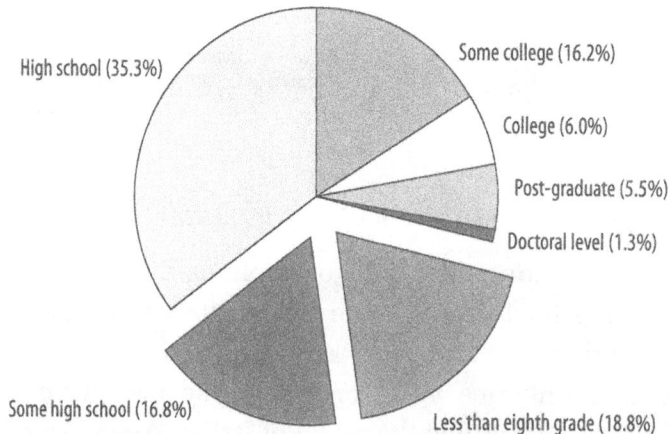

In Figure 3 we present the New York City data for Italian-American educational attainment. Here Italian Americans have: 1.4% doctoral level; 4.5% post-graduate level; 5.3% college only; 12.5% some college; 32.3% high school; 19.0% some high school; and 24.9% less than an eighth grade education.

FIGURE 3. *NYC Italian-American Educational Profile*

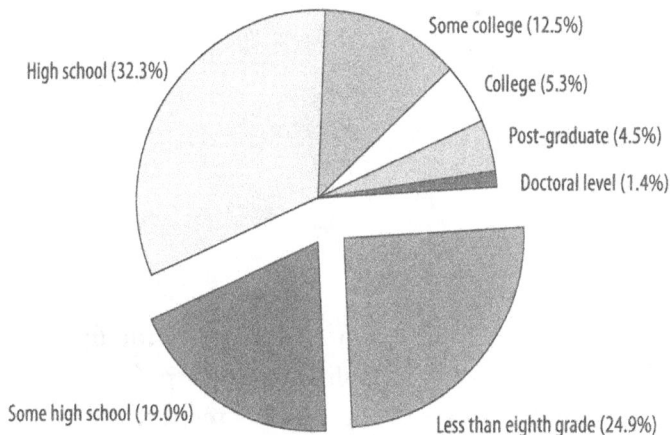

On further examination of these three charts, one starts to get a sense of the educational attainment trend for Italian Americans in the nation, state and the local New York City area. We see that outside of New York City, Italian Americans have higher educational attainment levels, both nationally and statewide, at the high school level and beyond, with many more Italian Americans going to college, graduating from college and going on to attend graduate schools. However, the doctoral level is consistent in the three geographical areas.

HIGH SCHOOL POPULATION BY RACE AND ETHNICITY

In Figures 4, 5, and 6 we present the high school population by race and ethnicity for the US, NYS, and NYC. Figure 4 shows that Italian Americans make up 5.5% of the national high school age population, which is comparable to Hispanics at 6.3% and less than Blacks at 13.3%.

FIGURE 4. *US High School Population by Race and Ethnicity*

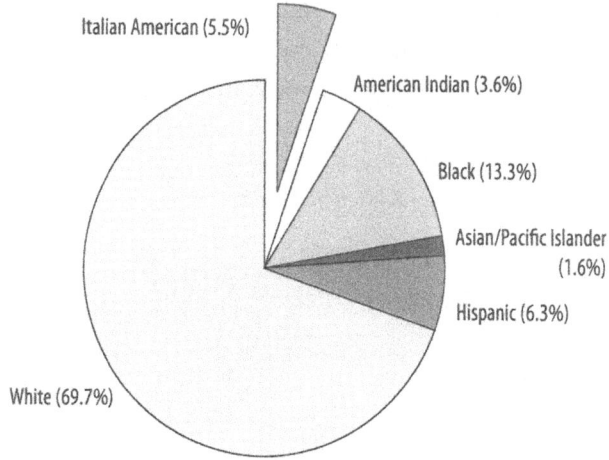

Italian American (5.5%)
American Indian (3.6%)
Black (13.3%)
Asian/Pacific Islander (1.6%)
Hispanic (6.3%)
White (69.7%)

In Figure 5 we find that Italian Americans made up 17.3% of the NYS high school age population, which is a larger piece of the pie than Hispanics or Blacks who have 9.0% and 14.8%, respectively.

FIGURE 5. *NYS High School Population by Race and Ethnicity*

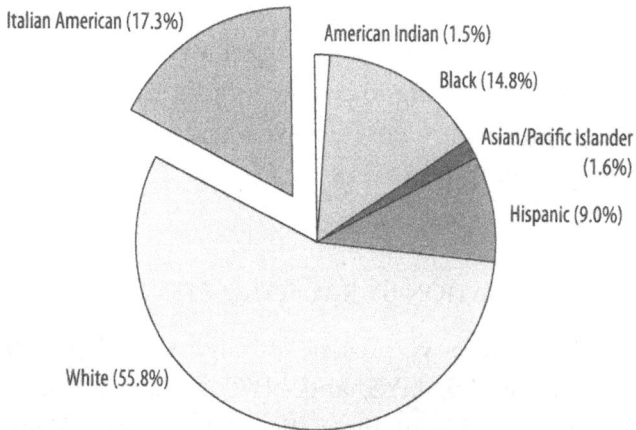

Italian American (17.3%)
American Indian (1.5%)
Black (14.8%)
Asian/Pacific Islander (1.6%)
Hispanic (9.0%)
White (55.8%)

In Figure 6 we find that Italian Americans make up 14.9% of the NYC high school age population. Even though this is a smaller piece of the pie than Hispanics (20.9%) and Blacks (29.8%), they make up a full one-third of the NYC high school White population.

FIGURE 6. *NYC High School Population by Race and Ethnicity*

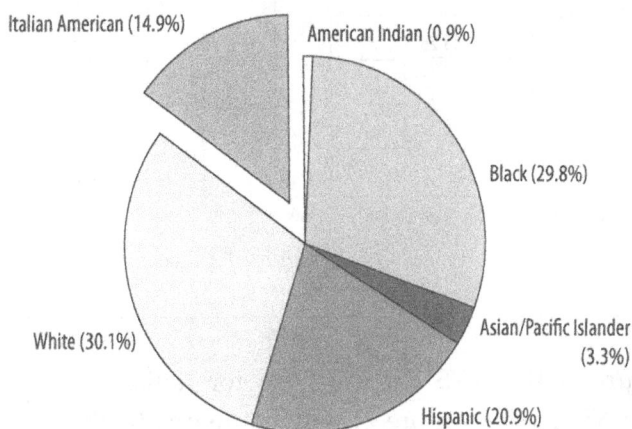

HIGH SCHOOL DROPOUT RATE INDICATORS

In Figures 7, 8, and 9 we present the four year high school dropout rate indicators by race and ethnicity for the US, NYS, and NYC. The bar-graphs in these figures were constructed utilizing 1980 census data based on responses of individuals who did not finish high school, grades nine through twelve. The census data was correlated with the 1987–1988 New York City Board of Education data in order to forecast Italian-American dropout statistics.

In Figure 7, the US dropout rate of Italian Americans is approximately 19.07%, which is less than other Whites and ranks fourth, comparable to American Indians. Hispanics have the highest dropout rate with Blacks second. Asian/Pacific Islanders have the lowest dropout rate.

FIGURE 7. *US High School Dropout Rate Indicator by Race and Ethnicity*

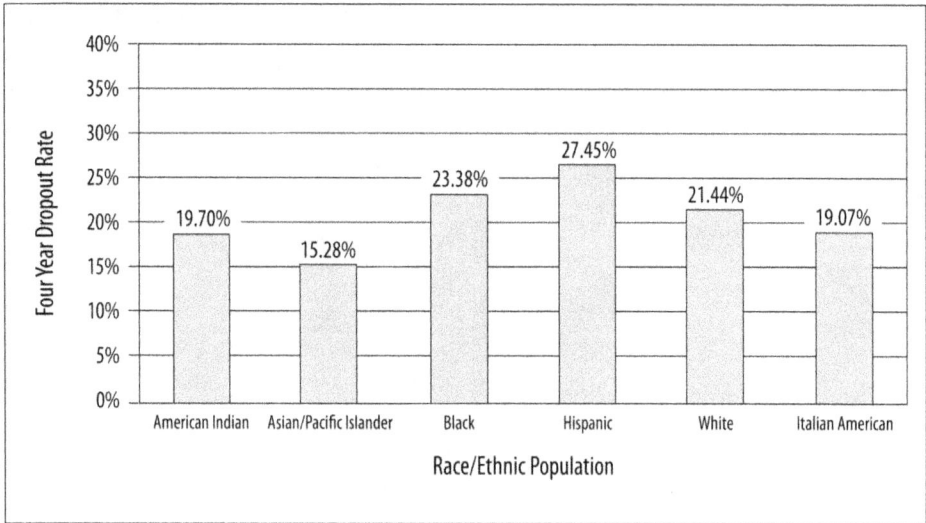

In Figure 8, the NYS dropout rate for Italian Americans decreases slightly, 18.65%, which more closely compares to the rest of the White population. Hispanics, again, have the highest dropout rate, with Blacks second and Asian/Pacific Islanders the lowest.

FIGURE 8. *NYS High School Dropout Rate Indicator by Race and Ethnicity*

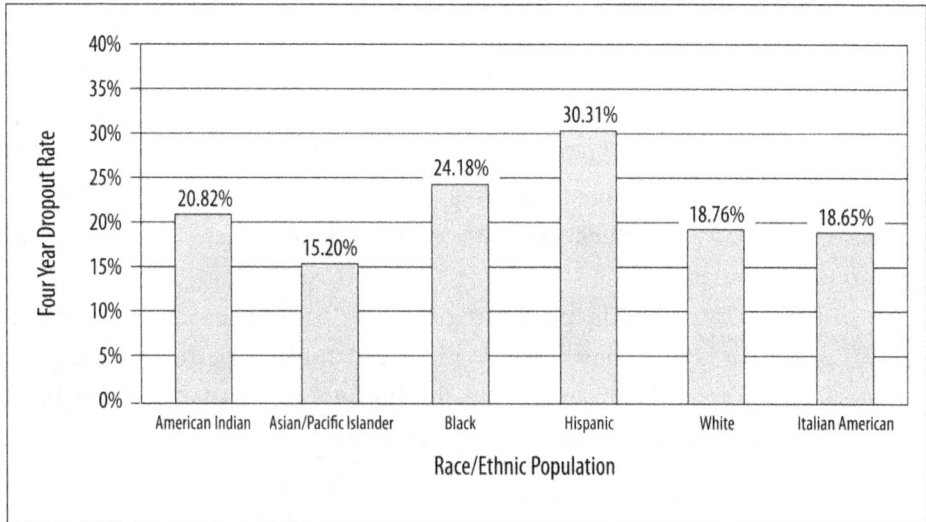

In Figure 9, which depicts the NYC high school dropout rate indicator by race and ethnicity, a different picture emerges for Italian Americans. Here they jump to the third highest dropout rate with 20.65%, or almost 21%, one out of five who do not finish high school. Hispanics again have the highest dropout rate with 31.78%; Blacks are second highest with 24.54%; American Indians are fourth with 18.89%; White are fifth with 18.55% and Asian/Pacific Islanders are the lowest again with 15.07%.

FIGURE 9. *NYC High School Dropout Rate Indicator by Race and Ethnicity*

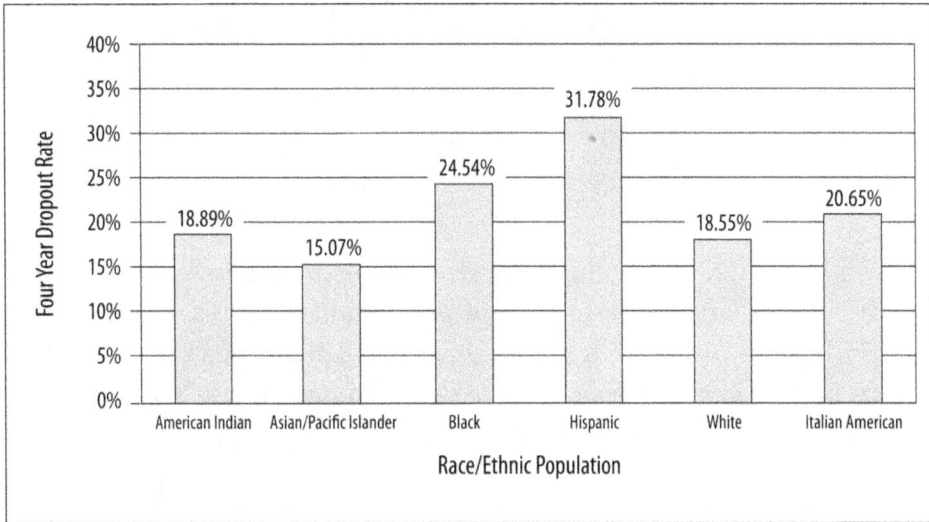

DEMOGRAPHIC ANALYSIS OF ITALIAN-AMERICAN HIGH SCHOOL DROPOUT RATES

We have conducted further research on the demographics of Italian Americans to understand these overall dropout rates. In Figure 10, pertaining to gender, we see that Italian-American males make up a greater number of the dropouts in NYS and NYC than they do in the US, where females represent the higher percentage.

FIGURE 10. *Italian-American High School Dropout Rate Indicator by Gender*

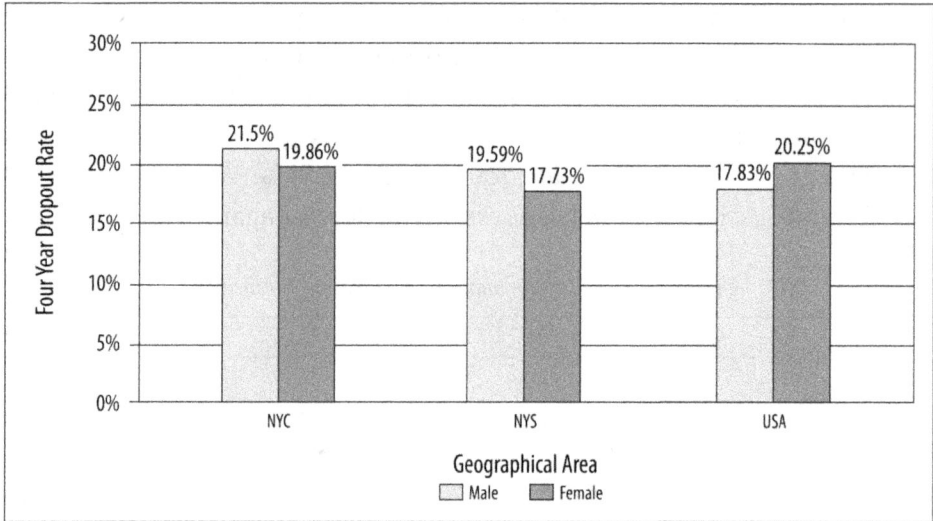

In Figure 11, which illustrates student generation, we see that the foreign born Italian-American student population in NYS and NYC is more likely to drop out of high school than their US born counterparts. However, in the US as a whole, the foreign born and native born have about the same high school dropout rate.

FIGURE 11. *Italian-American High School Dropout Rate Indicator by Student Generation*

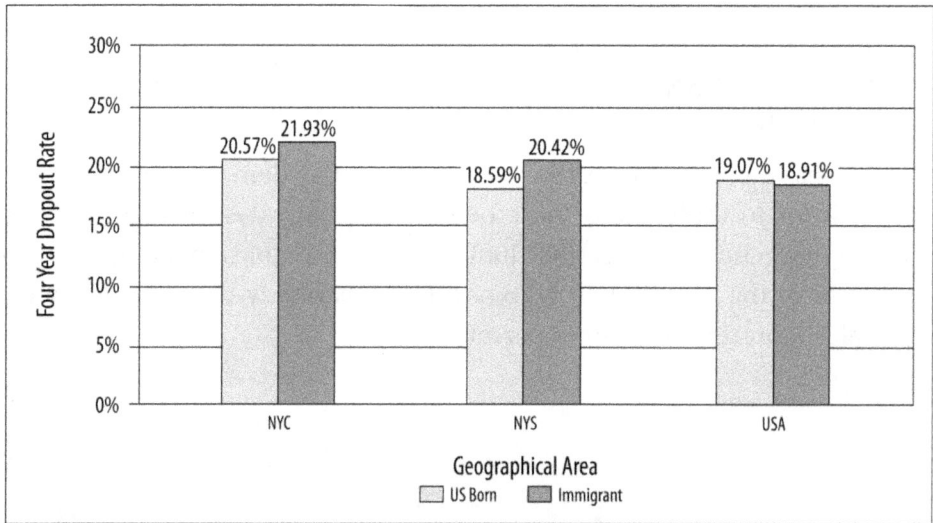

In Figure 12, head of household generation, we examine the dropout rate in relation to the head of household being born in the US or abroad. Italian-American students in NYS and NYC with a head of household born in the US have a higher dropout rate than those with a foreign born head of household. Again, in the US as a whole, the picture for both is about the same.

FIGURE 12. *Italian-American High School Dropout Rate Indicator by Head of Household Generation*

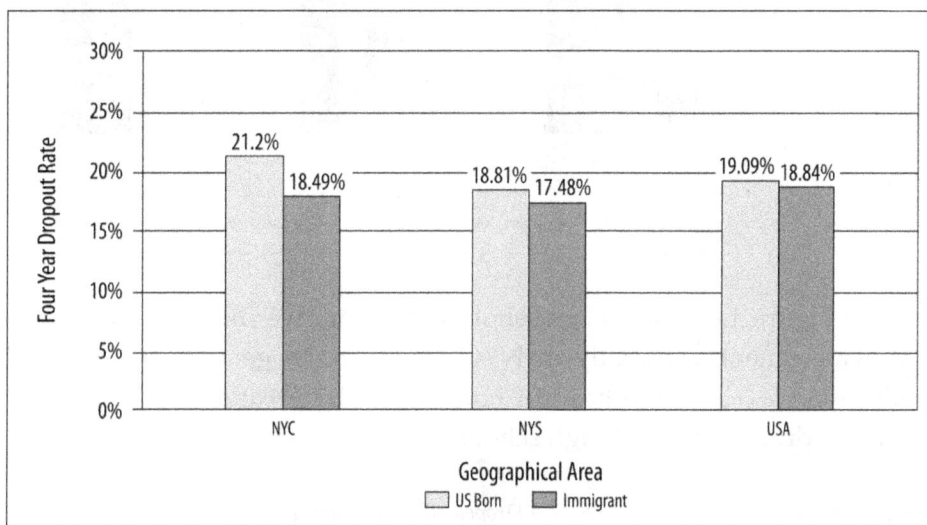

In Figures 13 and 14 we look at the Italian-American dropout rate with respect to family income and educational attainment levels. Then in Figure 15 we examine the combined effects of these two variables on the dropout rate.

In Figure 13, family income, we find that the highest dropout rate in NYC is in families reporting the lowest income level per year. Yet, outside of NYC (in NYS and the US), the dropout rate is higher in the middle income range. In general, however, we see an inverse relationship between the level of family income and dropouts — the lower the income the higher the dropout rate.

FIGURE 13. *Italian-American High School Dropout Rate Indicator by Family Income*

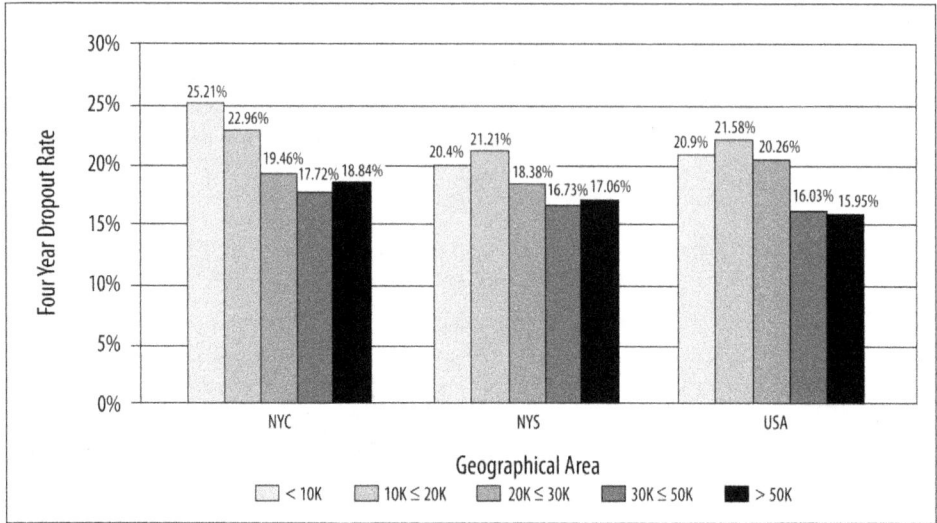

In Figure 14, head of household education, we find a similar pattern of achievement, especially in NYC and NYS. In general, the lower the education levels of the head of household, the greater the chance of the student dropping out of high school.

FIGURE 14. *Italian-American High School Dropout Rate Indicator by Head of Household Education*

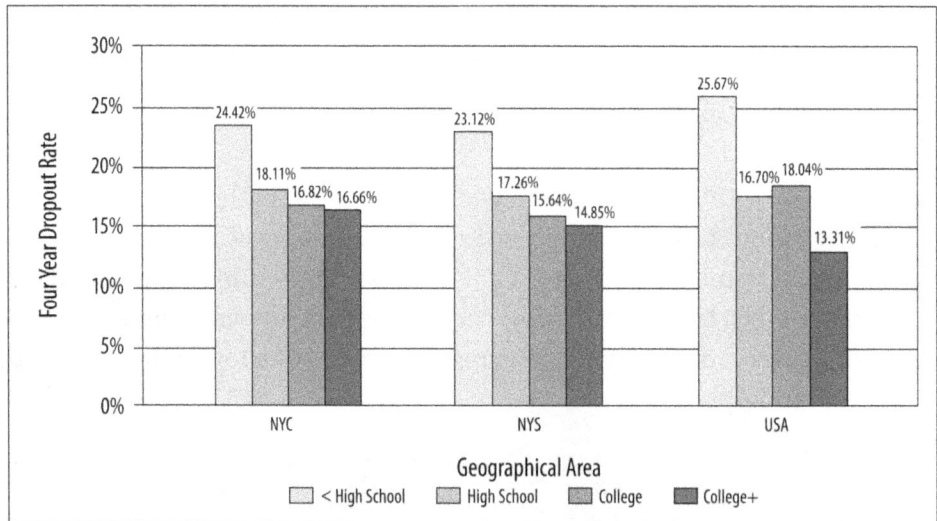

In the last graph, Figure 15, we find a consistent trend for the nation, state and city in terms of Italian-American dropout by combining factors related to lower income levels and parental lack of education. The lower the income and educational levels, the higher the dropout rate. In order to get a better understanding of this educational underclass we define this disadvantaged high school population as those students with a head of household earning less than $20,000 a year who has an educational achievement level of less than high school education. Nearly one out of three in this disadvantaged group do not complete high school compared to the almost one out of six in the advantaged group.

FIGURE 15. *Italian-American High School Dropout Rate Indicator, Disadvantaged vs. Advantaged*

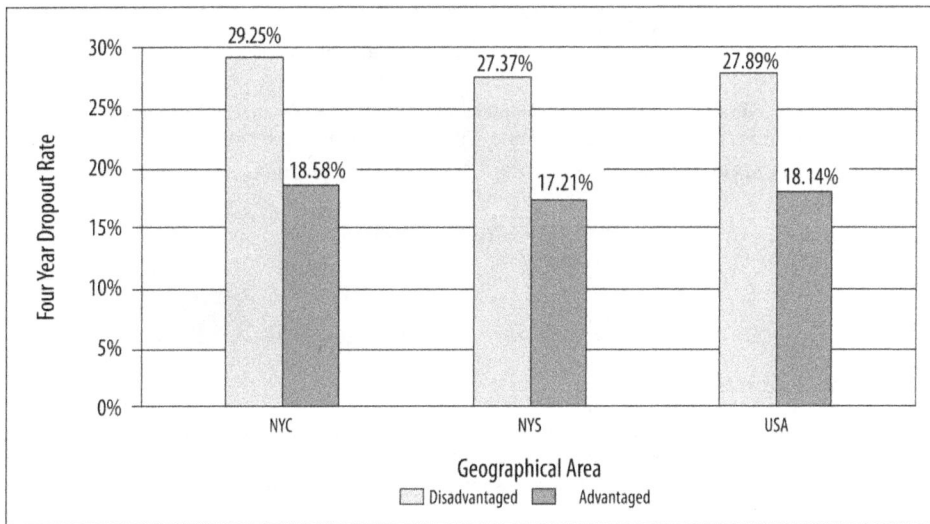

SUMMARY

In summary, the educational profile of Italian-American high school students that emerges is one that indicates that outside of NYC — in the US and the rest of NYS — Italian Americans have higher educational attainment levels. With respect to the high school dropout rate, Italian Americans are at, or below, the rest of the White population in the US and NYS. The one glaring exception is NYC, where one out of five Italian-American students do not complete high school, giving them the third highest dropout rate of 21%, with a substantial portion of this population dropping out of high school at a rate of one out of three.

Our research indicates that the profile of the Italian-American drop-out in New York City as well as New York State is: one who is likely to be male, of a lower income level, and from a multigenerational family lacking educational achievement.

This educational profile of Italian Americans has given us an initial understanding of the depth of the dropout problem. What is needed is an actual count of Italian-American achievement levels so that we can better target services for this population.

Notes

1. Remarks prepared for delivery at press conference on 1989 State Education Performance Chart, L. F. Cavazos, US Secretary of Education, May 1989.
2. Youth Policy, Monthly Report on National Youth Programs and Issues, Vol. 12, No. 1, January 1990.
3. Statistical Profile of Italian-American Educational Attainment: National, State and Local Trends, John D. Calandra Italian American Institute, City University of New York, April 1990.
4. Census of Population and Housing: 1980, US Department of Commerce, Bureau of the Census, Washington DC, 1983.
5. The Annual Dropout Report, 1987–1988, NYC Board of Education, Opperman and Gambert, Office of Research and Evaluation, April 1989.

Acknowledgements

We appreciate the coordination and administrative assistance provided by Institute research staff members Diane Galemmo and Luisa Bellaviti. We also want to thank Carmine Pizzirusso, John Virdone, and Jianxun Hu, from the Institute's research unit, who contributed to the data compilation, analysis, and reporting.

Stress Patterns in Adolescents:
A Focus on Italian Americans

PIERRE TRIBAUDI
NANCY L. ZIEHLER

ABSTRACT

A pilot study exploring stress patterns in urban adolescents was conducted in one New York City public high school with a diverse student population. One hundred sixteen students completed a demographic questionnaire and three instruments designed by the authors to measure levels of perceived stress ("Stress and Worry Questionnaire"), actual stress ("How Much Stress is in Your Life Questionnaire") and symptomatology ("Effects of Stress on Your Life Questionnaire"). The present article will focus on forty-two Italian-American students who identified their ethnicity as Italian American (IA) or of mixed Italian-American ancestry (MixIA). These students were divided into four groups according to gender and ethnicity: IA males, IA females, MixIA males and MixIA females. In general, although perceived stress scores were in the mild range for the majority of students, the results yielded very high actual stress scores and symptomatology scores. Perceived stress and actual stress seemed to vary according to gender; symptomatology seemed to vary according to ethnicity and gender. Gender and ethnicity appear to be salient factors in the lives of IA teens, as IA males were found to have the highest actual stress scores, while IA females had the highest perceived stress and symptomatology scores. The data also suggested distinct demographic and stress patterns among the four groups. Implications for counseling, program planning and future research are discussed.

INTRODUCTION AND RESEARCH OBJECTIVE

Stress is a fact of life and a universal experience. Multiple stressors and varying degrees of stress affect all human beings throughout the life span. Although each stage of growth is characterized by a unique set of developmental tasks, concerns and crises,[1] it does seem that adolescents have become an increasingly vulnerable group over the last few years. Media accounts of deadly school massacres, teen suicides, substance abuse, eating disorders and academic problems have raised the country's awareness of a group in dire need of attention and assistance.

Italian-American adolescents are no exception. In 1990, for example, it was reported that Italian-American high school students "were found to have the third-highest dropout rate in New York City at 20.65%, just behind African Americans at 24.54% and Hispanics at 31.78%."[2] In a subsequent cross-cultural comparison of high school students, Italian Americans had the highest percentage of all groups who expressed a desire not to attend college and the lowest aspirations for attaining a graduate or professional degree.[3] Although the general public seemed shocked by these findings, Italian-American educators had long suspected a problem masked by outdated research comparisons based on race. As early as the mid-1960s, for example, sociologist S. L. Washburn cautioned researchers that "racial classification tells us very little."[4] In other words, classifying data according to a raw, physiognomic, attribute variable does not have the capacity to enlighten researchers about the interior processes experienced by individuals. Ethnicity, on the other hand, is an internal process endowed with "the capacity to give meaning to race."[5]

Thus, in an attempt to highlight the importance of ethnicity in the lives of Italian-American youth, community leaders cited numerous sociocultural factors to account for their lagging educational mobility. These included life in isolated ethnic enclaves, family obligations and the media's negative stereotyping of Italian Americans.[6] While environmental and social context appear to exert a negative influence on the educational aspirations of this group, a crucial piece of the portrait remains noticeably absent from the literature. To date, the interior experiences of Italian-American high school students have yet to be examined. An exploration of internal processes, such as adolescent stress, might broaden our current understanding of Italian-American teens residing in NYC as well as the stressors that interfere with their educational progress.

The purpose of this study, therefore, was to identify stress patterns in Italian-American high school students in the following three areas: (1) perceived stress, (2) actual stress and (3) symptomatology. Based upon a transactional model of life stress, stress is defined in terms of a transaction between the person and the environment.[7] According to this perspective, perceived stress is a subjective perception of threat; actual stress is a particular event or set of events experienced by an individual; and adaptational response is the effect of stress on the individual, and/or the various symptoms that can develop as a result of stress. In this model, the same event may affect individuals differently with regard to perceived stress, actual stress, as well as the duration and intensity of symptoms.

A review of the adolescent stress literature revealed several limitations. For example, most studies that labeled themselves "multicultural" performed only standard data comparisons of gender and race. Although these studies attempted to examine ethnicity, race and ethnicity were used synonymously. Consequently, all Asian teens were treated as a unified group, as were all Black, Hispanic and White adolescents. Furthermore, cultural differences were not taken into account because culturally sensitive instruments were lacking in this body of literature.[8]

In order to overcome these limitations and obtain a more comprehensive view of the individual, the authors expanded the term "multicultural" beyond the usual race and ethnicity variables to reflect the "total" person. For the purposes of this study, "multicultural" also included racial/ethnic identity, gender, generation, acculturation level, language use, religion/spirituality, birth order, family educational level, college/career plans, hobbies/recreational activities, ways of dealing with stress and self-assessment. To capture each of these variables and also sensitize the instrumentation to include contemporary environmental stressors (such as fear of school violence, discrimination, poverty, language difficulties, or the spread of AIDS), the authors designed an extensive demographic questionnaire, including a global self-assessment of generalized equilibrium (see Appendix A) and three surveys. The "Stress and Worry Questionnaire" measures perceived stress and amount of worry (see Appendix B). The "How Much Stress is in Your Life Questionnaire," adapted from the Holmes and Rahe stress scale,[9] inventories and rates actual stressful events (see Appendix C). Finally, the "Effects of Stress on Your Life Questionnaire," a symptom checklist, measures the various effects of stress both during the past week and past year (see Appendix D).

This research project permitted an in-depth demographic analysis of a small group of Italian-American adolescents and how they perceive, experience, and deal with stress. (Further multicultural comparisons, based on the entire sample, will be provided in a future publication.) As there is little data to support the hypotheses, we explored the following research questions: (a) Does global self-assessment of generalized equilibrium differ by gender and Italian-American ethnicity? (b) Does perceived stress differ by gender and Italian-American ethnicity? (c) Does exposure to actual stressful events differ by gender and Italian-American ethnicity? (d) Does symptomatology differ by gender and Italian-American ethnicity?

METHOD

PARTICIPANTS AND PROCEDURES

The study took place in a large public high school, located within an Italian/Italian-American ethnic enclave of New York City. While Italians and Italian Americans comprise approximately 38% of the pilot population, the majority of the student body is ethnically and racially diverse. Participants for the study were 116 seniors enrolled in seven Health Education classes during the spring 1998 semester.

The entire project integrated both data collection and a service delivery session. During the data collection session students completed the demographic questionnaire and three surveys. Of the initial 116 students, 3 surveys were not returned and data from 4 students were excluded due to strong suspicion of invalid responses and/or being overly incomplete. The final sample consisted of 109 students.

One week following the survey administration, all participants were given results from the "How Much Stress is in Your Life Questionnaire" and provided with a stress management workshop. Individual consultation and counseling was made available to anyone who desired additional follow-up.

Out of the 109 students, 42 identified themselves as Italian American. These students were divided into four groups according to gender and ethnicity. Among those students who identified themselves as exclusively Italian American, there were 10 IA males and 15 IA females. The mixed groups included students who identified themselves as being of mixed ethnicity, including Italian American. There were 8 MixIA males and 9 MixIA females. Their ages ranged from 16 to 18, with the majority being 17 years old. (Five percent were 16 years old; 63% were 17 years old; 32% were 18 years old.)

INSTRUMENTS

Demographic questionnaire. A 38-item questionnaire covered standard background questions, such as date of birth, sex, GPA, as well as questions regarding country of birth for three generations to maximize accuracy of racial background, ethnic background and generational status for each student. In addition, a number of questions explored how students preferred to identify themselves as individuals and group members. Two major questions, open-ended in nature, dealt with coping strategies. The first of these (question #36) asked "What is/are your favorite hobby/ recreational activity(s), while the second (question #37) requested students to "list the ways you deal with stress." Students' responses to the coping questions were tallied and several categories emerged from the data.

The question pertaining to hobbies and recreational activities yielded eleven categories. Each category was assigned a name, as indicated below, based on the hobbies and activities that comprised that category. These categories included, (1) physical: sports and exercise; (2) emotional: being with family; (3) mental: reading and studying; (4) spiritual: helping others; (5) PEMS (a combination of physical, emotional, mental and spiritual): art, dancing, drawing, photography, music and writing, (6) talking: talking on the phone; (7) social: going to clubs, parties and hanging out; (8) entertainment: games, video games, television and movies; (9) sleep; (10) escapist: drug and cigarette use; and (11) other: going to the beach, building cars, computer use, cooking, playing with children, interest in girls, sex, shopping, stamp collecting, travel and working.

The question regarding ways students deal or cope with stress also yielded eleven categories. These included, (1) physical: sports, exercise and cleaning; (2) emotional: cry, get angry, punch self, punch others, punch walls and scream; (3) mental: reading and thinking; (4) spiritual: meditation and reflection; (5) PEMS: dancing, drawing, knitting, music and writing; (6) talking; (7) social: going out; (8) entertainment: video games, television and movies; (9) sleep; (10) escapist: drug use, eating and smoking cigarettes; and (11) other: biting nails, computer use, sex, shopping, showering, staying alone and working.

A global self-assessment of generalized equilibrium (see question #38) was intended to elicit students' overall perception of their internal feeling state. This question used a Likert scale to rate answers ranging from 1 (feeling very calm/relaxed) through 6 (feeling very tense/nervous).

Many other questions were included to allow for a more diverse and comprehensive analysis and cannot be dealt with in the present article.

Stress and Worry Questionnaire. This 80-item questionnaire was developed to measure the amount of anticipated and perceived stress/worry about concerns and experiences that may or may not have occurred. The questions addressed a wide span of issues including academic, social, sexual, emotional, psychological, health, environmental and religious/ spiritual concerns. Answers on a Likert scale ranged from 1 (indicating no stress/no worry) through 5 (indicating severe stress/extreme worry).

Possible scores on the "Stress and Worry Questionnaire" ranged from 80 to 400 points. Scores between 80 and 120 (with corresponding means between 1.0 and 1.5) indicated no or very mild stress/no or very little worry; scores between 121 and 200 (with corresponding means between 1.51 and 2.5) indicated mild stress/a little worry; scores between 201 and 280 (with corresponding means between 2.51 and 3.5) indicated moderate stress/some worry; scores between 281 and 360 (with corresponding means between 3.51 and 4.5) indicated considerable stress/a lot of worry; and finally scores between 361 and 400 (with corresponding means between 4.51 and 5.0) indicated severe stress/extreme worry. Raw scores and mean scores were obtained for each student and each question, while raw scores and the grand mean were also obtained for each profile group.

How Much Stress Is In Your Life Questionnaire. The present authors revised the Holmes and Rahe stress scale, a measure of middle-class stress in adulthood, to reflect stressful aspects of adolescent development in contemporary urban life. This 50-item inventory measured actual stressors and scored them with weighted points (5 to 100 points) for each life stress event that was experienced during the past year. Respondents were automatically given points for four events that are routinely experienced by all students: birthdays, holidays, exams and the first day of class. Thus, the range of possible scores was between 100 points to 1,985 points. Scores below 250 indicated low stress; scores between 250 and 349 indicated mild stress; scores between 350 and 449 indicated moderate stress; scores between 450 and 600 indicated high stress; and finally scores above 600 indicated very high stress. In general, it is widely accepted that the higher the level of stress, the greater the potential of being negatively effected by various symptoms.

Effects Of Stress On Your Life Questionnaire. This questionnaire is a symptom checklist designed to measure the various effects of stress both during the past week and past year. Twenty-eight symptoms are divided into 5 categories: physical, emotional, mental, spiritual and high risk. Physical responses to stress were assessed with questions concerning the following six symptoms: headaches, sleeping too much or too little, eating too much or too little, stomach ailments, rapid heartbeat and nausea and/or dizziness. Emotional responses to stress were assessed with nine questions that tapped various feelings: tension/nervousness, sadness, depression, apprehension, anger, excessive worry, irritability/annoyance, unwanted feelings and loneliness. Four questions pertaining to mental symptoms included: feeling very tired, lack of concentration, forgetfulness and having unwanted thoughts. Spiritual symptoms of stress were assessed with two questions: feeling alienated from others and feeling that life is meaningless. Finally, seven questions assessed symptoms typically associated with a high degree of risk: fear of losing control, hearing voices, suicidal ideation, irrational thoughts, irrational feelings, not feeling like oneself and paranoia.

For each of the five categories, overall totals and means were obtained. This article will only address symptoms experienced during the past year, as yearly patterns are inherently more enduring than transient symptoms obtained during the past week alone.

RESULTS

DEMOGRAPHIC PROFILE

This section will present demographic profiles of the four groups of Italian-American students subdivided according to gender and ethnicity: IA males, IA females, MixIA males and MixIA females. Since spatial limitations precluded a full-scale discussion of the numerous variables considered in the demographic questionnaire (see Appendix A), we have chosen to focus on select variables due to their relevance to both our work as counselors/cultural specialists and issues pertaining to this article. Each profile consists of fourteen variables illustrated in Table 1.

Italian-American males (IA males). One hundred percent of the IA male group identified their race as White and their ethnicity as Italian American. Although 90% were born in the USA and 10% were born in Italy, 66.7% indicated that they identified with the USA and 33.3% identified with Italy. When asked to choose between four preferences referring to terms of self-identification, 50% preferred to be identified by ethnic background exclusively, 20% preferred both ethnic and racial identification equally, 30% preferred neither ethnic nor racial identification and no one preferred to be identified by race alone. A subsequent open-ended question, which asked students to write how they preferred to be identified, yielded the following findings: 62.5% preferred to be identified by ethnic background, 25% preferred to be identified by their name and 12.5% preferred to be identified by personal qualities. Again, no one expressed a desire to be identified by racial background alone.

With respect to the use of primary and secondary languages, 80% reported using English as their primary language, while 20% use Italian. Sixty percent were most comfortable with the English language, 30% were comfortable with both English and Italian equally and 10% were most comfortable with Italian. As for their family of origin, 30% of their parents were USA born, while 70% were born in Italy.

The GPA mean score for IA males was 2.75; 100% indicated that they planned to attend college. Without exception, all group members selected the physical category as their favorite hobby/recreational activity. In terms of dealing with stress, they responded with a tie between the physical and other categories. Finally, on the global self-assessment of generalized equilibrium, a mean score of 2.7 for IA males fell within the range of feeling calm/relaxed to a little calm/relaxed.

Italian-American females (IA females). Like their male counterparts, all IA females identified their race as White and their ethnicity as Italian American. Also, relatively similar to the IA males, 93.3% were USA born and 6.7% were born in Italy. However, unlike the IA males, 91.7% identified with the USA, while only 8.3% identified with Italy. When asked to choose one of four terms relating to self-identification, the responses of IA females differed markedly from IA males, except for racial identification. Thus, 26.7% preferred to be identified by ethnic background exclusively, 33.3% preferred to be identified by both ethnic and racial background equally, 40% preferred neither ethnic nor racial self-identification and no one preferred to be identified by race alone. IA females also differed from IA males in their response to the open-ended follow-up question, where 44.4% wrote that they preferred to be identified by ethnic background, 11.1% preferred to be identified by their name and 44.4% preferred to be identified by personal qualities. Again, none of the IA female group expressed a preference to be identified by their racial background.

Primary language and comfort with language was reported as follows: 73.3% use English as their primary language, while 26.7% use Italian; 92.9% indicated that they were most comfortable using the English language, 7.1% reported equal comfort when using their bilingual skills (English and Italian) and none of the IA females felt most comfortable using Italian exclusively. Concerning their parents' country of birth, 46.2% of their parents were USA born, while 53.8% were born in Italy.

The GPA mean score for IA females, at 3.23, was considerably higher than their male counterparts and 100% planned to attend college. They selected the physical, PEMS and social categories equally for their favorite hobbies/recreational activities and chose the PEMS category most frequently as their preferred way to deal with stress. Finally, on the global self-assessment of generalized equilibrium, IA females attained a mean score of 3.5 indicating that they viewed themselves within the range of feeling a little calm/relaxed to a little tense/nervous. Among all the groups, this represented the highest mean score.

Males of mixed Italian-American ancestry (MixIA males). Concerning race and ethnicity, unlike the IA male and IA female groups, 87.5% of the Mix IA males identified their race as White and 12.5% identified their race as multiracial, while 100% identified their ethnicity as mixed. Although all group members were born in the USA, only 71.4% identified with the USA, while 28.6% identified with Italy. When asked to choose one of the four preferences that identify self, 25% preferred to be identified by both ethnic and racial background equally, 75% preferred to be identified neither by ethnicity nor racial background, and no one preferred to be identified by either ethnic or racial background exclusively. In the open-ended preference question, MixIA males again differed from the IA males and females, as only 25% preferred to be identified by ethnic background, 62.5% preferred to be identified by personal qualities and 12.5% preferred to be identified by name. No one expressed a preference to be identified by racial background.

Regarding language use and comfort using language, 100% use English as their primary language; 87.5% were most comfortable with English, 12.5% were most comfortable with Italian, and no one was comfortable with both English and a foreign language equally. Seventy-five percent of their parents were USA born, while 25% were foreign born.

The GPA mean score for MixIA males was 2.96. Unlike their IA male counterparts, only 75% planned to attend college. Similar to IA males, however, the mixed group selected the physical category most frequently as their favorite hobby/recreational activity and scored a tie between the physical and other categories for the way they preferred to deal with stress. Finally, a mean score of 3.0 on the calm/nervous continuum indicated that MixIA males viewed themselves as a little calm/relaxed.

Females of mixed Italian-American ancestry (MixIA females). Among this group, 88.9% identified their race as White, while 11.1% identified their race as Hispanic/Latino; all group members identified their ethnicity as mixed. All MixIA females were born in the USA and all identified with the USA. When asked to choose among one of the four preferences, 37.5% preferred to be identified by both ethnic and racial background equally, 62.5% preferred neither ethnic nor racial identification and no one preferred ethnic or racial identification exclusively. In the subsequent open-ended preference question, 14.3% preferred to be identified by ethnicity, 42.9% preferred to be identified by personal qualities and 42.9% preferred to be identified by their name. No one preferred racial identification.

Although 100% use English as their primary language, only 88.9% were most comfortable with it, while 11.1% were comfortable with both English and Spanish equally and no one was most comfortable with the exclusive use of a foreign language. Seventy-five percent of their parents were USA born and 25% were foreign born.

Very close to the GPA of IA females, the GPA mean score for MixIA females was 3.2. Unlike their IA female counterparts, however, only 88.9% indicated that they planned to attend college. MixIA females were also different from their female peers in that they chose the other category most frequently for their favorite hobby/recreational activity. The emotional category was selected most frequently as their preferred means of dealing with stress. Finally, with a mean score of 3.0 on the global self-assessment of generalized equilibrium, MixIA females rated themselves as a little calm/relaxed.

DEMOGRAPHIC PROFILE COMPARISON

The following section will highlight several group comparisons of the basic demographic data that stand out as noteworthy.

Race, country of origin and identification with the USA. All of the IA male and female students identified their race as White, while only 87.5% of the MixIA males and 88.9% of the MixIA females did so. In terms of country of origin, IA males and females had small percentages (10% and 6.7% respectively) who were born in Italy, while all of the MixIA students were

USA born. Both female groups identified with the USA at higher percentages than the two male groups.

Self-identification preferences. IA males indicated a preference to be identified exclusively by ethnic background at what seems to be a significantly higher percentage than all the other groups. In contrast, MixIA males preferred to be identified neither by ethnic nor racial background at higher rates than the other groups. It is also interesting to note that none of the groups preferred to be identified exclusively by racial background.

The open-ended preference question produced results beyond ethnic and racial background. IA males, once again, expressed a preference for identification by ethnic background at a higher percentage than all the other groups. Personal qualities were apparently important for MixIA males, as they expressed a preference to be identified by personal qualities at a higher percentage than all the other groups. MixIA females preferred to be identified by name at a higher percentage than all the other groups. Again, none of the groups expressed a preference for identification by racial background.

Language use. Only 80% of the IA males and 73.3% of the IA females use English as their primary language, while all of the MixIA males and females use English as their primary language. In addition, IA males yielded the lowest percentage of comfort with exclusive use of the English language, although they have the highest percentage of most comfort with both English and foreign language (Italian) equally. These results suggest that foreign language usage may be a greater part of the overall family life experience of IA students.

Parents' Country of Origin. IA males and females have significantly higher percentages of parents who were born in a foreign country (Italy) than either mixed group. The fact that 70% of IA males' parents were born in Italy may partially account for the IA male preference to be ethnically identified and their lower comfort level using English as their primary language.

GPA and college plans. Distinct gender differences were apparent in the GPA scores of all students. Females of both groups reported significantly higher GPA scores than males of both groups. The highest GPA mean score (3.23) was attained by IA females, who were very closely followed by MixIA females (3.20). The GPA mean score for MixIA males was 2.96, while the mean for IA males was the lowest at 2.75. It should also be noted, however, that the response rate for GPA was significantly lower for IA females. All IA males and females reported planning to attend college, while only 75% of the MixIA males and 88.9% of the MixIA females planned to attend college.

Favorite hobbies/recreational activities and ways of dealing with stress. Gender differences also occurred with respect to favorite hobbies/recreational activities and ways of dealing with stress. Physical outlets emerged as more important for males. Both male groups selected the physical category most frequently as their favorite hobby/recreational activity. In addition, both male groups selected two categories equally, physical and other, as their preferred method of dealing with stress. The female groups yielded different responses not only from the males, but also from each other on both questions.

Global self-assessment of generalized equilibrium. It is interesting to note that of the four groups, IA females reported the highest level of tension/nervousness (mean 3.5), while conversely, IA males reported the lowest level of tension/nervousness (mean 2.7). The mixed groups, both with a mean of 3.0, fell in between the IA males and females.

QUESTIONNAIRE FINDINGS

In order to answer the research questions, mean scores for the three instruments were calculated for each group of students. Table 2 contains the group mean scores for perceived stress, actual stress and symptomatology (the number of symptoms experienced frequently during the past year) according to gender and ethnicity.

Perceived stress. A comparison of mean scores indicated that all group means were located within the mild stress/a little worry range. IA females obtained the highest mean for perceived stress (183.1), followed by MixIA females (167.2), MixIA males (159.6) and lastly, IA males (155.9). In general, perceived stress tended to vary according to gender, as females obtained higher means than males.

Actual stress. In terms of actual stress, most students experienced high or very high levels of stress from actual life events. Of the four groups, three yielded very high levels of stress: IA males obtained the highest mean score (1039.5), followed by MixIA males (713.8) and MixIA females (698.9). Unlike their IA male counterparts, IA females reported the lowest mean score (542.7) for actual stress. While this mean represented the lowest of the four groups, it nevertheless indicated that IA females experienced a high degree of actual stress. In general, actual stress seemed to vary according to gender as group means were higher for males than females. It is interesting to note that although IA males achieved the highest actual stress mean, they yielded the lowest perceived stress mean. Conversely, while IA females registered the lowest actual stress mean, they produced the highest perceived stress mean.

Symptomatology. A comparison of mean scores for the number of symptoms frequently experienced during the past year revealed that IA females derived a mean of 17.1, indicating that they had experienced 61.1% of the 28 possible symptoms during the past year. IA males placed second with a mean of 14.9 or 53.2% of the possible symptom total. MixIA females followed with 11.7, which was 41.7% of the total possible symptoms, and MixIA males obtained 10.4 or 37.1% of the possible symptom total. In general, symptomatology seemed to vary according to both ethnicity and gender. Group means for IA females and males were significantly higher than those obtained by MixIA females and males. Symptom means for both groups of females, however, were higher than symptom means for males in both groups.

SUPPLEMENTAL DATA ANALYSES

Several in-depth supplemental analyses were conducted to explore possible patterns, including group similarities and differences in perceived stress events, actual stress events and symptomatology.

Perceived stress events. Table 3 presents the percentages of students in each of the five perceived stress categories on the "Stress and Worry Questionnaire." No one reported severe stress/extreme worry and very few (11.1%) reported considerable stress/a lot of worry. The bulk of students perceived themselves as having mild stress/a little worry.

Additional analyses based on mean rankings of perceived stressors revealed distinct patterns among the four groups. The five perceived stressors rated most frequently by IA males were: (1) getting a sexual disease including AIDS, (2) becoming successful or not, (3) the future in general, (4) graduating from high school and (5) completing questionnaires like this one.

The perceived stress concerns ranked most frequently by IA females were: (1) failing a class, (2) becoming successful or not, (3) overall physical appearance, (4) being raped and (5) being a high school student.

The top rankings among MixIA males were: (1) becoming successful or not, (2) getting a sexual disease including AIDS, (3) the future in general,

(4) graduating from high school and (5) being a high school student.

The top five perceived stress concerns for the MixIA females were as follows: (1) becoming successful or not, (2) going to college, (3) the future in general, (4) failing a class and (5) being healthy/being raped.

The following specific items also stand out for consideration as they highlight some of the similarities that emerged in the data. For example, in terms of specific perceived stressors, all four groups selected "becoming successful or not" as one of their main concerns. In fact, IA males and females chose it as their second most frequent concern, while MixIA males and females chose it as their most frequent concern. Academic and future life concerns were also rated frequently by each of the four groups.

On the other hand, there were also some very interesting differences among the four groups, including gender differences, in perceived stressors. For example, each group selected at least one item as a frequently ranked stressor, while the other groups did not even select that particular item within their top twenty concerns: IA males selected "completing questionnaires like this one;" IA females chose "being sexually harassed;" MixIA males picked "working;" and the MixIA females selected "committing a crime." In terms of gender differences, both male groups ranked "getting a sexual disease including AIDS" much higher than the female groups, while both female groups ranked "your overall appearance" much higher than both male groups.

For the most part, ethnic, racial and cultural concerns were not perceived as stressors, since students indicated no more than mild stress/a little worry about these issues. There were no apparent group differences in the following items: (a) ethnic, racial and/or cultural concerns in general; (b) people not understanding your culture; (c) where your parents were born; (d) where your grandparents were born; and (e) your place of birth. Although questions regarding "being discriminated against" and "being effected by racism" also fell into the mild stress/a little worry range, these items yielded somewhat higher mean scores across all groups than the items mentioned above. Of the four groups, MixIA males indicated that they were "effected by racism" to a greater degree than the others.

Further gender differences emerged for select perceived stressors. Females perceived much higher stress than males on items concerning "your family life in general" and "violence in general" even though all scores remained in the mild stress/a little worry category. In addition, IA females seemed to be more concerned about religious/spiritual issues than all the other groups and, in fact, were the only group to score in the moderate stress/some worry category regarding "the meaning of life."

Actual stress events. Table 4 illustrates the percentage of students in each of the five possible stress levels on the "How Much Stress is in Your Life Questionnaire." It is interesting to note that, with the exception of the MixIA female group, the largest percentage of each group scored above 600 indicating a very high level of stress. Especially striking is that all IA males scored above 600, while in contrast, all other groups had at least some percentage of students distributed across each of the five stress level categories. Although three groups were in the very high actual stress category and one group was in the high category, students did not perceive themselves as stressed individuals according to their perceived stress mean scores.

Further analyses revealed distinct patterns among the four groups based on the top percentage rankings of actual stress events. Of the IA male group, 100% experienced stress from change in amount of homework/study habits and arguments/conflicts with friends; 90% were stressed by arguments/conflicts with boyfriend/girlfriend and having a vacation. The overall profile of IA males indicated that they were the only group to experience all of the possible actual stress events.

Among IA females, 73.3% experienced stress from arguments or conflicts with friends, while 66.7% were stressed by change in eating habits and change in amount of homework/study habits.

MixIA males indicated that 87.5% were stressed over a big night out on the town and change in amount of homework/study habits; 75% experienced stress from minor illness/injury, arguments/conflicts with boyfriend/girlfriend and arguments/conflicts with friends.

The entire MixIA female group was stressed by change in eating habits, while 88.9% experienced minor trouble at school and arguments/ conflicts with family.

The following specific actual stress scores are a cause for concern: IA males reported the highest rate of being a "victim of discrimination" (30%); IA females scored second (20%); while, in contrast, MixIA females came next (only 11.1%) and none of the MixIA males indicated being discriminated against. Strikingly, a high percentage of IA males (80%) reported having a "minor violation of the law" followed by the MixIA males (50%); both female groups scored relatively low percentages on this item (MixIA females 11.1% and IA females only 6.7%). Even more striking and alarming is the fact that 60% of the IA males reported having a "major violation of the law," while no other student from any other group responded yes to this question. In addition, IA males (30%) were the only group to report being "suspended from school."

Symptom categories and symptomatology. Symptoms were further analyzed to determine if there were any notable group patterns in the frequency of physical, emotional, mental, spiritual and high-risk symptoms, as well as for specific symptoms experienced during the past year. Table 5 presents a comparison of the mean scores and percentages for each of the four groups.

In order of frequency, IA males experienced 62.5% of the mental symptoms; 61.7% of the physical symptoms; 55.6% of the emotional symptoms; 42.9% of the high-risk symptoms; and 35% of the spiritual symptoms.

IA females reported having 77.8% of the emotional symptoms; 67.8% of the physical symptoms; 61.7% of the mental symptoms; 56.7% of the spiritual symptoms and 35.2% of the high-risk symptoms.

MixIA males experienced 56.3% of the mental symptoms; 47.2% of the emotional symptoms; 33.3% of the physical symptoms; 25% of the spiritual symptoms and 19.6% of the high-risk symptoms.

MixIA females had 55.6% of the mental symptoms; 50% of the physical symptoms; 45.7% of the emotional symptoms; 27% of the high-risk symptoms and 22.2% of the spiritual symptoms.

A comparison of the symptom categories revealed that IA females had the highest number of symptoms and the highest percentage of physical, emotional and spiritual symptoms. IA males reported the highest percentage of mental and high-risk symptoms. MixIA males reported the lowest number of symptoms and the lowest percentage of physical and high-risk symptoms, while MixIA females had the lowest percentage of emotional, mental and spiritual symptoms.

In terms of symptomatology, the top symptoms experienced by IA males were as follows: 90% reported sleeping a lot or too little and feeling very angry. IA females indicated that 93.3% had frequent headaches, felt very angry and very tired during the past year. Of the MixIA males, 87.5% felt very angry and 75% felt very tired. MixIA females indicated that 88.9% felt very tired and 77.8% were sleeping alot or too little and also felt irritable/annoyed.

Experiencing high levels of actual stress does not automatically imply

risk, especially if students experience themselves as relatively calm/ re-
laxed and perceived stress/worry is relatively mild. How students deal
with stress is ultimately what really counts. Therefore, both the number of
symptoms and the specific type of symptoms experienced are the factors
that provide a more complete picture. In addition to the top symptoms
mentioned above, the following percentages regarding each group's response to six symptoms of particular concern further reinforces the seriousness of the overall results. IA males reported: afraid of losing control of
myself (70%), feeling depressed (60%), feeling tense/nervous (60%), not
feeling close to other people (40%), feeling you do not want to live (30%)
and feeling like there is no meaning to life (30%). IA females reported: feeling depressed (86.7%), feeling tense/nervous (86.7%), feeling like there is
no meaning to life (60%), not feeling close to other people (53.3%), feeling
you do not want to live (40%) and afraid of losing control of myself
(33.3%). The symptom percentages for MixIA males were as follows: feeling depressed (50%), feeling tense/nervous (50%), afraid of losing control
of myself (37.5%), not feeling close to other people (37.5%), feeling like
there is no meaning to life (12.5%) and feeling you do not want to live (0%).
MixIA females reported: feeling tense/nervous (55.6%), feeling depressed
(33.3%), afraid of losing control of myself (22.2%), feeling you do not want
to live (22.2%), not feeling close to other people (22.2%) and feeling like
there is no meaning to life (22.2%).

SUMMARY

Although a larger sample, multiple administration sites and statistical
analyses were preferable, the intent of this pilot study was exploratory in
nature. Despite these limitations, however, the data revealed distinct
findings. Ethnic and gender differences emerged across the groups in
terms of self-assessment ratings, specific concerns, issues and symptomatology, as well as distinct stress patterns.

In terms of the global self-assessment of generalized equilibrium,
dramatic gender differences surfaced between the IA males and females.
IA males assessed themselves as the most calm/relaxed group and the
females as the most tense/nervous group. As opposed to the extreme
scores of the IA groups, gender differences did not emerge among MixIA
males and females. Both MixIA groups reported feeling a little calm/ re-
laxed and their scores fell in between the IA male and female groups.

Perceived stress scores resulted in gender differences as both female groups scored higher than their male counterparts, although all groups fell within the mild stress/a little worry category. Once again, the scores for the MixIA groups fell in between the IA groups.

The amount of actual stress across the four groups is cause for concern. IA females had the lowest actual stress scores, however their mean score for actual stress was still in the high stress range. All other groups fell into the very high stress category. The scores of MixIA males and females were located between the IA groups, continuing a pattern of ethnic differences.

Symptomatology, including severity of symptoms and overall number of symptoms experienced during the past year, was reported at alarmingly high percentages. As stated earlier, symptomatology seemed to vary according to ethnicity and gender. IA students reported higher symptom percentages than their MixIA counterparts, while both female groups reported higher percentages than the male groups. In contrast to the pattern mentioned above, the mean scores for MixIA students were not located in between IA male and female mean scores. The MixIA students, however, continued to attain similar group scores, while IA males and females continued to report more significant gender differences in their scores.

A number of interesting relationships developed among the questionnaires. First, the results yielded a progression of severity across the questionnaires for most groups with scores increasing from their global self-assessment, to their perceived stress, to actual stress and, finally, their symptomatology scores. Second, in general, there was a positive relationship between global self-assessment and perceived stress scores. Third, there was an inverse relationship between the global self-assessment and perceived stress ratings as compared to the actual stress experienced by adolescents in their everyday lives. For example, IA males viewed themselves as the most calm/relaxed group and reported the lowest perceived stress scores, even though they had the highest amount of actual stress. IA females, on the other hand, assessed themselves with the highest degree of tension/nervousness and perceived stress, but reported the lowest actual stress scores. Fourth, except for the IA female group who had the highest symptomatology mean score, there was a positive relationship between actual stress scores and symptomatology. Taken together, the relationships among the instruments suggest that IA males and females were least realistic in their self-assessment ratings. Furthermore, IA males seem to use denial to a greater extent than all other groups.

Finally, highlights of each group's unique characteristics are as follows: IA males had the lowest scores on global self-assessment of generalized equilibrium and perceived stress, while they had the highest scores on actual stress as well as the highest percentage of mental and high risk symptoms in comparison to the other groups. They reported a preference to be identified exclusively by ethnic background, had the lowest GPA scores and the highest percentage of "escapist" ways of dealing with stress.

The IA females scored the highest on global self-assessment of generalized equilibrium and perceived stress, while they had the lowest actual stress scores (just the opposite of the IA males), the highest number of overall symptoms experienced during the past year, and the highest percentage of physical, emotional and spiritual symptoms in comparison to the other groups. Although they expressed considerable stress/a lot of worry about "failing a class," more so than any other group, IA females reported having the highest GPA scores. In addition to having the highest percentage of spiritual symptoms among the groups, IA females had the highest percentage of concern about religious/spiritual issues and also had the highest percentage rankings for depression and suicidal ideation.

The MixIA males had the lowest number of symptoms experienced during the past year, and the lowest percentage of physical and high-risk symptoms. They expressed a preference to be identified by personal qualities rather than by ethnic or racial identification. In addition, MixIA males scored third on perceived stress regarding being discriminated against and were the only group reporting no one actually having been a victim of discrimination, yet had the highest perceived stress score on being effected by racism. Finally, MixIA males also reported the highest percentage of actual stress with sexual concerns/difficulties at what appears to be a significant difference from the other groups.

For MixIA females, there appeared to be a relationship between their most frequent way of dealing with stress, which was in the emotional category, and the fact that they reported the lowest percentage of emotional symptoms of the four groups. They also had the lowest percentage of spiritual symptoms. Furthermore, they preferred to be identified by personal name at what appears to be a significant difference from the other groups. MixIA females had the highest percentage of actual stress on having minor trouble at school, while they also had the highest mean score for concern about committing a crime on the perceived stress questionnaire.

DISCUSSION AND RECOMMENDATIONS

As adolescent development commonly unfolds with bouts of great turbulence and stress, high scores were expected. We did not anticipate, however, scores to soar sky high; nor did we expect so many students to be deleteriously effected by perceived stress, actual stress events and symptomatology. Given these results, together with the tragic current events that have occurred within school settings across the country, it seems clear that students are experiencing serious problems and that these problems are not being adequately addressed in school settings.

We can probably agree that the process of educating adolescents is complex and multifaceted. To complicate the issue even further, the world has changed exponentially in recent years, yet education has not kept pace with our emerging individual and societal needs. For example, acquiring information and a broad knowledge base, developing critical and analytical thinking, and the ability to discuss and communicate effectively have always been targeted components of learning. Education has not, however, focused enough on students' emotional and psychological growth. We believe that the current climate calls for additional learning opportunities that can be applied to everyday life, such as creativity and interpersonal skills. Now, more than ever, it seems that non-traditional studies, such as human relations training, diversity training and stress management need to be routinely incorporated into academic life. Although there has been some progress in these areas, much more needs to be done.

It is obviously beyond the scope of this article to address the spectrum of educational issues with their concomitant solutions. However, some suggestions are worth noting. The authors recommend revisiting the concept of prevention. Prevention is not a new concept, just one that has been greatly neglected in recent years. More specifically, what seems to be needed is primary prevention. Primary prevention attempts to address issues before they ever become problems. Secondary prevention deals with problems that have already emerged and strives to resolve or at least keep them from escalating. The role of tertiary prevention is to minimize the quality and quantity of the current and potential new problems. Ideally, services and programs should address and offer all three levels of prevention. Of course, a major problem has been the historical lack of both private and public resources for these services. Funding priorities must be re-evaluated for the sake of future generations.

In relation to the results of this study, some specific preventive measures are recommended. First, programming that promotes personal growth and facilitates multicultural awareness, as a primary method of prevention, can be implemented through classroom or small group discussions, focused workshops, recreational activities, field trips, special events and mentoring. Secondary and tertiary levels of prevention can be addressed through a combination of individual academic, career and personal counseling, as well as through specialized groups and workshops, such as stress reduction, negotiation/mediation skills and anger management.

The results of this study also suggest the need for further research in the area of multicultural stress patterns. It is recommended that more detailed research be conducted throughout the NYC school system which would include: instrument validation studies, a larger sample, broader diversity in terms of the geographic, ethnic and racial mix of students, multiple administration sites and the use of statistical methods.

Since the authors firmly believe that service delivery is an integral part of praxis, research and practice, a follow-up stress management workshop is recommended. Students identified as high-risk can also be offered optional consultation, referral services and other services as deemed appropriate. Finally, in an additional component, the research results can be shared and discussed with school staff and parents to foster better understanding of the issues and help with program development.

CONCLUSIONS

Distinct demographic and stress patterns emerged across the four groups examined in this study. Although there were also similarities in terms of elevated mean scores on questionnaires and select variables, there were, in fact, greater gender and ethnic differences in the specific experiences of perceived stress, actual stress and symptomatology. Based on the results of this pilot study, Italian Americans and Italian Americans of mixed ancestry seem to be groups needing attention and services beyond what is currently provided. Italian-American students, in particular, present themselves as high-risk teenagers. One consequence of being in a high-risk group, for example, is the elevated dropout rate of Italian-American high school students. Although self-motivation and aspiration levels are certainly contributing factors to their dropout rate, it is possible that these are not the primary problem. More specifically, the authors would like to suggest that perhaps stress levels and symptomatology are at such high levels that these students simply cannot function effectively and achieve to their potential.

The patterns that emerged in this research indicate that adolescents experience stress differentially and that overall program planning and counseling services must address issues of diversity. Although basic counseling principles suggest an individualized approach, sensitivity to multicultural patterns and issues can only foster increased effectiveness in counseling and program planning.

TABLES

TABLE 1. *Select Demographic Profile Summary*

	IA MALES	IA FEMALES	MIX IA MALES	MIX IA FEMALES
White	100.0%	100.0%	87.5%	88.9%
Hispanic/Latino	0.0%	0.0%	0.0%	11.1%
Multiracial	0.0%	0.0%	12.5%	0.0%
Ethnicity	100.0%	100.0%	100.0%	100.0%
USA born	90.0%	93.3%	100.0%	100.0%
Foreign born	10.0%	6.7%	0.0%	0.0%
USA identification	66.7%	91.7%	71.4%	100.0%
Foreign identification	33.3%	8.3%	28.6%	0.0%
Prefer race identification	0.0%	0.0%	0.0%	0.0%
Prefer ethnic identification	50.0%	26.7%	0.0%	0.0%
Both equally	20.0%	33.3%	25.0%	37.5%
Neither	30.0%	40.0%	75.0%	62.5%
Open-ended race id.	0.0%	0.0%	0.0%	0.0%
Open-ended ethnic id.	62.5%	44.4%	25.0%	14.3%
By personal qualities	12.5%	44.4%	62.5%	42.9%
By personal name	25.0%	11.1%	12.5%	42.9%
Primary language English	80.0%	73.3%	100.0%	100.%
Primary language foreign	20.0%	26.7%	0.0%	0.0%
Comfort language English	60.0%	92.9%	87.5%	88.9%
Comfort language foreign	10.0%	0.0%	12.5%	0.0%
Comfort both equally	30.0%	7.1%	0.0%	11.1%
Parent USA born	30.0%	46.2%	75.0%	75.0%
GPA mean	2.75	3.23	2.96	3.20
College plans	100.0%	100.0%	75.0%	88.9%
Hobby/recreation	Physical	Multiple	Physical	Other
Deal with stress	Physical/other	PEMS	Physical/other	Emotional
Calm/nervous mean	2.7	3.5	3.0	3.0

TABLE 2. *Questionnaire Mean Scores*

	IA MALES	IA FEMALES	MIX IA MALES	MIX IA FEMALES
Perceived stress	155.9	183.1	159.6	167.2
Actual stress	1039.5	542.7	713.8	698.9
Symptoms past year	14.9	17.1	10.4	11.7

TABLE 3. *Perceived Stress Questionnaire Percentages*

	IA MALES	IA FEMALES	MIX IA MALES	MIX IA FEMALES
(1) 80-120: very mild stress/very little worry	20.0%	0.0%	37.5%	22.2%
(2) 121-200: mild stress/ a little worry	70.0%	60.0%	37.5%	55.6%
(3) 201-280: moderate stress/some worry	10.0%	40.0%	25.0%	11.1%
(4) 281-360: considerable stress/a lot or worry	0.0%	0.0%	0.0%	11.1%
(5) 361-400: severe stress/extreme worry	0.0%	0.0%	0.0%	0.0%

TABLE 4. *Actual Stress Questionnaire Percentages*

	IA MALES	IA FEMALES	MIX IA MALES	MIX IA FEMALES
(1) Below 250: low stress	0.0%	6.7%	0.0%	0.0%
(2) Between 250-349: mild stress	0.0%	26.7%	12.5%	0.0%
(3) Between 350-449: moderate stress	0.0%	6.7%	0.0%	33.3%
(4) Between 450-600: high stress	0.0%	13.3%	25.0%	33.3%
(5) Above 600: very high stress	100.0%	46.7%	62.5%	33.3%

TABLE 5. *Symptom Category Mean Scores and Percentages*

	IA MALES		IA FEMALES		MIX IA MALES		MIX IA FEMALES	
	MEAN	%	MEAN	%	MEAN	%	MEAN	%
Physical symptoms (6)	3.7	61.7%	4.1	67.8%	20	33.3%	3.0	50.0%
Emotional symptoms (9)	5.0	55.6%	7.0	77.8%	4.3	47.2%	4.1	45.7%
Mental symptoms (4)	2.5	62.5%	2.5	61.7%	2.3	56.3%	2.2	55.6%
Spiritual symptoms (2)	0.7	35.0%	1.1	56.7%	0.5	25.0%	0.4	22.2%
High risk symptoms (7)	3.0	42.9%	2.5	35.2%	1.4	19.6%	1.9	27.0%
Total Symptoms (28)	14.9	53.2%	17.1	61.1%	10.4	37.1%	11.7	41.7%

APPENDIX A

DEMOGRAPHIC QUESTIONNAIRE

Today's Date: _____

1. Name of School: _____

2. Please check one: ☐ Freshman   ☐ Sophomore   ☐ Junior   ☐ Senior

3. Please check one: ☐ Male   ☐ Female   4. Date of Birth: _____   Age: _____

Please list the country where the following family members were born (leave blank if not sure):

5. Your mother's mother: _____   6. Your mother's father: _____   7. Your mother: _____

8. Your father's mother: _____   9. Your father's father: _____   10. Your father: _____

11. In what country were you born? _____

12. What is your racial background? _____

13. What is your ethnic background? _____

14. Do you prefer to be identified by your (please check one):
   ☐ Racial background   ☐ Ethnic background   ☐ Both equally   ☐ Neither

15. What country are you most comfortable identifying with? _____

16. How do you prefer identifying yourself? _____

17. What language(s) is/are spoken at home? Primary _____ Secondary _____

18. What language(s) are you most comfortable speaking? _____

19. How long have your parents lived in the USA? _____

20. How long have you lived in the USA? _____

21. What is your religious background? _____

22. Do you attend religious services (either in the community or at home)?   ☐ Yes   ☐ No

23. Is your family religious?   ☐ Yes   ☐ No   ☐ Not sure

24. Is your family spiritual?   ☐ Yes   ☐ No   ☐ Not sure

25. Do you consider yourself to be religious?   ☐ Yes   ☐ No   ☐ Not sure

26. Do you consider yourself to be spiritual?   ☐ Yes   ☐ No   ☐ Not sure

27. Do you live with: ☐ Both parents ☐ Mother ☐ Father ☐ Other relatives ☐ Friends ☐ other

28. How many brothers do you have? _____   29. How many sisters do you have? _____

30. What is your birth order? _____   ☐ I have a twin   ☐ I am an only child

31. Do you plan to go to college?   ☐ Yes   ☐ No   ☐ Not sure

32. What is your GPA? _____

33. Do you know what your major will be?
   ☐ Yes (please specify) _____   ☐ Not sure   ☐ Not going to college

34. Do you know what job/career you will choose? ☐ Yes (specify) _____ ☐ Not sure

35. What is the highest school grade reached by your: Mother _____ Father _____ Siblings _____

36. What is/are your favorite hobby/recreational activity(s)? _____

37. List the ways you deal with stress: _____

38. Do you consider yourself to be (please check one):   ☐ Very calm/relaxed ☐ Calm/relaxed
   ☐ A little calm/relaxed ☐ A little tense/nervous ☐ Tense/nervous ☐ Very tense/nervous

APPENDIX B

STRESS AND WORRY QUESTIONNAIRE

Please circle the number that best describes how intense you feel about and react to the following:

1	2	3	4	5
NO STRESS (no worry)	MILD STRESS (a little worry)	MODERATE STRESS (some worry)	CONSIDERABLE STRESS (a lot of worry)	SEVERE STRESS (extreme worry)

1. Being a high school student	1	2	3	4	5
2. Your relationship with your mother	1	2	3	4	5
3. Not having enough friends	1	2	3	4	5
4. Can't afford everything you want to buy	1	2	3	4	5
5. Being discriminated against	1	2	3	4	5
6. Becoming successful or not	1	2	3	4	5
7. The meaning of life	1	2	3	4	5
8. Failing exams	1	2	3	4	5
9. Your relationship with your father	1	2	3	4	5
10. Dating	1	2	3	4	5
11. Working	1	2	3	4	5
12. Ethnic, racial and/or cultural concerns in general	1	2	3	4	5
13. Graduating from high school	1	2	3	4	5
14. Whether you believe in "God" or a "Supreme Being" or not	1	2	3	4	5
15. Taking exams	1	2	3	4	5
16. Your parents don't get along with each other	1	2	3	4	5
17. Being accepted by others	1	2	3	4	5
18. Where your parents were born	1	2	3	4	5
19. Going to college	1	2	3	4	5
20. Your religion	1	2	3	4	5
21. The future in general	1	2	3	4	5
22. Family arguments and/or conflicts	1	2	3	4	5
23. Having or not having a boyfriend/girlfriend	1	2	3	4	5
24. Getting a job	1	2	3	4	5
25. Where your grandparents were born	1	2	3	4	5
26. Choosing a career	1	2	3	4	5
27. Having or not having world peace	1	2	3	4	5
28. Failing a class	1	2	3	4	5
29. People not understanding who you are as a person	1	2	3	4	5
30. Having sex or not	1	2	3	4	5
31. Living in the USA	1	2	3	4	5
32. Being physically abused	1	2	3	4	5
33. Having enough time and/or space to study	1	2	3	4	5
34. Being healthy	1	2	3	4	5
35. Your social life in general	1	2	3	4	5
36. People not understanding your culture	1	2	3	4	5
37. The environment	1	2	3	4	5
38. Having good study skills	1	2	3	4	5
39. Your relationship with classmates	1	2	3	4	5

40. Being sexually harassed	1	2	3	4	5
41. Living in New York	1	2	3	4	5
42. Getting sick and/or injured	1	2	3	4	5
43. Committing a crime	1	2	3	4	5
44. Your relationship with teachers	1	2	3	4	5
45. Smoking cigarettes	1	2	3	4	5
46. Your family life in general	1	2	3	4	5
47. Your place of birth	1	2	3	4	5
48. Your relationship with friends	1	2	3	4	5
49. Violence in general	1	2	3	4	5
50. Not having enough fun	1	2	3	4	5
51. Being pressured to do things you don't want to do	1	2	3	4	5
52. Being effected by racism	1	2	3	4	5
53. Being the victim of a crime	1	2	3	4	5
54. Having arguments with your boyfriend/girlfriend	1	2	3	4	5
55. Whether you "belong" or not	1	2	3	4	5
56. Religious/spiritual concerns in general	1	2	3	4	5
57. Getting into a fight	1	2	3	4	5
58. Your overall physical appearance	1	2	3	4	5
59. Your relationship with your brothers and sisters	1	2	3	4	5
60. Having enough food to eat or not	1	2	3	4	5
61. Being raped	1	2	3	4	5
62. Drinking alcohol	1	2	3	4	5
63. Your school life in general	1	2	3	4	5
64. Pregnancy (yourself or your partner)	1	2	3	4	5
65. Having difficulty with the English language	1	2	3	4	5
66. Having arguments and/or conflicts with friends	1	2	3	4	5
67. Choosing the best college for me	1	2	3	4	5
68. Being "attractive" or not	1	2	3	4	5
69. Getting a sexual disease including AIDS	1	2	3	4	5
70. Using drugs	1	2	3	4	5
71. Your weight	1	2	3	4	5
72. Having arguments and/or conflicts with teachers	1	2	3	4	5
73. Spiritual issues	1	2	3	4	5
74. Your relationship with your boyfriend/girlfriend	1	2	3	4	5
75. Being liked by people in general	1	2	3	4	5
76. Being emotionally abused	1	2	3	4	5
77. Becoming your "own person"	1	2	3	4	5
78. Financial worries in general	1	2	3	4	5
79. Enjoying life	1	2	3	4	5
80. Completing questionnaires like this one	1	2	3	4	5

Please feel free to add any other concerns/worries not listed:

_____

_____

APPENDIX C

HOW MUCH STRESS IS IN YOUR LIFE?
✔ Please check each event that has happened to you during the past year:

1. ☐ Big night out on the town	26. ☐ Outstanding personal achievement
2. ☐ Birthday	27. ☐ Arguments/conflicts with teachers
3. ☐ Minor trouble at work	28. ☐ Change in job responsibilities
4. ☐ Minor trouble at school	29. ☐ Change in amount of homework/study habits
5. ☐ Minor violation of the law	30. ☐ Change in living environment
6. ☐ Minor illness or injury	31. ☐ Change in personal habits
7. ☐ Holidays	32. ☐ Beginning or ending a job
8. ☐ Family reunion	33. ☐ First day of class
9. ☐ Change in amount of family contact	34. ☐ Victim of discrimination
10. ☐ Change in recreational activities	35. ☐ Change of financial situation
11. ☐ Vacation	36. ☐ Arguments/conflicts with boyfriend/girlfriend
12. ☐ Attending different church/synagogue	37. ☐ Arguments/conflicts with friends
13. ☐ Change in eating habits	38. ☐ Gain of a new family member
14. ☐ Change in sleeping habits	39. ☐ Change in health of a family member
15. ☐ A special project at work	40. ☐ Fired from work
16. ☐ A special project at school	41. ☐ Suspended from school
17. ☐ Got teased/made fun of	42. ☐ Sexual concerns/difficulties
18. ☐ Attending a different school	43. ☐ Arguments/conflicts with family
19. ☐ Change in amount of free time	44. ☐ Separation/divorce of parents
20. ☐ Change in social activities	45. ☐ Severe personal illness or injury
21. ☐ Increased/decreased dating	46. ☐ Pregnancy (yourself or your partner)
22. ☐ Participated in a fight	47. ☐ Major violation of the law
23. ☐ Victim of a crime	48. ☐ Breakup with boyfriend/girlfriend
24. ☐ Exams	49. ☐ Death of a close friend
25. ☐ Failing a class	50. ☐ Death of a close family member

The above checklist has been adapted from the Holmes-Rahe Stress Test by Pierre Tribaudi.

APPENDIX D

WHAT ARE THE EFFECTS OF STRESS ON YOUR LIFE?

✔ Please check which of the following you have experienced:

DURING THIS PAST WEEK	FREQUENTLY DURING THIS PAST YEAR
1a. ☐ Having a headache	1b. ☐ Having a headache
2a. ☐ Feeling tense/nervous	2b. ☐ Feeling tense/nervous
3a. ☐ Feeling sad	3b. ☐ Feeling sad
4a. ☐ Feeling depressed	4b. ☐ Feeling depressed
5a. ☐ Sleeping a lot or too little	5b. ☐ Sleeping a lot or too little
6a. ☐ Eating a lot or too little	6b. ☐ Eating a lot or too little
7a. ☐ Feeling afraid something bad will happen to you	7b. ☐ Feeling afraid something bad will happen to you
8a. ☐ Feeling very angry	8b. ☐ Feeling very angry
9a. ☐ Feeling very tired	9b. ☐ Feeling very tired
10a. ☐ Lack of concentration	10b. ☐ Lack of concentration
11a. ☐ Having stomach problems	11b. ☐ Having stomach problems
12a. ☐ Worrying a lot	12b. ☐ Worrying a lot
13a. ☐ Feeling irritable/annoyed	13b. ☐ Feeling irritable/annoyed
14a. ☐ Forget things easily	14b. ☐ Forget things easily
15a. ☐ Having unwanted thoughts	15b. ☐ Having unwanted thoughts
16a. ☐ Having unwanted feelings	16b. ☐ Having unwanted feelings
17a. ☐ Feeling lonely	17b. ☐ Feeling lonely
18a. ☐ Afraid of losing control of myself	18b. ☐ Afraid of losing control of myself
19a. ☐ Having a fast heartbeat	19b. ☐ Having a fast heartbeat
20a. ☐ Hearing voices	20b. ☐ Hearing voices
21a. ☐ Feeling you do not want to live	21b. ☐ Feeling you do not want to live
22a. ☐ Having irrational thoughts	22b. ☐ Having irrational thoughts
23a. ☐ Having irrational feelings	23b. ☐ having irrational feelings
24a. ☐ Feeling nauseous and/or dizzy	24b. ☐ Feeling nauseous and/or dizzy
25a. ☐ Not feeling close to other people	25b. ☐ Not feeling close to other people
26a. ☐ Not feeling like yourself	26b. ☐ Not feeling like yourself
27a. ☐ Feeling like people are out to hurt you	27b. ☐ Feeling like people are out to hurt you
28a. ☐ Feeling like there is no meaning to life	28b. ☐ Feeling like there is no meaning to life

Notes

1. E. H. Erikson, *Childhood and Society* (New York, 1963).

2. J. V. Scelsa, "Missed Opportunities," *Ambassador: National Italian American Foundation Quarterly* (Spring, 1991), 17-19.

3. D. Carielli, "Aspirations of NYC Public and Parochial High School Students and Their Parents' Level of Education," *Newsletter: The John D. Calandra Italian American Institute* (Spring, 1992), 2-3.

4. S. L. Washburn, "The Study of Race," in A. Rose and C. Rose, Eds., *Minority Problems* (New York, 1965), 329

5. S. D. Johnson, "Toward Clarifying Culture, Race and Ethnicity in the Context of Multicultural Counseling," *Journal of Multicultural Counseling and Development*, 18, (1990), 41-50.

6. Scelsa, "Missed Opportunities."

7. B. S. Dohrenwend and B. P. Dohrenwend, Stressful Life Events: Their Nature and Effects, (New York, 1974) and R. S. Lazarus and S. Folkman, *Stress, Appraisal, and Coping* (New York, 1984).

8. H. M. Perlow and C. A. Guarnaccia, "Ethnic and Racial Differences in Life Stress Among High School Adolescents," Journal of Counseling and Development, 75, (1997), 442-450; and E. P. Copeland and R. S. Hess, "Differences in Young Adolescents' Coping Strategies Based on Gender and Ethnicity," *Journal of Early Adolescence*, 15, (May, 1995), 203-219.

9. T. H. Holmes and R. H. Rahe, "The Social Readjustment Rating Scale," *Journal of Psychosomatic Research*, 11, (1967), 213-218.

Italian-American Youth and Educational Achievement Levels: How are we doing? (Revised)*

VINCENZO MILIONE
CIRO T. DE ROSA
ITALA PELIZZOLI

During the last twenty years there has been an explosion in technology that has significantly altered the way we live. With the advent of computers, cell phones and the Internet, today's mode of communication has enhanced societal knowledge and has made the world an even smaller place. The high-tech world has changed the face of the industrial complex, and promises to continue to define the global landscape for the foreseeable future. This surge in twenty-first century technology requires, more than ever, that our nation's future workforce possess the skills necessary to earn a living in an emerging global market. In efforts to better understand the future career and occupational possibilities of Italian Americans, one needs to first examine the role that educational attainment has played in the lives of Italian-American students.

Not long ago, the Italian neighborhoods of New York City, similar to ethnic enclaves found in other large cities, were insulated by actual or imagined borders that served to limit the perception of occupational possibilities. These enclaves of first and second generation Italians were generally inhabited by workers from every facet of the building trades, mom-and-pop shops, and city employees in varying blue-collar jobs. The focus for many Italian-American youngsters was not on the world of academia but on the role models they saw within their family and neighborhood on a daily basis. The neighborhood, comprised of an eight or ten block radius, was not just broad avenues but one's town to police, protect, and reside in with those familiar to them. Outsiders were viewed as suspect

---

* At the time the initial research was conducted, in the year 2002, the 2000 US Census was not available. The 1990 US Census was used to project the year 2000 Italian-American high school population. This revised edition uses the now available year 2000 census estimate of Italian-American high school population. The research results using 2000 census data do not change the conclusion that Italian Americans by the year 2000 had among the lowest high school dropout rates in New York City.

and not to be trusted until they proved otherwise. These conditions very much resembled a residual *paese* mentality maintained by the immigrants to sustain those aspects of daily life deemed essential for survival in a new culture. The familiarity of the territory gave Italian youth a real sense of belonging to a close-knit community comprised of grandparents, aunts, uncles, cousins and *paesani* living within walking distance. This arrangement afforded a sense of proprietorship regarding the neighborhood while reinforcing the precepts of familial unity as a very important aspect of their lives. Perhaps another reason why Italian youth opted for jobs that did not require them to go beyond the limits of their neighborhood, or consider educational options outside their city, was allegiance to their family and by extension the Italian community.

The fact that familial role models did not go to work in a shirt and tie was less important to Italian youth than one's ability to contribute economically to their family's well being. Thus, Italian youth worked in a variety of industries. For example, many families owned their own businesses and sons worked in the family meat market or grocery store. Others were employed as shop stewards in the bricklayers union or as tradesmen earning as much as thirty dollars an hour. In addition, family members were often employed in the transit department and were able to offer assistance with the city test. All of these respectable blue-collar jobs added to the perception that the completion of high school was not a pressing necessity.

The Italian-American family may have also contributed in part to this perception. Parental lack of knowledge about formal education and the benefits of such did not outweigh the extrinsic rewards of employment. The family's financial situation, coupled with parental values, did not encourage children toward higher education. Often it was the case of children knowing very little about educational opportunities and parents knowing less. In addition, peers were not positive role models since they too were not interested in higher education.

More recently, the educational achievement issue may also have been compounded by the negative stereotype of Italian Americans in the media. Films such as *The Godfather* and *Saturday Night Fever* depict Italians as anti-educational and anti-intellectual. Their glamorous portrayals of wise guys serve as negative role models for Italian-American youth. Italians are depicted as gangsters having strong family ties and men of honor who are observed by youngsters in their neighborhoods. For a time, such individuals became the model to emulate because they were successful without having attended college and, more importantly, they commanded respect because they were feared. This again reflects the parochial nature of many Italian enclaves in urban areas and New York City in particular.

The sociocultural factors discussed above, woven into the fabric of everyday neighborhood life, resulted in an educational achievement problem among Italian-American youth. By the mid-1980s, however, community leaders began to articulate their concerns and many organizations rallied to address the multifaceted issue. For example, programs were created to depict a positive portrait of the Italian experience in America. The Commission for Social Justice, the anti-defamation arm of the Order Sons of Italy in America, embarked on a nationwide program in the early-1990s to profile famous Italian Americans who were influential in all spectrums of American life. Speakers were dispatched to discuss the achievements of Italians, Italian Americans and Italy's contribution to the world.

In addition to nationwide endeavors, local services geared toward the individual needs of students were established. Mentoring programs such as the Calandra Institute's AMICI Project[1], in conjunction with the NYS Mentor Program (founded by Mrs. Matilda Cuomo, former First Lady of the State of New York), were implemented to provide middle school children with an array of services including tutoring, career development, and the support of a caring mentor. As an adjunct to mentoring, parents of mentees were offered workshops to address a variety of parenting issues. Sponsored by the Calandra Institute, outreach counseling programs assisted high school students who were unfamiliar with higher education, raising their awareness of programs offered by the City University of New York. Other community organizations, such as NIAF and the Columbus Citizens Foundation, created scholarship programs to support students as they embarked upon college.

The media coverage given to these initiatives generated discourse and discussion that was communicated into Italian households. Neighborhood residents finally began to realize that, without a strong educational foundation, the career development of Italian-American youth would be significantly affected. This movement inspired Italian Americans to address the problem that, in New York City, their teenagers had the third-highest dropout rate of 21%.

DATA COLLECTION, METHOD, AND ANALYSIS

The data used in this study was obtained from the New York City

Department of Education (formerly the Board of Education) and the United States Census Bureau. In 1978, New York City public schools began collecting high school non-completion data. The data collected included all students who did not complete high school. In 1986, non-completion data was analyzed vis-à-vis the following affirmative action race categories: American Indian, Asian, Black, Hispanic and White. Italian-American high school non-completion rates were not calculated.

Additional data was extracted from the 1980 US Census. This decennial survey consisted of a sampling of one out of twenty households, or a 5% sample. Every ten years a sample of Italian Americans receives a census data questionnaire. In addition, approximately one out of twenty Italian Americans receives a long survey questionnaire. All Italian Americans receive a short questionnaire; however, Italian Americans can only identify themselves as "white." On the longer survey questionnaires, there are specific sociodemographic questions regarding the respondent's ethnic ancestry and in 1980, ancestry data was reported in the Census Bureau's survey through self-identification that included multiple ancestries. Respondents who identified Italian as one of their ancestral roots (first or second entry) were counted in the Italian-American population. It is through this ancestry question that Italian Americans were identified within the education system and in varying career fields.

In 1990, the Calandra Institute developed the High School Dropout Indicator Model (HSDIM) utilizing the 1980 census data and 1977–80 New York City Board of Education dropout statistics. The 1980 census data reported information on the highest grade attained and completed including 18 to 21 year old respondents that did not complete school included among the cohorts of dropouts from 1977 to 1980.

For each census respondent, the highest educational grade completed was identified. Respondents who did not complete grades 9–12 were considered potential high school dropouts. In order to approximate a four year high school cohort peer group, respondents between 18 and 21 years old were included. This cohort group would have attended high school from ages 15 to 18 years old in 1977 to 1980. In addition, the 18 to 21 year old group would also include those who may have completed their high school grades at a later age beyond 18 years. The 18 to 21 year old group is the best cross-sectional profile of respondents who completed high school on time as well as those respondents who completed high school after the age of 18.

Additional data for the Calandra HSDIM was collected and summarized from the NYC Board of Education for racial minority groups and the White population. Such data included the number of dropouts in grades 9 through 12, and the number of students enrolled in these grades predominantly within the ages of 15 to 21. In the 1980s more than 13% of the high school population was between 18 and 21 years old. The Calandra HSDIM calculated the annual survival rate that represents the probability of the high school population persisting in school within each year of high school. Over the four years of high school the projected survival rate is defined as an average yearly rate multiplied by itself four times.

The Board of Education reported the four year projected dropout percentages for minority groups that included Alaskan Native/American Indian, Asian/Pacific Islander, Hispanic, and Black (non-Hispanic) students. The four year projected dropout percentage was also calculated for White (non-Hispanic) students. The Calandra HSDIM estimated a statistical correlation between the percentage of students that did not complete high school as reported in the census data and summary counts of high school dropouts reported by the Board of Education (see Scelsa and Milione for modeling descriptions, pp. 243*ff*).

ITALIAN AMERICAN HIGH SCHOOL DROPOUT

On April 30, 1990 a conference was co-sponsored by the Calandra Institute, the Italian American Studies Committee of the United Federation of Teachers, and the New York State Governor's Office for Ethnic Relations, entitled "The Education of Italian-American Youth," that focused on Italian-American high school dropouts. Scholars, educators and guidance personnel recognized that many Italian-American students were not completing four years of high school. The Calandra Institute collaborated with the New York City Board of Education to estimate the non-completion rate of Italian-American high school students as compared to other racial and ethnic student populations being reported.[2]

Not surprisingly, the data confirmed the educational community's perception that one out of five Italian-American students entering ninth grade did not receive a high school diploma due to premature termination of their studies.[3] This resulted in Italian Americans having the third highest dropout rate in New York City after Hispanic and Black high school students (see Figure 1).

FIGURE 1. *New York City High School Dropout Rates, 1988*

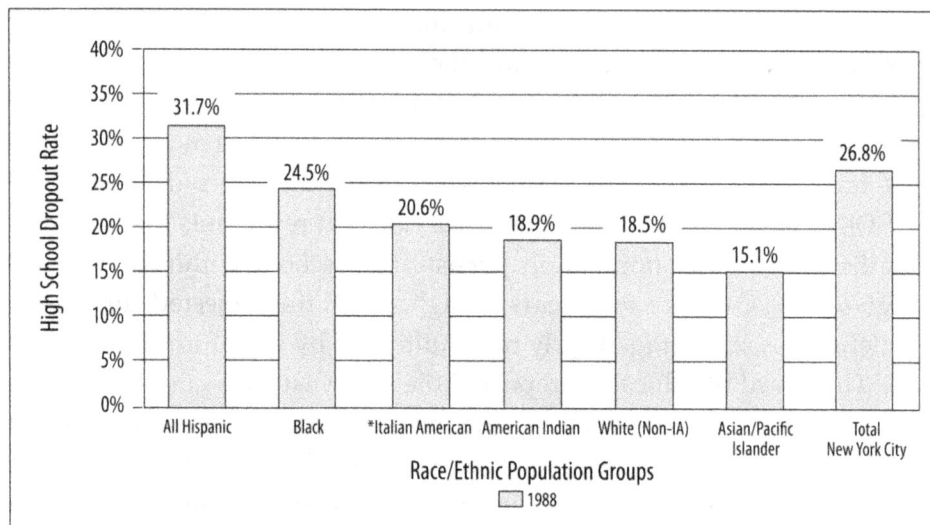

*Calandra Institute high school dropout rate indicator based on 1980 and 1990 census data on high school educational achievement levels and New York City Board of Education four year high school dropout rates.

In response to these alarming statistics, the Italian-American community acted swiftly to develop initiatives in efforts to foster higher education and articulation to college. During the same time, as research findings were being disseminated to the Italian-American community, the Calandra Institute, in conjunction with the Board of Education, created programs targeted to students at risk of prematurely terminating their studies. The Institute sponsored outreach counseling programs in various city high schools that provided psychosocial and educational support to Italian-American youth and their parents.

Guidance services offered in the schools included: mentoring programs, positive image campaigns, scholarship opportunities, parent-education workshops and college information.[4] Throughout the 1990s, programs and efforts facilitated by the Calandra Institute, the Italian-American educational community, and concerned others cohesively articulated the value of education and student development. Such constituencies inspired a range of programs and interventions in an attempt to ameliorate the high school dropout phenomenon.

Using a decade of data available from the New York City Board of Education, the Calandra Institute was able to estimate Italian-American high school dropout patterns throughout the 1990s.[5]

Figure 2 depicts the trend in the NYC Board of Education high school dropout rates from 1978 to 2000 for the total population. These dropout rates are defined by the percent of entering ninth grade students who exit the school system and do not return to complete a high school diploma within four years. High school dropout rates went from a high of 47.3% in the late 1970s to 19.3% in 2000.[6]

FIGURE 2. *New York City High School Dropout Rates, 1978–2000*

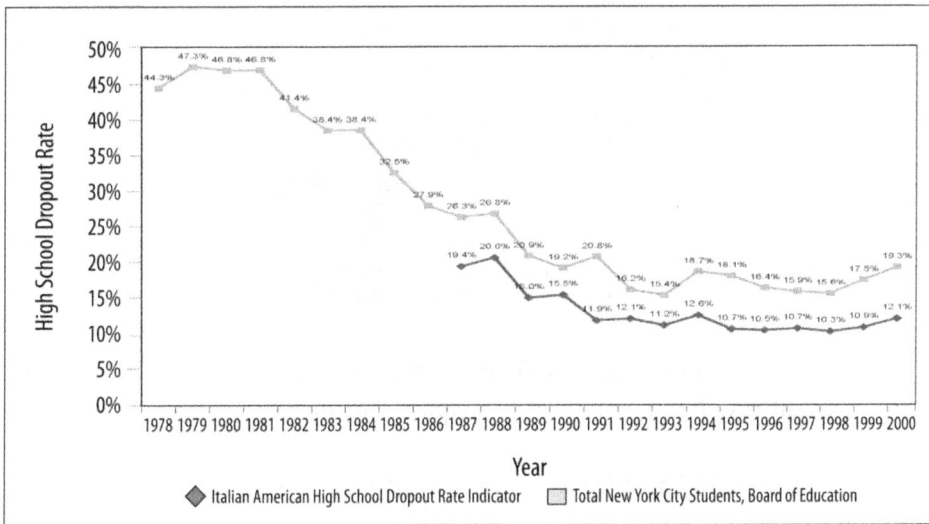

It should be noted that it was not until 1986 that the Board of Education started to report high school dropout rates by racial categories (American Indian, Asian, Black, Hispanic and White). The Italian-American high school dropout rate was estimated using the race and ethnicity dropout pattern and census data of Italian-American student education achievement levels from ninth to twelfth grades.[7]

Figure 2 also depicts the Italian-American high school dropout rate indicators from 1987 to 2000. In 1988 nearly 21% of incoming ninth graders terminated their studies within the next four years, giving Italian Americans the third-highest dropout rate after Hispanics and Blacks. In 2000, the Italian-American dropout rate decreased to nearly 12%. This was the most significant decrease of all racial and ethnic groups.

Figure 3 illustrates the changing dropout rate between 1988 and 2000 for differing racial and ethnic populations. In the year 2000, Italian-American students had the lowest dropout rate after Asian and White (non-IA) students.

FIGURE 3. *New York City High School Dropout Rates, 1988 vs. 2000*

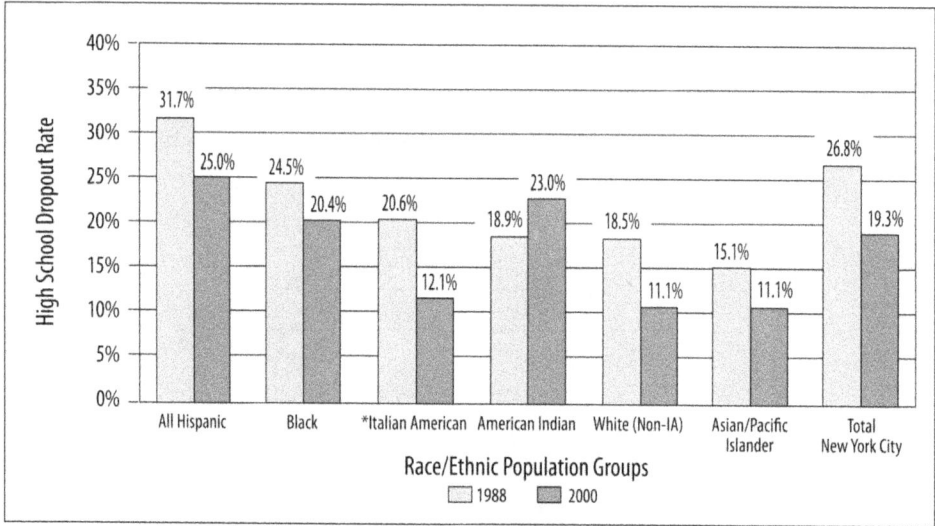

*Calandra Institute high school dropout rate indicator based on 1980, 1990 and 2000 census data on educational achievement levels and New York City Board of Education four year high school dropout rates.

Figure 4 compares Italian-American and Hispanic students. The highest dropout rate has been among Hispanic students.

FIGURE 4. *New York High School Dropout Rates, Italian American vs. Hispanic*

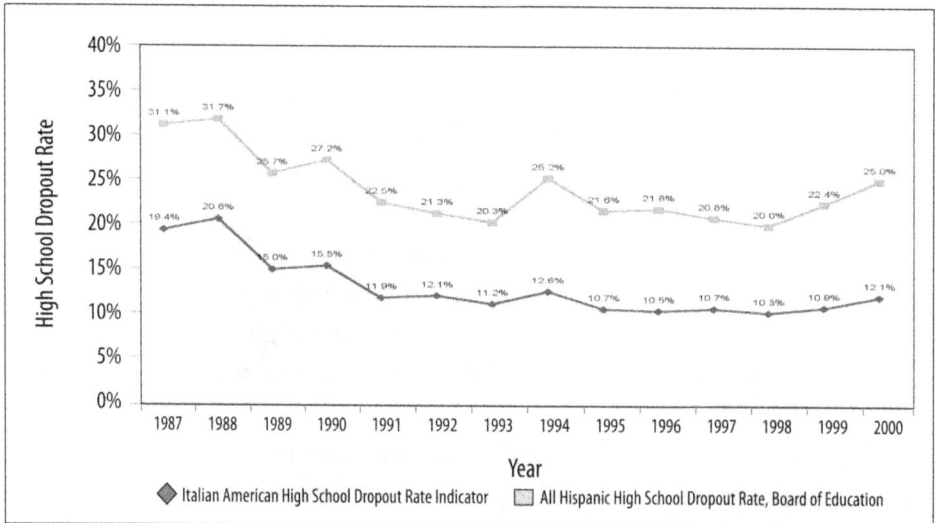

Figure 5 compares Italian-American and American Indian students. American Indian students had the second-highest dropout rate at 23%. In 1988 the dropout rate for this group was lower than that of Italian Americans.

FIGURE 5. *New York City High School Dropout Rates, Italian American vs. American Indian*

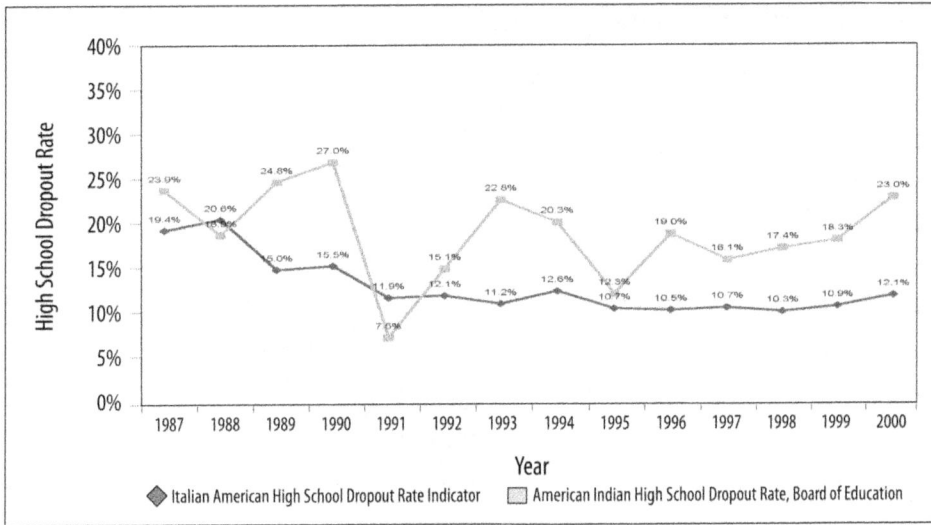

Figure 6 compares Italian-American and Black students. In the 1980s, the high Italian-American dropout rate was similar to the dropout rate of Black students. In 2000, the dropout rate for Italian Americans was significantly lower than the dropout rate for Black students.

FIGURE 6. *New York City High School Dropout Rates, Italian American vs. Black*

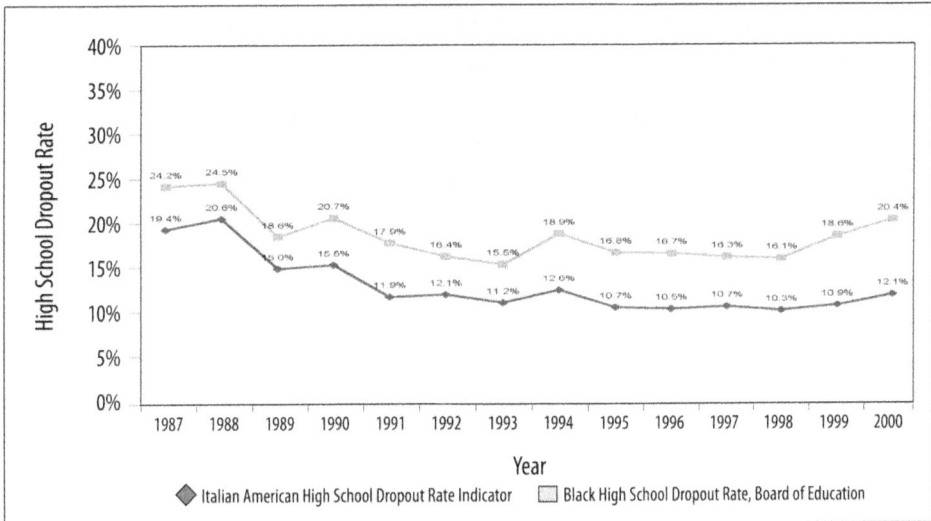

Figure 7 compares Italian Americans and other White (non-Italian American) students. While other Whites had consistently lower dropout

rates than Italian Americans in the 1980s, the difference in dropout rates for other Whites and Italian Americans narrowed in the 1990s.

FIGURE 7. *New York City High School Dropout Rates, Italian American vs. White (non-Italian American)*

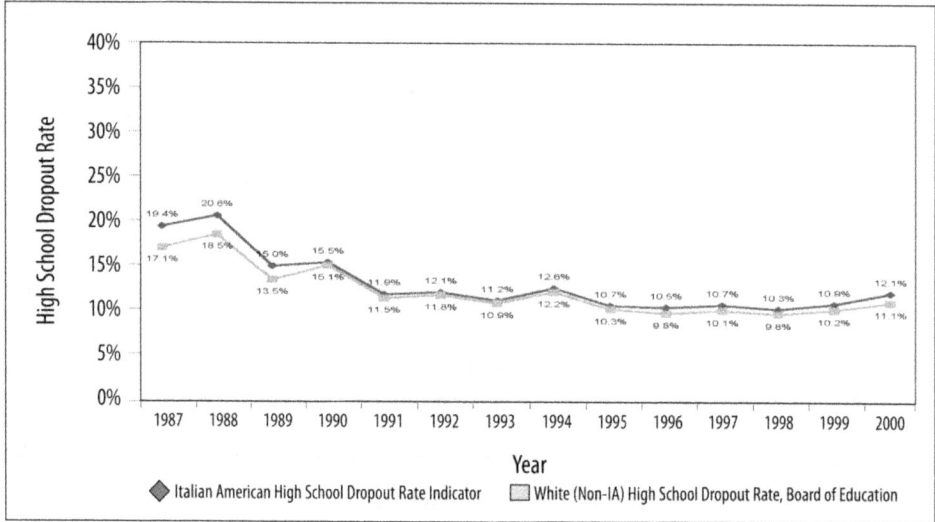

Figure 8 depicts Italian American and Asian/Pacific Islanders. Asian students dropped out significantly less than Italian-American students in the 1980s. The dropout patterns of the two groups were similar through out the 1990s. In 2000, the difference between Italian-American students and Asian students was significantly reduced.[8]

FIGURE 8. *New York City High School Dropout Rates, Italian American vs. Asian/Pacific Islander*

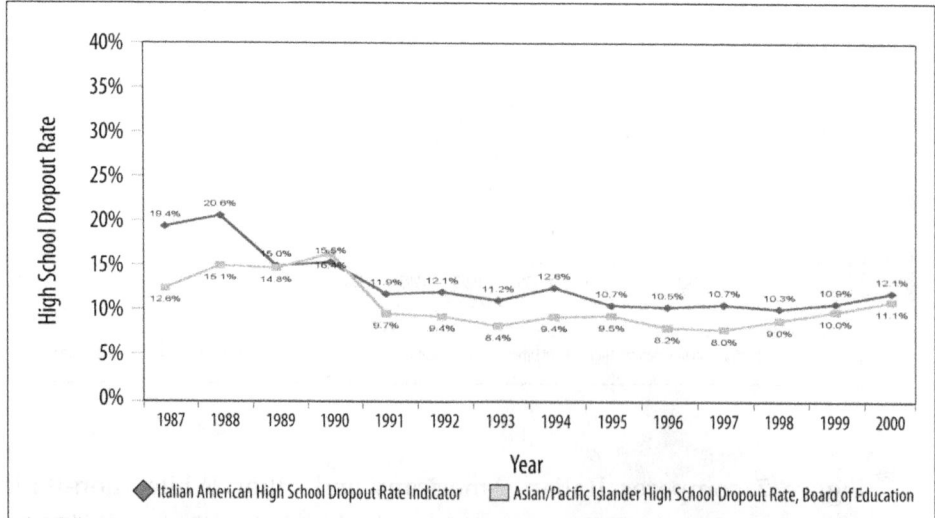

ITALIAN AMERICAN HIGHER EDUCATION ACHIEVEMENT

HIGH SCHOOL GRADUATES

The changes in Italian-American high school dropout rates from the 1980s to the 1990s are reflected in the overall educational achievement levels of the New York City Italian-American community in this period between 1980 and 1990. Figure 9 shows that Italian Americans with less than a high school degree decreased more than other population groups from 44% to 30%.[9]

FIGURE 9. *Less Than High School Education, 1980 vs. 1990 New York City Education Achievement*

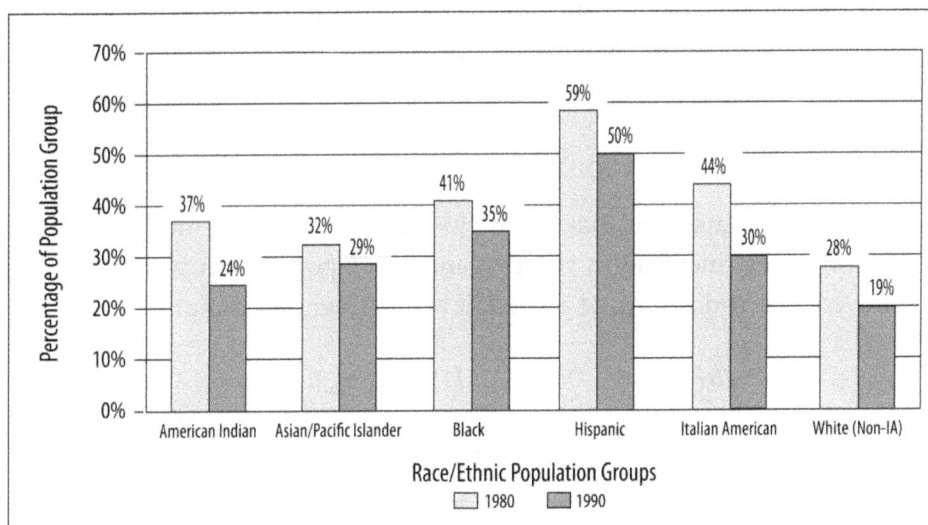

Note: 21 years of age or older.

It is important to note that Italian-American high school dropout rates were at a low of 10.5% in 1996 but have slightly increased until the year 2000. Hopefully, the increase will not continue to the high points of the 1980s. In fact, recent reports by high school educators and Calandra Institute counselors indicate concern that Italian-American youth appear to be prematurely terminating their high school studies.

It could be argued that many social factors are affecting these growing numbers. Some believe that our school system is on the verge of collapse and not able to retain students due to an inability to successfully meet the psychoeducational needs of students. In addition, there are a growing number of young students who have lost faith in our educational system because teachers are overwhelmed with extraneous duties, thus reducing their time and ability to effectively respond to student concerns and impart a meaningful educational process.

In addition, since many households function with both parents working full time, leaving children without guidance and supervision may also contribute to a lack of academic connection and integration. Finally, since the divorce rate in America has become epidemic, many youngsters are without a father figure to instill a paternal work ethic and cannot contemplate the notion of education under very stressful circumstances within their family. All too often students have to work and/or leave school to help contribute to family income. Certainly, these are just some of the issues affecting the increase in the dropout rate of Italian-American students. Other ethnic and racial groups are also encountering a rise in dropout rates due to similar issues.

UNIVERSITY/COLLEGE STUDIES

Figure 10 illustrates that, from 1980 to 1990, Italian Americans had the second largest increase in the percentage of population having attained some college and above, 24% to 37%, after American Indians.

FIGURE 10. *Some College and Above, 1980 vs. 1990 New York City Education Achievement*

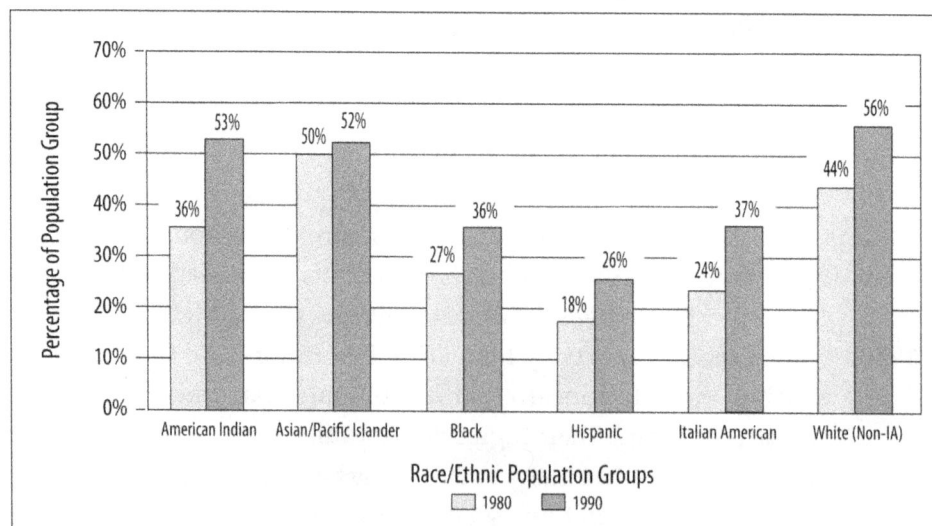

Note: 21 years of age or older.

GRADUATE STUDIES

As shown in Figure 11, however, when Italian Americans are compared to other groups (minority and other whites) regarding college and advanced graduate degree attainment, Italian Americans continue to lack graduate education although they are slightly ahead of the minority populations reported.

FIGURE 11. *Higher Education Achievement, 1990 New York City (All Race and Ethnic Populations)*

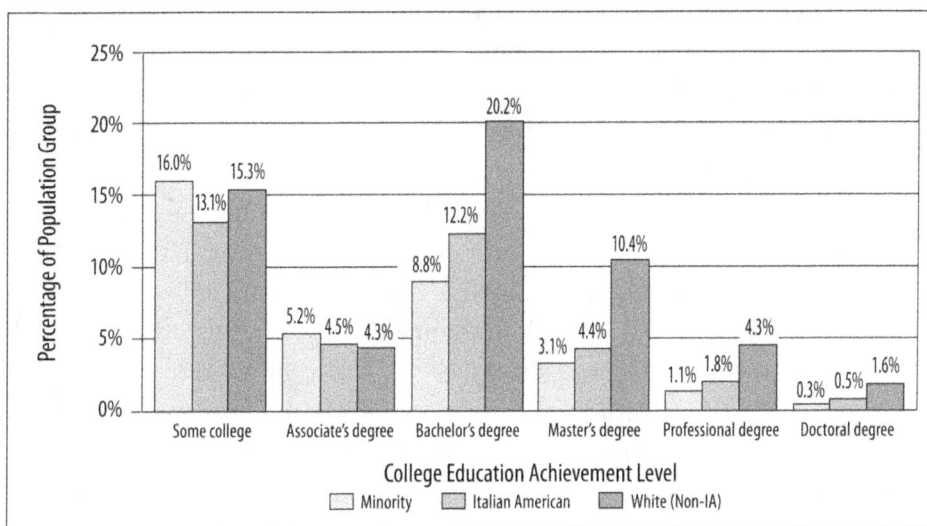

Note: 21 years of age or older.

The next census will provide an opportunity to assess improvements in the college achievement levels of Italian Americans. It appears, however, that the efforts that were exerted on behalf of at-risk high school students in the 1990s should be applied to contemporary Italian-American college students to increase interest in graduate education.

It is interesting to note that while the ranks of Italian-American college students are increasing, there is a disproportionate gap in graduate education achievement levels, even when it is increasingly obvious that an undergraduate degree is not what it was a decade ago. There is evidence that an advanced degree is now becoming the entry-level requirement in many career fields. The question is, how do we instill the need for graduate and professional education so that Italian-American students will be able to effectively compete in their chosen professions?

The answer is fundamentally the identical approach taken in the 1980s that insured that the high school dropout rate of students would decline from 21% to the present rate of nearly 12%. Mentoring and counseling programs that make our students aware of the importance of advanced degrees, and highlight the advantages of post-graduate degrees, are necessary. Organizations such as the Order Sons of Italy in America, Unico National and the National Italian American Foundation, that were in the forefront of programs that provided generous scholarships for high school students to attend college, must now make scholarships available to qualified students for graduate school.

Certainly, families must embrace the idea that the new millennium requires their children to make informed choices regarding higher education. This can be accomplished by making information about careers and graduate studies available to students and parents through school and community-based programs. Now that Italian-American high school graduates wish to proceed to college, it is imperative that they receive career guidance to help them choose the institution that will best serve them, and the path that will allow them a chance to utilize their particular interests and abilities. These strategies must also be used to help students who want to attend graduate school. How many bright young Italian-American men and woman missed the opportunity for graduate study at an Ivy League university because they were not able to afford it or were not aware of their academic potential as it applied to a particular career?

SUMMARY

During the past twenty-five years we have seen a marked change, for the better, in the dropout rate among Italian-American students in our large urban areas, as well as throughout the entire country. This is particularly evident in those households where both parents attended college and have moved from a lower to middle class lifestyle.

Italian-American high school dropout rates were highest in the 1980s, reaching 21%. The Italian-American community's outreach efforts to encourage students to complete high school were successful in lowering high school dropout rates in the 1990s. By the year 2000, Italian-American students had among the lowest dropout rates of all groups measured by the New York City Board of Education at 12%, comparable to other White (non-Italian) and Asian students. A slight increase in the Italian-American high school dropout indicator in 1996, however, cautions that outreach efforts should continue so as to avoid the inordinately high dropout rates of the 1980s.

Between 1980 and 1990, college achievement levels also drastically improved, with significant increases in the population having some college or graduate level studies. During the 1990s, although progress was made with college attendance, Italian Americans lagged behind other Whites (non-Italian Americans) in regard to graduate education levels.

The authors contend that it is important to continue the aggressive mentoring, counseling, positive image and outreach programs to Italian-American high school and college students. Furthermore, expansion of the outreach counseling programs for Italian-American college students is needed to facilitate career decision-making, college retention and graduation. In addition there is a strong demand to provide mentoring and scholarship incentives for college and graduate studies.

Students today may not be aware of the historical and often conflictual relationship between Italian-American ethnicity and educational attainment. Much of this began to change when their parents, who were the beneficiaries of outreach programs, began to recognize the importance of education. And, as the parents became more educated, their views regarding the value of education changed from traditional perceptions of blue-collar work in the neighborhood to professional and white-collar career opportunities in the new millennium. Hopefully, their children will realize that a formal education can help them reap the rewards our system affords to those who are able to compete in a changing workplace and global economy.

Notes

1. Ziehler, N. L. (1990). "AMICI: The Italian American Mentoring Project." Unpublished manuscript, John D. Calandra Italian American Institute, City University of New York.

2. Scelsa, J. V. and Milione V. (1990). "Statistical Profile of Italian American Educational Attainment National, State and Local Trends." Paper presented at the Education of Italian American Youth Conference, State of New York Governor's Office of Ethnic Relations, Due Casa Una Tradizione Project of the International Partnership Program United Federation of Teachers, AFL-CIO Italian American Studies Committee, at the Graduate School and University Center, City University of New York, April 30, 1990.

3. Scelsa, J. V. and Milione, V. (1990). "Statistical Profile of Educational Attainment Including High School Dropout Rate Indicators for Italian-American and Other Race/Ethnic Populations: United States, New York State, and New York City." In H. E. Landry (Ed.) *Annual Conference of the American Italian Historical Association, Vol. 23, To See the Past More Clearly: The Enrichment of the Italian Heritage* (pp. 1–18). Austin, Texas: Nortex Press.

4. Scelsa, J. V. (1991). "Missed Opportunities." Ambassador: National Italian American Foundation Quarterly, (Spring 1991), 17–19.

5. Opperman and Gambert, (2001). The Annual Dropout Report, 1987–2000. NYC Board of Education, Office of Research and Evaluation, April 1989–April 2001.

6. Milione V. (2002). "Italian American High School Dropout Rate: Where Are We Now?" Paper presented at the New York Conference of Italian American State Legislators, Albany, NY, June 2002.

7. Census of Population and Housing: 1980, 1990. US Department of Commerce, Bureau of the Census, Washington DC, 1983, 1992.

8. Milione V. and Pelizzoli I., (2003). "Student Academic Achievement: A Comparison Between Italian and Asian Americans." Paper presented at the Asian American Conference on Education: Challenges and Perspectives, Baruch College, May 2003. www.aaari.info. (workshop 2B).

9. Milione V. (1996). "The Changing Demographics of Italian Americans in New York State, New York City and Long Island: 1980 and 1990." The Italian American Review, 5.2, 133–154.

Index

www.ingramcontent.com/pod-product-compliance
Lightning Source LLC
Chambersburg PA
CBHW080230270326
41926CB00020B/4190